THE DISCURSIVE FIGHT OVER
RELIGIOUS TEXTS IN ANTIQUITY

RELIGION AND NORMATIVITY
VOLUME 1

THE DISCURSIVE FIGHT OVER RELIGIOUS TEXTS IN ANTIQUITY

Edited by Anders-Christian Jacobsen

Acta Jutlandica
Theological Series

Aarhus University Press |

The discursive fight over religious texts in antiquity
Religion and normativity vol. 1
© Aarhus University Press and the authors 2009

Cover, design and typesetting by Jørgen Sparre
Printed by Narayana Press, Gylling
Printed in Denmark 2009

ISBN 978 87 7934 427 5
ISSB 0065 1354 – Acta Jutlandica
ISSN 0106 0945 – Theological Series

Published with the financial support of
Aarhus University Research Foundation
The Learned Society in Aarhus
The Theological Faculty at Aarhus University

Aarhus University Press
Langelandsgade 177
DK-8200 Aarhus N
www.unipress.dk

INTERNATIONAL DISTRIBUTORS:
Gazelle Book Services Ltd.
White Cross Mills
Hightown, Lancaster, LA1 4XS
United Kingdom
www.gazellebookservices.co.uk

The David Brown Book Company
Box 511
Oakville, CT 06779
USA
www.oxbowbooks.com

TABLE OF CONTENTS

PREFACE

In 2005 the Faculty of Theology, Aarhus University, chose as its research priority area *Religion and normativity*. This research priority area builds on existing research on topics covered by the faculty's strengths, and is divided into three themes:

Theme 1: The discursive fight over religious texts
Theme 2: Bible and literature – receptions and transformations of the Bible
Theme 3: Religion, politics, and law.

The research priority area has contributed to a deeper understanding of the role played by religion in defining past and present cultures and societies. Its participants have compared Judaism, Christianity, Islam and antique religions in the light of exegetical, historical and systematic perspectives. In a contemporary context, they have explored whether religion is still normative.

The result of their research is presented in a three-volume work entitled:

The discursive fight over religious texts in antiquity, Religion and normativity, Vol. 1, ed. by Anders-Christian Jacobsen.

Receptions and transformations of the Bible, Religion and normativity, Vol. 2, ed. by Kirsten Nielsen,

Religion, politics, and law, Religion and normativity, Vol. 3, ed. by Peter Lodberg.

The three editors wish to express their sincere thanks to the participants in the research area for many stimulating discussions during the research period, and for their contributions to these three volumes.

The Faculty of Theology, Aarhus University, has provided excellent working conditions and financial support, for which we are most grateful.

Thanks are also due to Aarhus University Press for taking care of the publishing in a very professional way.

Finally we wish to thank the University Research Foundation and Det Lærde Selskab (the Learned Society) Aarhus for financial support.

Anders-Christian Jacobsen, Peter Lodberg, Kirsten Nielsen
Aarhus, April, 2009

INTRODUCTION

As mentioned in the preface, in this book a group of scholars from (or with strong connections to) the Faculty of Theology at Aarhus University, Denmark present some of the results of a research project named 'The discursive fight over religious texts in antiquity'. This project has been running since the beginning of 2007. Before that the same group of scholars (more or less) conducted another project entitled 'Critique and Apologetics – Jews, Christians and Pagans in antiquity'. These projects have been conducted under the framework of a research seminar with the title 'Antiquity and Christianity' which was opened in 1999. This book thus provides a taste of the research in the field of 'Antiquity and Christianity' which has now been conducted in organised form at the Faculty of Theology in Aarhus over the past ten years.

The project 'The discursive fight over religious texts in antiquity', which is mirrored in this book, has focused on the factors that played a role in the development of a normative Christian corpus of scripture, and Christianity's response to various interpretations of this canonical corpus. Christianity developed from being a charismatic movement to becoming institutionally more organised. The close relationship between Judaism and Christianity changed, and Christianity manifested itself as a separate religion. The development of a number of alternative interpretations of Christianity also generated a demand for an authoritative collection of texts, binding doctrines etc.

This institutionalisation and a variety of more anonymous processes have influenced the canon of Christian scriptures. Many texts were already used at church services and in teaching, which also contributed to the formation of the Christian canon. Another characteristic feature is that religious groups have consolidated their identity and thus distanced themselves from other religious and social groups by favouring certain collections of texts. Some texts were considered to have a greater degree of truth than others. This meant that certain texts were perceived as generating the norms and values for the religious group's ethics and world view. Eventually, the development of liturgical uses of the texts and the social process of using them to form identities meant that these texts contributed to the shaping of the criteria that legitimised their own normative status.

This development included a shift from oral to written tradition. Written narrative cannot be adjusted to the same extent as oral narrative to meet the expectations of its audience, and this tends to cause dissonance between the values and views of ancient texts and the values and views of readers in a subsequent age. To overcome this disagreement and to justify the normative role of the text, it became necessary to develop special interpretation strategies.

In particular three factors which influenced these processes should be mentioned:

1) Christianity's relation to Judaism:
How did the relationship between ancient Christianity and Judaism affect the Christians' perception of biblical texts and their interpretation? How did the Jewish canonisation of certain texts and the Jewish debate about which texts belonged to this canon influence the Christian debate? How did the fact that Christians were also using scriptures of Jewish origin influence the formation of a canon of Christian writings? The contributions of Anders Klostergaard Petersen, Else K. Holt, Bart Vanden Auweele and Jörg Ulrich address these questions in different ways.

2) Christianity's relation to ancient Greco-Roman culture:
How did the relation to Greco-Roman culture in general contribute to the formation of a Christian literature, and to what extent was this literature shaped by an idea of Christian written tradition as an alternative basis for a new culture? How have the ancient Greco-Roman texts affected Christianity? These issues include the use of both Greek philosophy and Greek mythology and iconography. The contributions of Jesper Hyldahl, Karla Pollmann, Gitte Lønstrup and Anders-Christian Jacobsen discuss these questions, among other things.

3) Christianity's development towards orthodoxy:
In the first stage of the Christian era (1st-3rd centuries) the conflict between the church's main-stream and heterodox interpretations (e.g. Montanism and Gnostic currents) was due to disagreement about the fixation of the scripture and its canonical status and interpretation. The Nag Hammadi sources have helped to shed light on these discussions between orthodoxy and heresy. The same can be said about the ancient discussions about the provenance of ancient texts. The age and the origin of texts played an important role for their normative and canonical status. The discussions about the definition of the Christian biblical canon ended in the 4th century. After that the discussion concentrated on how to interpret the canonical scriptures. This development towards orthodoxy often included 'fights' between different groups – Jews and Christians, various currents of early Christianity etc. Most often these 'fights' were 'discursive'. However, from time to time they also had more corporeal aspects. The biblical canon was not defined without struggle.

This book consists of thirteen contributions which cover many of the topics which have been studied in the research project entitled 'The discursive fight over religious texts in antiquity'. However, it was not our intention to include all the topics which we have worked on. Consequently, these contributions should be seen together with other books and articles which have been or will be published as results of the project. The contributors to this book have largely been allowed to decide their own themes and titles. Notwithstanding this fact, the contributions are quite coherent and represent almost all the main aspects of the project. This mirrors the high degree of communication and discussion enjoyed by the research group over the years. The book has two main parts: The first part deals mainly with theoretical aspects (but always including examples of empirical material). And the second part consists of more detailed studies of empirical material (but always bearing relevant theories in mind).

In the first essay in this book Anders Klostergaard Petersen tries to define what the canonisation and authorisation of texts mean. His basic argument is that canonisation and authorisation are attempts to limit the production of new interpretations and new meaning (to constrain the semiotic riverrun). He takes his point of departure in the current Danish cultural debate, which has been greatly influenced by the government's publication of a variety of canons such as a cultural canon, a historical canon etc. Here canonisation means defining what is good and what is bad, what is important and what is unimportant, etc. Against this background Klostergaard Petersen finds that the concept of canonisation tends to be understood in a much too narrow sense in biblical exegesis and related areas of scholarship. Klostergaard Petersen says that: 'So I concur with the attempt made in an article by Jonathan Z. Smith to broaden the concept of canon to designate a much more prevalent cultural element.' According to Smith and Petersen, canonisation is not only a question of defining a corpus of texts as normative and authoritative for a religion or a religious community. Texts and books are not the only things that can be normative. However, Petersen concentrates on what happens when authority is attributed to texts, and furthermore on the different ways in which authority can be attributed to texts. Petersen answers the first question as follows:

To allot authority to a text is to ascribe it a semiotic privileging and, therefore, culturally regulating function. It is a way of extracting elements or stages from the cultural production – or in the case of religions, from the theological *Wirkungsgeschichte* – by elevating them to a semiotic foundational status.

Petersen's answer to the second question is that authority can be attributed to texts in different ways, for example on the basis of the content of the text, because of the reader's interpretation of the text, or because of the use of the text as an artefact. Finally, Petersen discusses how the concept of 'canon' should be defined. Petersen wants to widen this concept, and understands the concept of 'canon' to mean lists of authors or texts which are taken to be authoritative in their respective areas. This is the modern literary concept of 'canon'. According to Petersen, this concept can also be found in antique traditions including early Christianity and Judaism. With his broad introduction to concepts of authority and canonicity, Petersen sets the stage for the following contributions, which all in one way or the other discuss the use of these concepts in antiquity.

Jesper Hyldahl discusses how texts gain authority and normativity, and how the relations between canonical and non-canonical texts should be understood. So he continues the theoretical discussions which were begun by Petersen. In order to understand the differences and the interplay between these groups of texts, Hyldahl describes the development from oral to written tradition. The writing down of oral traditions gave them a fixed and unchangeable form which was related to the past. At the same time, readers were given the chance to analyse these traditions critically because they had them in front of them as an unchangeable object. Another development followed from this, namely a process leading towards the canonisation of various text corpora. These developments began in relation to the Homeric tradition, but were repeated in Judaism and Christianity. One of the difficult questions which resulted from this process was how to relate these fixed past traditions to the present time. If texts became 'old' in the sense that they became irrelevant for readers, they lost their importance and authority and were forgotten. Hermeneutics was needed, and was provided by the Stoics (among others) and further developed by Jewish and Christian exegetes. What status do these interpretations then have? This is the next question which Hyldahl poses. According to Hyldahl, interpretations of normative texts and text corpora gain a certain kind of normativity of their own. Hyldahl labels this process 'mutual authorisation'. According to Hyldahl, the openness of the biblical canon is what makes new interpretations and thus adjustments to new circumstances possible. If the canon was not open to such new interpretations, it would have lost its authoritative status a long time ago.

Karla Pollmann writes about 'Normativity, ideology and reception in pagan and Christian antiquity'. In her contribution she suggests a number of helpful definitions which widen the perspectives of Petersen's and Hyldahl's contributions further, and which (in combination with these contributions) form a very useful foundation for the more empirically oriented contributions in part II. Pollmann starts by suggesting the following definition of the concept of normativity:

Normativity can be defined as the claim to form an absolute standard, a 'rule' (*norma*) with overall validity. It does not refer in a descriptive way to reality as it is, but in a prescriptive way to reality as it ought to be. Thus, it comprises statements with a prescriptive aim of how to act correctly, in the form of precepts, prohibitions, and duties. Such norms are not absolute, but depend on cultural and historical contexts; thus they change during history, although the norms themselves claim absolute, 'transcendent' validity.

In continuation of this definition of normativity, which is supported by many examples from antique literature and philosophy, Pollmann defines canonisation as the process through which certain texts are picked out because their content is taken to be normative for a certain community. If a certain group of texts is claimed to be canonical and normative in a strong sense which includes prescriptions both for ethical and moral life and for the belief of the community, the beliefs of such a community will become an ideology. Religion can thus turn into ideology if its norms are so strong that they exclude any other opinions and interpretations of life and belief. Even though Christianity most often defines itself as being in opposition to ideologies, there have been several examples of very strong interpretations of Christianity which actually tend to turn Christianity into an ideology. Pollmann illustrates this with examples from early Christian literature, taking Ambrosiaster as a main example.

Jakob Engberg writes about how ancient discussions about the provenance of texts influenced their normative and canonical status. The foundation of this discussion is the ancient idea that 'the older is the better'. If one could show that a text was old, this was a good argument for ascribing it a strong normative and canonical status. And if it could be shown that a text was written recently, this was a good way to deprive it of normativity. Combined with this idea, the question of authorship was important. If it could be shown or rendered probable that a text was composed by an important (and ancient) figure like an apostle or prophet, this was a strong argument for the normativity of the text. If such an important authorship could not be shown it had the opposite effect, namely that the text could not claim any normative status. The normative status of a text was, as also shown by Karla Pollmann, the key to obtaining a place in the biblical canon. Using the discussion about the status of the Revelation of John and the discussion about which gospels should be included in the canon as his main examples, Jakob Engberg shows how these ideas worked in the process of defining the Christian biblical canon. Engberg thus manages to unearth some of the most important principles for ancient canon building.

Gitte Lønstrup deals with the construction of memory as a way to create normativity. She describes how Constantinople was constructed as the 'new Rome' through the creation of monuments, feasts etc. which 'remembered' the architecture and public life in the 'old Rome'. Lønstrup expresses the process of memory construction as follows:

Through the manner of this appropriation, Constantinople simply became Rome, as I shall argue later in this paper. In the process of becoming 'Rome', Constantinople's leaders created a distinctive social and cultural memory that not only likened new Rome to old Rome, but also surpassed and superseded the Rome on the Tiber.

Using old sources from the centuries immediately after Constantinople was built, Lønstrup manages to show that the outline and the architecture of Constantinople were deliberately constructed as a 'copy' of Rome. Lønstrup then tests the idea that Constantinople was built on seven hills like Rome. The question is whether this distinct idea was originally part of the 'new Rome ideology' or a later idea invented by modern scholars. In fact Constantinople does not have seven hills, and Lønstrup shows that the historians writing at the time when Constantinople was made capital of the Roman Empire did not make this claim, either. However, the idea came up much later in the eighth century. Modern scholars in the 19th and 20th centuries, however, transferred the idea back to the Late Antique period even though they never managed to find the idea expressed in the ancient sources. Thus Lønstrup shows that there was a very effective memory-construction going on in the centuries immediately after the foundation of Constantinople – and that this memory-construction continued in later centuries – even among modern scholars.

Else Kragelund Holt's contribution is the first in the second part of the book, which deals with normativity and canon building in relation to specific ancient texts. Holt reflects on concepts of authority in relation to biblical exegesis. Being an Old Testament scholar, her reflections have their basis in the study of authority in the Old Testament, more precisely in the Book of Jeremiah. According to the Book of Jeremiah the prophet has his authority from God, who communicated this authority to the prophet by calling him a prophet (for instance). Being invested with divine authority, the prophet was divided from the people. The prophet spoke on behalf of God to the people. The prophet spoke the word of God. According to Holt, it was not until very recently (the 1980s) that this divine authority of the Old Testament prophets was challenged in modern biblical exegesis by historical criticism. So what is the normative theological meaning of prophets and prophetical texts – if any? According to Holt, the meaning of the texts is now restricted to the meaning which the individual reader brings into the text. The prophetic texts from the Old Testament can thus no longer claim to have any inherent normativity. Finally, Holt describes an emerging situation in the theological and exegetical environment: the ways of North-American and European biblical scholarship are parting. Owing to prevailing conservatism, the theological environment in North America is still able to invest the prophetic texts with authority, while European biblical scholarship is much more secularised and therefore unable to count these texts as normative. This description of the current situation in biblical exegetical scholarship could easily provoke quite a lot of discussion.

René Falkenberg writes about a text called *Sophia of Jesus Christ*. This text has been handed down in two versions, both in Coptic. Furthermore, the *Sophia of Jesus Christ* is a rewritten extension of another text called *The Letter of Eugnostos*. The *Sophia of Jesus Christ* is thus a good example of how early Christians reused existing texts and corrected and expanded them in order to make them useful for the needs of the community to which the author / editor belonged (cf. Hyldahl's contribution). Falkenberg shows how the original text – the *Letter to Eugnostos*, which concentrated on describing a heavenly cosmic system – was expanded so the new or rewritten text also dealt with soteriological questions related to the created cosmos. Furthermore, the two versions of the *Sophia of Jesus Christ* – the rewritten text – describe these soteriological questions in different ways and from time to time only through implicit hints. For this reason Falkenberg compares the soteriological content of the *Sophia of Jesus Christ* with soteriological passages from other Coptic texts from the Nag Hammadi corpus. In this way Falkenberg is able to reconstruct a soteriological process with three stages. The first stage concerns cosmogony, the second concerns anthropogony, and the third concerns the time of the revelation dialogue in which the author of the *Sophia of Jesus Christ* receives revelations and instructions. Falkenberg's contribution is thus an interesting example of how the rewriting of texts can revive old texts in a new context where new meaning is needed.

Analysing Justin's *Dialogue with the Jew Trypho*, Jörg Ulrich approaches the canon debate in its earliest stage in the mid-second century. At this time the biblical canon was not yet fixed, although the main framework had been set (cf. Pedersen's contribution, which deals with the final stage in the building of the Christian canon). Although some Christians and Jews protested, one of the things which was clear to many Christians and Jews in the mid-second century was that they shared normative texts – the Jewish Bible, which would be called the Old Testament by Christians somewhat later. The discussion between Justin and Trypho was thus not about whether the text under discussion was canonical or apocryphal, as is the case later on in the discussion among Christians about the definition of the New Testament canon (cf. again the contribution of Nils Arne Pedersen). From the fact that both recognised the same texts as normative, the question of the interpretation of these texts was raised (the theme addressed by Hyldahl). Trypho and Justin accept that the Old Testament texts are normative. And from that position they try to convince each other of the truth of their respective interpretations. However, Justin and Trypho are unable to reach any consensus. The reason for this, according to Ulrich, is that they do not share hermeneutical premises. For Justin most of the texts, which were later canonised in the New Testament, were normative for his interpretation of Moses and the Prophets. The same was the case for the figure of Jesus Christ. Justin thus read Moses and the Prophets in the light of Christ. According to Trypho, this meant bringing something foreign into the texts under discussion. In addition to this major disagreement about hermeneutical preconditions, the *Dialogue* shows that Justin and Trypho also disagree with regard to minor questions such as the reliability of different versions of the LXX.

Anders-Christian Jacobsen discusses normative structures in Origen's exegesis. Origen's exegesis of the Bible is often characterised as 'allegorical'. Whatever label we put on his exegesis, it is characterised by the idea that the text of the Bible has several levels of meaning. This leads unavoidably to the question of whether (and how) such texts with several levels of meaning can be interpreted in a way which preserves their meaning. Some ancient theologians and modern scholars claim that the results of Origen's allegorical exegesis are totally random. In his contribution to this book, Anders-Christian Jacobsen shows that Origen's allegorical exegesis leaves room for much creativity of interpretation, but that the creativity of the interpreter is still controlled by a hierarchy of norms controlling the interpretation. So the creedal formulations, the apostolic tradition, the Bible itself, philosophical traditions and rhetorical procedures are all to some extent normative for the exegetical work of Origen. It becomes clear that from Origen's own point of view his exegesis is fully controlled by these norms. This means that Origen regards these norms as strong guidelines for his biblical interpretation. However, seen from outside these norms do not seem to be particularly strong because Origen largely constructs them himself and often goes beyond the limits that he has set himself.

Bart Vanden Auweele asks the question of how the Song of Songs – a text about human erotic love – has become a part of the biblical canon. According to Auweele, recent exegesis has realised the importance of the text's poetic character: 'As a poem, a dialogue and a grotesque, the Song offers several interpretations and solicits its readers to the highest degree.' Other modern exegetes stress that the normative meaning of the Song of Songs depends on an intertextual reading in which other parts of the canon lend meaning to the text. Others again stress that on its own and at the literal level, the text finds its meaning as a critique of an excessively spiritualised understanding of love, of the relation between woman and man etc. Many of the same ideas can be found in ancient exegesis. According to ancient sources, there has been no real discussion of whether the Song of Songs should be included in the canon or not. This is true of both Jewish and Christian tradition. At the same time, it seems to be obvious to the exegetes that the text must be treated allegorically or metaphorically – the same type of exegesis which Origen used. Auweele uses Gregory of Nyssa's exegesis of the Song of Songs as an example. According to Gregory, the Song of Songs is part of the canon and is thus normative for Christians. To understand the text, it is necessary to enter into the erotic way of thinking. The erotic desire which is described in the text is an expression of how humans should desire God. The three books which are attributed to Salomon (cf. Engberg's thesis about the importance of ancient authorship) – Proverbs, Ecclesiastes and the Song of Songs – describe the erotic journey in which the soul must participate to be near to God. Despite many differences between the ancient and modern exegesis of the Song of Songs, interpreters seem basically to agree that the Song of Songs is a poetic text which must be interpreted metaphorically or allegorically in order to take its place in the biblical canon. As a canonical and thus normative text, the Song of Songs is still open to a wide variety of interpretations. According to Auweele, this does not compromise the normativity of the text.

Nils Arne Pedersen addresses one of the core questions in the scholarly debate about the formation of the New Testament canon: When was the New Testament canon consisting of twenty-seven writings established and accepted throughout most of the ancient church? Pedersen argues that the 39th *Festal Letter* of Athanasius from Alexandria is a milestone in this process. Thus he rejects recent attempts to argue that the New Testament canon was already defined in the middle of the second century. Claiming the importance of Athanasius' *Festal Letter*, Pedersen reveals what the letter tells us about the motives of Athanasius in producing the canon list and about Athanasius' arguments for constructing the list as he does. In continuation of this point, Pedersen tries to explain why Athanasius' canon was victorious as the normative New Testament canon. According to Pedersen, Athanasius' most important motive for 'closing' the New Testament canon was to isolate the Melitians as heretics. One way of achieving this involved showing that they used unauthorised writings (ἀπόκρυφα) which were not part of the New Testament canon. To do this, Athanasius first had to define the normative canon. However, Pedersen thinks that during the conflict with the Arians Athanasius had already defined his New Testament canon, and that the arguments from Scripture were even more important in this conflict. It has been argued that the success of Athanasius' canon was due to the almost 'worldwide' circulation of this part of his 39th *Festal Letter*. Pedersen, however, thinks that Athanasius' personal authority was more important for the success:

'Here I think we should look to the fact that Athanasius won for himself an authority which was not only bound up with his office or his direct power. He was the man who never compromised and who suffered for what he believed in. The same reasons that made him a saint after his death made his canon a success'.

Jennifer Hart sheds light on the process of canonisation from a non-Jewish and a non-Christian perspective. In her essay she traces the influence of Islam on the formation of a normative Mandaean text corpus. This is an exciting and important theme in its own right, but the fact that this formative process runs through more or less the same decades and centuries as the formation of the Jewish, Christian and Islamic canons makes it even more important and interesting. Hart's fundamental thesis is that exposure to Islam had a formative impact upon the Mandaean move towards canonisation. Among the various types of Mandaean literature two works are of special importance: the *Ginza* and the *Book of John*. The Ginza is constructed out of numerous individual works which predate the Ginza itself. Parts of the Ginza are much older than Islam (3rd century C.E.), but other parts reveal a rather profound knowledge of Islam and show how the Mandaeans tried to incorporate an awareness that Islam was a possible threat to their own religious life. Hart suggests that even the construction of the Ginza as a book is a result of the Mandaeans' awareness of the important role which normative scriptures played in the development and spread of Islam. This suggestion is supported by the chronological information which can be extracted from the lists of scribes and copyists attached to most *Ginza* manuscripts. This information reveals that the earliest versions of the *Ginza* date to approximately 650 to 700 C.E. – the period in which Islam established its rule in the Mandaean homeland. Like the *Ginza*, the *Book of John* demonstrates that the Mandaeans were well acquainted with Islam and even involved in some kind of theological dialogue with them. As a conclusion to her investigations of the two most important Mandaean texts, Hart says that:

It should hardly be dismissed as coincidental that within a generation or two of encountering a religion that valued highly the possession of a foundational book, the focus of Mandaean literature should shift from a loose library of disconnected texts to a collection of obviously collated, purposefully structured and thoughtfully named books.

Carmen Cvetkovic explores the influence of the Church Fathers, especially Augustine, on Bernard of Clairvaux's and William of St Thierry's so-called 'mystical theology', i.e. the union of the soul with God. In this last essay in the book, we thus turn our attention to the question of the normative role of ancient text in later centuries. Cvetkovic defends the thesis that Bernard and William regarded the tradition of the Church Fathers as normative for their own interpretations; but the tradition leaves room for various opinions and interpretations. For both Bernard and William, the biblical foundation for this 'mystical theology' is 1 Cor 6: 17: *Qui adhaeret Domino, unus spiritus est.* As the first step, Cvetkovic describes how Augustine understands the union of the soul with God. According to Augustine, the 'unus spiritus' means the union of two spirits of different natures – God and Man. This is a union of will, not of substance. Only when the Bible says 'unum' without any specification, such as in Jn 10:30 (I and the Father are one), does it mean union of the same nature. In this way Augustine preserved the ontological gap between divine and human nature. Bernard follows Augustine in using 1 Cor 6:17 as a key text for his 'mystical theology'. In the same way as Augustine, he also claims that the unity between the Son and the Father is different from the unity between God and the human soul. According to Bernard, the union between God and the human soul is a union of will. Bernard adds that this union is established through love. This can also be found in Augustine – even introduced by means of the same biblical quotations. The most important addition made by Bernard is that this union has to be experienced. William uses the same technical terms as Augustine and Bernard, namely *unum* and *unus spiritus*. But he differs from them in that he does not attach *unum* strictly to the divine unity. The human soul can also be what God is. The difference between the Father, the Son and the human soul is that the Father and the Son are divine by nature, whereas the human soul can be made divine only by grace. Taking the idea a step forward to indicate that the unity between the soul and God is established by love, William claims that love is identical with the Holy Spirit. This identification between love and the Holy Spirit is a famous Augustinian idea. However, Bernard does not use this idea. This shows that Bernard and William differ in their reception of Augustine.

After this overview of the contents of this book, it may be relevant to ask the question: 'Why waste the taxpayer's money on old stuff like this?' As Klostergaard Petersen's discussion of the Danish government's recent canon projects shows, these kinds of questions are not as uncommon in a Danish context as they were earlier. Many people not involved in historical or theological scholarship have realised the importance of such studies. Studies like this provide important knowledge about the historical, cultural and religious foundation of modern societies, which is acknowledged by many as being of great importance for the welfare of society. At this general level, studies of foundational texts and text corpora are of great importance. In addition, such studies are also important for historical and theological scholarship as a way to provide more detailed and better theoretically based knowledge about the processes which led to the establishment of the text corpora which are fundamental for Judaism, Christianity and other religions. Even though historical studies of the processes of canonisation and other historical-critical studies have been going on for decades and in fact centuries, there are still strong tendencies among theologians to accept ancient 'myths' about the formation of the biblical canon which prevent these theologians from addressing questions about the normative foundation of theological studies in a proper way. It is not the aim of this book to do away with or relativise the question of religious normativity, but we hope to contribute to a more complex understanding of what religious normativity is.

Before ending this introduction, one practical issue must be mentioned. In order to reduce the length of the bibliographies, the editor has decided not to include primary sources in the bibliographies. In most cases it is not necessary to consult particular editions of the primary sources or particular translations of these sources. The reader can use the versions which she has at hand. If particular editions are needed, or if the sources can only be found in old editions or editions which are difficult to find for any other reasons, bibliographical information is provided in the footnotes.

Finally, it is important for me to thank my good colleagues for the efforts and the energy which they have invested in the writing of these essays – a fair reflection of all the hard work which the members of this research group have invested in the studies of 'Antiquity and Christianity' for the past ten years.

*The discursive fight over religious texts
in antiquity – theoretical perspectives*

CONSTRAINING SEMIOTIC RIVERRUN
– DIFFERENT GRADATIONS AND UNDERSTANDINGS OF CANONICITY AND AUTHORITATIVE WRITINGS

Anders Klostergaard Petersen

The aim of this essay is to examine what it entails to say that a text is authoritative and, secondarily, to discuss how the ascription of authority to particular writings is related to the larger phenomenon of canon formation. Since different understandings of canonicity exist, which often tend to be conflated with each other, it is important to analyse the different conceptions in order to discuss their relationship. At the same time, it is crucial to consider various understandings and gradations of authoritative writings, since the notion of an authoritative text is a notoriously difficult and slippery concept. I shall argue that the allotment of authority to particular writings and the corresponding endeavour – although situated at a higher level of complexity – to select particular groups of writings as culturally prescriptive intrinsically relate to each other. I shall also contend that both activities embody different attempts to impose constraints on the ongoing processes of sign production, that is, the attribution of authority to a particular writing or the selection of a particular list of texts as culturally normative represent different forms of semiotic closure.

Contemporary examples of canonisation

When we initiated the Århus research project on the Discursive Fight over Religious Texts in Antiquity two years ago, a younger colleague, Kasper Bro Larsen, had already prepared the way for the project by elaborating a comprehensive list of relevant litera-ture that could help us in our studies of the subject.[1] Retrospectively, I have sometimes thought about this list as an example of some of the problems that confront us when trying to understand the entailments of terms such as 'canonical' and 'authoritative'. What is the status of such a bibliographical catalogue? Is it reasonable to ascribe it canonical significance, and if so what is meant by the term canonical? To what extent is it meaningful to think of such a list in terms of authority?

Before addressing these questions, I shall point to another recent example that serves to set the stage for the subsequent discussion of different gradations and un-derstandings of canonicity and authoritative writings. For the past couple of years the

---

[1]   Kasper Bro Larsen's list is an extended and updated version of the annotated bibliography found in van der Kooij and van der Toorn 1998 and compiled by J.A.M. Snoek (1998, 435-506).

Danish cultural debate has been almost obsessed by a quest for canons. In 2004, the Danish Minister for Culture, Brian Mikkelsen, a member of the Conservative Party, launched a grandiose project to compile a cultural canon. By the spring of 2005, the minister had appointed seven canon committees, the number corresponding to the seven main art forms under the auspices of the Danish Ministry of Culture (architecture, visual arts, design and crafts, film, literature, music, and dramatic arts).[2] To the scholar of antiquity, the resemblances to ancient canonical lists, which similarly enumerated the ten most important rhetors, the nine best lyric poets, the five best tragic poets, the seven miracles of the world etc. are striking (Cancik 2003, 117). The members of each committee were commissioned to jointly select 12 works of Danish art, which they considered 'to provide outstanding artistic experiences – for us today, but also for previous generations and for those who will come after us' (http://www.kum.dk/sw37439.asp).

The elaboration of such lists is surely not an entirely innocent endeavour. It resembles the attempts of children to draw up lists of their preferred friends. Listing is a way of expressing one's preferences by selecting the chosen ones and concomitantly excluding others from the good company. Since the project was bound to create misunderstandings and criticism, the homepage of the Ministry makes it clear that the endeavour is not part of a national mobilisation project, since the selected works 'should also illustrate that Danish art and culture have come into being in interplay and interaction with European and international trends' (ibid.). Nevertheless, the aspect of national identity formation and the concomitant attempt to enhance cultural coherence is difficult to ignore: 'In other words, the works must be "indispensable", i.e. works of art that cannot be disregarded if we want to define what is characteristic and distinctive about Danish culture' (ibid.). In other words, canon making may be a way of establishing identity markers that serve to define what it means to be part of a particular culture or group.

In the same vein, the homepage provides several concise answers in the form of bullet points to the question of why a cultural canon needs to be compiled. The first point asserts that the canon will: 'contribute to a lively cultural debate by acting as a yardstick for quality – a yardstick that will obviously be constantly challenged and discussed.' The second point states that the canon will 'give citizens an easy introduction to Danish art and culture and hopefully also inspire them to immerse themselves further in the individual art forms.' The canon should present 'a competent, qualified suggestion of the elements of Denmark's cultural heritage that are valuable, of good quality and worth preserving for our descendants.' It should 'make us more aware of who we are and give us more information on the cultural history of which we are part.' At the same time, the canon is urgent, because it will 'give us reference points and aware-

---

2   At a later point in the process, the chairmanship of the canon project decided that an additional canon aimed specifically at children's books should be drawn up. Similarly, it was decided sometime during the project that the canon pertaining to music should be divided into two canons, the first covering 12 pieces of so-called score music, and the other including the same number of compositions, but from the domain of popular music.

ness of what is special about Danes and Denmark in an even more globalised world.' Finally, the homepage asserts that the canon will 'strengthen the sense of community by showing key parts of our common historical possessions' (ibid.).

In this manner, it is obvious that canon formation is an intrinsic part of identity forging, as well as being a means of fighting against cultural oblivion, as pointed out constantly by Jan Assmann (2006, 65-68). It is a way of creating a normative past by selecting a particular group of works that should be binding for the present and determinative for the future course. The canon project was launched owing to an imagined or real threat to Danish culture and the social coherence of Danish society. Globalism is regarded as a threat to Danish cultural identity and national coherence. To scholars of antiquity, it is hardly surprising that the selection of authoritative lists of art and the formation of canons are frequently enmeshed in politics, whether such canons are educational or more general in nature. The construction of a canon may be a way of exerting and controlling influence, just as it may be a way of inscribing oneself into a laudable past whose impact should be acknowledged in the present by the subordinates' ascription of authority to the ruling house. We know, for instance, that the Homeric poems presumably underwent a process of standardisation during the Pisistratean rule of sixth-century Athens, enabling the Athenian state to gain control over the writings, just as they became an integral part of the Panathenaic festival (cf. Finkelberg 2003, 91).

Correspondingly, the point of time at which the Danish Minister of Culture initiated the canon project was hardly coincidental. It was simultaneous with a so-called foundational "debate of values" called for by the then newly re-elected government consisting of the Conservative Party and the Liberals. Simultaneously, this debate was part of a larger and on-going discussion about the number of immigrants and refugees in Denmark, the role of Islam in Danish society, the status of Muslim citizens in Danish culture etc. Leading politicians – tacitly or explicitly – endorsed the view that Islam as a religion was incompatible with human rights and modern Western democracy, as it had allegedly developed from the traditions of ancient Greece and nascent Christianity. Parallel to the explicitly stated threat of globalism, the presence of Islam in Western societies was held to be a threat to Western democracy. It is this particular situation which provided the background for the Danish canon debate, although this debate did not stop once the various cultural canons had been finally fixed.

After this project, the government instigated two additional initiatives. The different arguments put forward for the cultural canons mentioned above strongly underline a relationship between historical awareness and the sense of sharing a distinctive cultural identity. So it was hardly surprising that the next canon was concerned with the teaching of history in the Danish primary school system (comprising third to ninth grade). In 2006, the Minister of Education appointed a commission that was asked, among other things, to present a canon for the teaching of history. In their final report, the commission emphasised that:

the canon for the discipline of history must make it clear that the discipline is a culturally foundational field from which the pupils obtain a common cultural historical background. The obligatory canonical points must ensure that all young people leaving the Danish primary school have a common font of knowledge and insight which not only strengthens the use of the past in a societal context, but also constitutes the foundation for their continued education (www.uvm.dk/o6/documents/historie_ooopdf).[3]

Unlike the canons published by the Ministry of Culture, this canon comprised 29 points which were not limited to Danish history only. The canon embodies a list of highlights regarded as determining the development of current Western identity. The obligatory points proposed include: Tutankhamon, Emperor Augustus, the Westphalian Treaty, and the Siege of the Bastille among a number of crucial events pertaining to Danish history. Here we may also note an important relationship between canonical texts and the educational system, which is also a prevalent feature in the way canons functioned in the Graeco-Roman ancient world.

The latest canon – published in January 2008 – is a so-called canon of democracy, following in the wake of the Danish cartoon crisis (the now herostratically famous publication in 2005 of 12 cartoons depicting the prophet Muhammad by the Danish newspaper *Jyllands-Posten*). Once again, there is no attempt on the homepage of the Ministry of Education to conceal the agenda behind the initiative. The homepage makes it blatantly clear that: 'the Government wishes to strengthen the knowledge of Danes of the principles of freedom and representative government on which Danish society is based' (http://www.uvm.dk/o8.dk.htm?menuid=6410). On publication of the canon, the Danish Minister of Foreign Affairs, Per Stig Møller of the Conservative Party, emphatically stated that:

the promotion of democratic institutions and the strengthening of democratic principles are among the most important priorities for Danish foreign policy. Our engagement is rooted in Demark's own democratic history and traditions. All this is and may appear self-evident, but we are currently experiencing at home and abroad that the values of democracy are being attacked. This situation increases the need to clarify and specify the preconditions and content of democracy, and it is my hope that the canon will be used both in teaching and in the current debate (ibid.).

Similarly, the Minister of Culture, Brian Mikkelsen, endorsed the view that:

the canon of democracy will support us and provide us with a common basis, so that we are not seduced by anti-democratic ideological currents. In the battle against any form of fanaticism, democracy is our strongest weapon (ibid.).

3   I am responsible for the translation of this and the subsequent quotes into English.

Like the canon of history, the canon of democracy was not limited to Danish examples only. There was also an explicit emphasis in advance on social coherence, with a view to ensuring that the canon consisted of 'those events, thinkers and writings which have had a particular influence on attitudes regarding the freedom of the individual, the social coherence of society, and the development of Danish democracy' (ibid.).

The cultural pervasiveness of canonisation processes

These examples make it conspicuously clear that canon formation and the ascription of authority to particular events or writings are not a phenomenon belonging solely to the past. In fact, they seem to be a vital and indispensable element in the current cultural debate too. This is an important point, because in biblical scholarship and related disciplines the examination of canonicity and the formation of canons are often limited to the discussion of canons in terms of religions only, and particularly those religions that traditionally have been designated religions of the book.[4] Even if we widen the discussion of authoritative writings and canonicity to include another important scholarly strand, i.e. the talk about canons in literary studies, we would hardly grasp the comprehensiveness and pervasiveness of the phenomenon. So I concur with the attempt made in an article by Jonathan Z. Smith to broaden the concept of canon to designate a much more prevalent cultural element.

In Smith's understanding, the occurrence of canons is not confined to written cultures only. It is a ubiquitous element intrinsic to culture – whether written or oral, past or present.[5] Common, for instance, to the principles governing human food is the fact that each culture selects a particular number of foods, which it can subsequently vary in an infinite number of ways:

A given foodstuff represents a radical, almost arbitrary, selection out of the incredible number of potential sources of nutriment that are at hand; but, once the selection is made, the most extraordinary attention is given to the variety of its preparation. That is to say, *if food is a phenomenon characterized by limitation, cuisine is a phenomenon characterized by variegation* (1978, 15).

The same relationship pertains to religion, since the prime object of study for the historian of religion is 'those dimensions of the theological endeavour that are concerned with canon and its exegesis' (17). Smith specifies the theological *Wirkungsgeschichte* of a given religious tradition as 'the radical and arbitrary reduction represented by the notion of canon and the ingenuity represented by the rule-governed exegetical enterprise to apply the canon to every dimension of human life,' which is 'that most

---

4   The phrase 'religions of the book' is coined based on the Quranic concept 'people of the book' (*ahl al-kitāb*), which is found in several Surās and refers to the different groups that all possess sacred writings, see 2,109; 9,29, for instance.

5   Another opinion can be found in the essay written by Jesper Hyldahl below. Hyldahl claims that the phenomenon of canonisation is a result of the shift from orality to literacy.

characteristic, persistent and obsessive religious activity' (18). In this manner, cuisine is parallel to the exegetical enterprise, and canon making is comparable to the selection of a limited number of foodstuffs that may be infinitely varied.

According to Smith, canon formation is the last element of a tripartite sequence which comprises the preparation of lists, catalogues, and finally canons. Whereas lists are characterised by the sheer enumeration of names or events, catalogues represent an attempt to impose order on lists – but both are open-ended. They have neither a necessary beginning, nor an end. Their duration is entirely determined by the attention of their compiler or the use for which they have been produced (19). From this perspective, it is obvious that the bibliography by Kasper Bro Larsen mentioned above is a catalogue and not a canon, since canons in Smith's understanding are primarily characterised by formal closure. The same applies to the alleged canons produced under the auspices of the Danish government during recent years. They are catalogues and not canons, since they are – in principle – open-ended. This, however, has not prevented the government from referring to them as canons.

Before we enter the discussion of different conceptions of canon, however, I would like to emphasise another important point in Smith's argument. He highlights the fact that the closure of the canon results in the emergence of an ingenuous hermeneutical activity – a phenomenon well-known to historians of religion, since almost every codification of sacred writings has prompted correspondingly fervent activity in the creation of commentaries to secure the right interpretation and the continuous extension of the sphere of the authoritative texts. Smith emphasises that it is the role of the interpreter 'to continually extend the domain of the closed canon over everything that is known or everything that is' (23). However, this makes it expedient to clarify the relationship between the canon and its subsequent application to all aspects of life.

Whereas Smith's focus is on the principal relationship between the closure of the canon and the subsequent outburst of various forms of hermeneutical activity that canonically attempt to map the world, I shall concentrate on the relationship between the two in terms of authority. Additionally, I shall take this as a clue to widen the discussion to a more general examination of what it entails to attribute authority to particular writings. The idea is that intrinsic to every formation of a canon is a more basic cultural mechanism that has to do with the ascription of authority to particular interpretations at the expense of others. In this manner, canon formation and the allotment of authority to particular texts represent different ways of controlling the continuous processes of *semiosis*. In lieu of this perspective, it also may prove possible to bring together not only the different conceptions – past and present – of canonicity into a common understanding of the term, but also different aspects pertaining to the attribution of authority to particular writings.

Canonisation as semiotic closure

The catalogue in Smith's understanding may well represent a pre-stage to canon formation, but at the same time it may also – as witnessed by the various canonical catalogues
discussed above – be a way of imposing semiotic constraints on the cultural process.
To select a certain group of writings and ascribe to them canonical status is to argue
that they should somehow be exemplary for ongoing cultural development. It is this
particular aspect that I want to highlight, and that I think points to the pervasiveness of
attributing authority to particular writings. It may occur in the full terms of formation
of a canon understood as the formal selection of a fixed set of writings, or on a minor
scale in terms of the ascription of authority to one particular text, but both phenomena
reflect the attempt to control or exert influence on the processes of culture.

My point is not to argue that the elevation of texts or groups of writings to authority
necessarily represents a deliberate attempt to control the semiotic process. It may well
be so in the cases of formal selection, but the much more frequent informal selections
of textual canons or writings – determined by their extensive use – do not represent
conscious attempts to impose constraints on the *semiosis*. They are simply reflecting
processes of selection, which for various – and often not entirely lucid – reasons prefer
some writings instead of others. From an external perspective, however, it is obvious
that the selection of some writings rather than others reflects a semiotic process by
which some interpretative choices have been favoured at the expense of others.

I do not think this understanding is contradictory to Smith's argument, but it slightly
rephrases it and widens his conception at two points. First, it makes it abundantly clear
that any ascription of authority to a particular writing is a reflection of those semiotic
mechanisms which on a larger scale lead to the formation of canons. To allot authority to a text is to ascribe it a semiotic privileging and, therefore, culturally regulating
function. It is a way of extracting elements or stages from the cultural production – or
in the case of religions, from the theological *Wirkungsgeschichte* – by elevating them to
a semiotic foundational status. Second, I think it is beneficial to weaken the clear-cut
distinction Smith makes between canon formation and subsequent exegesis by a greater
acknowledgement of the transitional nature of the hermeneutical activity that is bound
to succeed processes of canonisation.

As is well-known from the Hebrew Bible, texts that originated as hermeneutical activity in response to authoritative writings may, in the continuous process of
infinite *semiosis*, themselves become the object of canonisation and, subsequently,
themselves provoke new instances of exegetical activity. Deuteronomy and the Books
of Chronicles are illustrative examples. This phenomenon, however, is not limited to
particular writings, but pertains to textual corpora as well. The codification of the
Mishnah at the turn of the third century, for instance, is a comparable case in which an
original hermeneutical activity is elevated to the status of a canon. True, the Mishnah
does not become part of the Hebrew Bible, but what about the relationship between
canon and subsequent hermeneutical activity in the case of the New Testament? Here
the *deuterosis*, as the phenomenon has been elegantly designated by Guy Stroumsa

(1998, 18), not only becomes part of a canon, but is given the predominant role over its predecessor. Additionally, if we narrow the focus to the simplest form of exegetical activity taking place in response to an authoritative writing, there is ample evidence that derivative writing (although being formally regarded as secondary to its literary antecedent) is in practice given the role of a canonical key to interpretation. This is reminiscent of the time-honoured distinction in Protestant theology between *norma normans* and *norma normata*, which ascribes the decisive role to the biblical texts, but in practice gives interpretative privilege to the subsequent confessional writings.

These examples point to another important aspect. Just as the processes of sign production are infinite, because every interpretation will lead to the production of new signs which will in turn provoke everlasting chains of new *semiosis*, the same applies to the recurrent attempts to control sign production by establishing regulating principles. The point is not to extrapolate canonisation from the general processes of *semiosis*, of which it is obviously an inherent part, but to specify its nature in the cultural process. In fact, the riverrun of *semiosis* entails the corresponding construction of sign-controlling dams, or in other words different processes of canonisation.

Although sign producers seldom acknowledge this, the selection of a canon or the attribution of authority to a particular writing reflects an attempt to intervene in the semiotic process by creating a closure. But it cannot prevent the continuous riverrun. Consequently, the constant attempts to create new semiotic barriers constitute an unacknowledged recognition of the vain fight against the uncontrollable evolution of continuous sign production. The so-called 'Canon in Canon' debate of 20th century Protestant theology is a telling example. It grew out of the historical awareness that the New Testament canon far from guaranteeing the particular Lutheran understanding of Scripture which the theologians behind the debate endorsed, actually prompted (even within their own interpretative community) confessional and unrestrained forms of interpretation. By arguing like Ernst Käseman (for instance) that 'the principle of the justification of the godless is the kernel of all Christian proclamation and, therefore, also of Scripture, which under no circumstances must be relinquished' (1970, 405, my translation), is a desperate attempt to prevent the inevitable process of infinite *semiosis*.

There is one final point that I would like to emphasise before discussing different gradations of authority. It is the so-called 'legal fiction', which is, at least in the realm of religious texts, a prevalent feature and important for the examination of textual authority. The term refers to the fact that although exegetes are supposed faithfully to extend the impacts of canonical writings by developing appropriate hermeneutical strategies, they often fail to admit the alterations which they *de facto* add to such canonical writings (Smith 1978, 24, with reference to Henry Maine). This is, of course, an inevitable element of the continuous processes of *semiosis*. Interpretation is bound to result in the production of new signs, but often scholars tend to forget that an interpretation of an authoritative text may well claim to be secondary with regard to its antecedent, but simultaneously it may – without admitting it – attempt to usurp the discursive space of its predecessor.

For instance, it has often been said that as a piece of rewritten Scripture the Book of Jubilees does not pretend to challenge the authority of its literary predecessors (Gen – Ex 12), since it obviously borrows its claim to authority from them. Being orchestrated as a revelation spoken by God (ch. 1) and the Angel of Presence reading from the heavenly tablets (ch. 2-50) to Moses, I think it is difficult to overlook the book's attempt to surpass its literary antecedents with regard to authority. It is true that the book does not discredit the alleged authority of the narratives upon which it relies, but it purports to reflect an understanding that is superior to the one found in its predecessors. Arguably, one can claim – more irenically – that the book is a supplement to the revelation already embodied by its antecedents (Brooke 2005, 98), but if a complementary aspect is needed to truly acknowledge the revelation contained in them, it is also suggested that the authoritative writings are deficient unless they are supplemented by this secondary writing.[6] The same holds true for the Temple Scroll, which in the form of a rewriting of the Torah from the end of Exodus through the end of Deuteronomy purports to reflect direct divine speech, just like the Book of Jubilees.

Florentino Garzía Martínez may be quite right when he argues that:

> the essential features of its (the *Temple Scroll*) relationship to the Mosaic *Torah* are that it does not seek to be an alternative nor a complement, but as being the only valid interpretation, and that it is this element that determines its literary genre (2000, 930).

On the other hand, this formal observation tends to underestimate the fact that by its exegesis the Temple Scroll *de facto* usurps the discursive space of its predecessors. Like Deuteronomy, which as its Latinised Greek name suggests is a second collection of laws based on the rewriting of law material originating in Exodus, Leviticus and Numbers, the Temple Scroll groups law material derived from its predecessors, and by orchestrating it as divine speech attributes to itself an authoritatively superior position. This is also reminiscent of the relationship between the different gospels of the early Christian tradition. They, too, attempted to usurp the discursive space of their predecessors without admitting that they were doing so. Tacitly, the Gospel of Matthew, for instance, purports to be an improved version of the Gospel of Mark owing to its rewriting and addition of new material. The same holds true for the Gospel of John, which also claims to be a superior gospel to the Synoptics thanks to rewriting, restructuring and the addition of new material.

Different gradations of textual authority

It is frequently argued that texts do not have authority unless people are prepared to allot it to them. That may well be true from a particular perspective, but it is not a full explanation, at least not in the sphere of religion, where some writings purport

---

6   For an extensive discussion of the authority of this writing, see Najman 1999.

to possess a special authority regardless of whether this authority is acknowledged or not. We have already referred to cases like the Book of Jubilees and the Temple Scroll, which both claim in different ways to be revelatory discourses. Although it is not intrinsic to religious writings to make such allegations, some do. For instance, when Paul disclaims ultimate responsibility for the creation of the letter at the beginning of Galatians by arguing that he is acting as an apostle 'not from men nor through man, but through Jesus Christ and God the Father' (Gal 1:1), the text ascribes authority to itself regardless of the intended audience's acknowledgement of this authority. Obviously, the writing presupposes that the intended audience shares this interpretation, but it cannot guarantee this reaction from its first recipients. Nor can it control any later receptions of the text.

In a different context, Kierkegaard uses the same rhetorical strategy – although in a far more complex manner in the pseudonymous orchestration of Johannes Climacus – in the *Philosophical Fragments*. The Kierkegaard of the *Fragments* is, in the figure of Climacus, an apostle who – like Paul – disclaims responsibility for his own statements by attributing authorship to the realm of the divinity (Petersen 2004, 55-58). Notwithstanding this disclaimer of responsibility for the discourse, Kierkegaard's tractate has not yet attained religious authoritative status, although naturally this has not prevented it from being acknowledged as part of the canon of Western philosophy.

Correspondingly, during the late Hellenistic period in particular the Neoplatonists claimed that the Homeric Songs were of divine origin, which made them an obvious choice for allegorical readings. The poems were thought to embody a deeper meaning pertaining to nature and the fate of the soul, to which one could gain access by subjecting them to allegorical readings (Lamberton 1986, 21). Although it might be misleading to speak of Homer – as common knowledge would have it – as 'the Bible of the Greeks' (for instance, Finkelberg 2003, 91), Homer was acknowledged by some as divine (*theios*). But this is not how the Homeric poems are perceived today. This is an important point, because it documents the social-relational nature of textual authoritativeness. Writings which were once ascribed religious authoritative status may lose that position at a later point in time, and may (in another cultural context) be interpreted in secular terms only. The opposite is of course also possible, and this is well-known in the cultural sphere. Works of art once regarded as pre-eminent parts of the cultural canon may eventually fall into oblivion. However, this does not prevent them from reappearing again at a later point in time and being included in the cultural canon once again.

Textual authority, however, is not only related to content and social acknowledgement by text users. It may also relate to form. If one particular form is authoritatively prevalent in a given culture, one way of ascribing authority to one's composition is by clothing it in that specific authoritative literary form. Perhaps this is even more so in cases when an exemplary form is further developed. Genre bending is an indication that the author wants to take the form to a hitherto unsurpassed level by slightly changing the literary paradigm of the predecessors. To do so is, of course, also to assert that one is capable of developing the existing literary models to new heights.

However obvious it is to discuss textual authority in terms of content, form and social acknowledgement, it would be misleading to narrow the discussion to this triangle only. Another important aspect pertains to the artefactual status of some writings. It may not be particularly prevalent, but simultaneous with or subsequent to their acknowledgement as authoritative writings certain texts are also revered as artefacts. The two dimensions are not necessarily contradictory to each other. The manner in which the Torah scroll is treated in the synagogue liturgy, for instance, where it is venerated both as an artefact and as a text regarded as the revelation of God, is a telling example. Here the two different aspects mutually enforce each other. There are comparable uses of the Bible as a sacred writing in the Orthodox churches as well as in the Roman Catholic Church. In other instances, however, a transition takes place which removes the focus from the text as such to its composition as an artefact, which may be attributed magical significance and therefore used in divinatory contexts. When, for instance, Homeric verses or biblical writings are turned into mantic instruments in the context of astragalomantics or rhapsodomantics, such a transition has taken place (van der Horst 1998, 151-66). It is not the text as such that is interpreted, but by means of divinatory manipulation excerpts taken from them become the medium of divine information which is regarded as conveying important directives to the mantic practitioner (see Petersen, forthcoming).

As already stated, there need not be a discrepancy between the two aspects, but the variety of gradations of authority makes it expedient to raise the question of what it means in a particular context to say that a specific writing is attributed authority. Regardless of the different aspects by which writings may be attributed authority, I shall nevertheless contend that they all mirror an attempt – whether deliberate or not – to impose constraints on the ongoing semiotic processes. Their authority is a reflection of their ascribed regulating function – whether by form, content, social acknowledgement or artefactual status – to determine the future processes of *semiosis*. They are meant to be determinative by their purported control over the continuous semiotic riverrun. From my perspective, canon formation is a further development of the same cultural mechanism to establish a closure of the uncontrollable semiotic processes. We shall, therefore, now proceed by turning our attention to the phenomenon of canon formation.

Different contemporary understandings of canonicity

If we return for a moment to the cultural canons of the Danish Ministry of Culture discussed above, it is interesting to see how the accompanying text defines canon as:

a collection of works which has become accepted and designated as the best or most genuine of its kind. For example, the texts of the Old and the New Testaments are the canon of the Christian church; the texts have been chosen as the best of many, many sacred texts. A canon can be used as a benchmark or a model, if for example, we want to assess the quality of something. And it can also offer guidance and provide bearings if we want to acquaint ourselves with something new. In other words, a canon contains the most important and most distinguished elements within its designated area (http://www.kum.dk/sw37439.asp).

Such an understanding of canonicity is fully compliant with the way the notion of canon is used in contemporary literary studies, where it designates a prescriptive list of reading for educated people; but the notion is distinctly different from the use of the concept in biblical studies and its affiliated disciplines. Here canonical and canon traditionally designate a clearly demarcated and closed corpus of writings with a textually fixed or, as a minimum, relatively stable wording, to which nothing can be added, and from which nothing can be detracted.[7] In addition, it is often surmised within this strand of scholarship that a canon is the product of a conscious decision, by which an authoritative body – be it political, religious or both – at a particular point in time has taken a firm decision on which texts to include and (equally significantly) which to exclude from the canon. It is easy to see how a particular understanding of the Christian formation of the New Testament canon lurks behind the notion.

Whether or not this conception is adequate for the assessment of Christian canon formation I shall leave open,[8] but it has definitely caused problems for the appraisal of the Rabbinic formation of a Jewish canon.[9] As long ago as the early 1960s, J.P. Lewis exposed the myth of the alleged Council of Jamnia – purportedly held around 90 CE and surmised to be the decisive point for the closure and determination of the Jewish canon – as a scholarly construct without historical foundation (Lewis 1964, 125-32). Despite his exposure of the 'Jamnia myth', the impact of this understanding continues to be reverberated by scholarly attempts to make a meeting at the Academy of Yavneh the decisive turning point for the closure and determination of the Jewish canon. In recent years, the problems pertaining to an understanding of Jewish formations of canons in lieu of a particular conception of the processes that led to the formation of the New Testament canon have grown even greater. During the past three decades and, particularly, in the wake of the general release of the unpublished Cave 4 material from Qumran in 1991, there has been a growing chorus of scholars who (based on its anachronistic nature) question the use of terms such as Bible and canon as appropriate for the study of Second Temple Judaism. Robert Kraft, for example, has rightly called

---

7   See, for instance, Talmon 2002, 12, and Brooke 2007, 81. A comparable notion with this understanding is found in Eugene Ulrich's distinction between a more broad and a more strict conception of canon, where the former designates notions of traditional, sacred texts attributed authority, and the latter includes the wider notions of a reflexive, articulated decision that specific texts and not others belong to a special category and are binding for all believers for all time (1999, 55).

8   For a critical assessment, see Markschies 2003, 192f.

9   Cf. Stern 2003, 229f, who maintains that: 'Further, it (sc. canon) is a literary term that is quintessentially Christian, and therefore almost inevitably bound to be problematic if applied to Jewish tradition. Most models of the *process* of canonisation are modelled upon the history of the Christian canon, that is, as being largely the result of a process of exclusion and as having been determined significantly, if not exclusively, by ideological/ theological considerations.' For a careful and recent appraisal of the formation of the Bible in Rabbinic Judaism, see Alexander 2007, and, particularly, his concluding seven theses, 79f.

attention to the fact that well into the fourth century there was no Bible in the sense of a set of sacred writings organised in physically unified collections. Prior to Constantine there is no evidence of single codices containing all the Scriptures that Eusebius and Athanasius considered authoritative (2007a, 10f.). In addition, the variegated textual material from the Dead Sea Scrolls (encompassing not only the texts found in 11 caves in the vicinity of Khirbet Qumran, but also the additional textual finds from the Judean Desert) bear witness to several facts that call the use of the terms canon and Bible prior to the late 1st century and early 2nd century CE into question.

First, it has become increasingly clear that we are facing a considerably more complex situation with regard to what was once recognised as 'biblical' writings among Jewish groups of antiquity. At the time of their composition, many texts which we have been accustomed to categorise as either apocryphal or pseudepigraphic may well have been regarded by some Jewish groups as being on a par with (if not surpassing) the allegedly biblical texts. Second, whereas a majority certainly considered many of the so-called biblical writings as authoritative during the last part of the Second Temple period, the writings had not yet developed into a closed set which was considered canonical. Nor had their wording been conclusively fixed. Third, it has become much more difficult to distinguish between reworkings or rewritings of biblical texts and the biblical writings proper, since the borders between these different categories are less evident than they have often have been regarded as being (Petersen 2007, 299-302). Additional arguments could easily be listed to question the use of the terms biblical and canonical with regard to an adequate assessment of Second Temple Judaism, but this will suffice to emphasise the anachronistic problems pertaining to the notions. The problematic nature of the terms has led Robert Kraft to call for a moratorium on the use of the term canon, even with regard to the pre-4th century:[10]

While there are no simple solutions and it may not be practical to eliminate the word "canon" from our scholarly language, perhaps it is appropriate to ask for a more reflective use of "canon" terminology in the study of the pre-4th century period – even a moratorium on its use – while we struggle towards more adequate and accurate modes of expression (2007b, http://ccat.sas.upenn. edu/rs/rak/SBL2007/canon. Cf. also Ulrich 1999, 54-61).

What has been said about the problems of using the term canon with regard to the study of Judaism prior to the 4th century CE also pertains to the examination of ancient Greek and Roman literature. Canon defined in terms of 'a reflexive, articulated

---

10   Unlike Kraft, I do not find it particularly problematic to speak of canon with regard to various forms of Judaism from the time of the late 1st to the early 2nd century CE, but that, of course, depends upon one's understanding of the term canon. Kraft's understanding seems heavily dependent upon a Christian coloured conception, which entails that the formation of a canon is the result of a deliberate decision taken by an official authoritative body. With regard to Rabbinic Judaism, see Alexander 2007, 72: 'The Rabbis established their canon of Sacred Scripture around 200 CE when the residual areas of doubt, such as the Song of Songs and Qoheleth, were finally resolved, and, indeed, a "Second Testament" (the Mishnah), which held the hermeneutical key to the "First", was promulgated.'

decision that specific texts and not others belong to a special category and are binding for all believers for all time' (Ulrich 1999, 55) is a Christian concept which is difficult to use outside and prior to the Christian context of the 4th century.[11] However, it is – as already indicated – expedient to move beyond this more narrow understanding of canonicity if we want to use the term as a cross-cultural category, and, secondarily, if we want to acknowledge those historical elements that eventually led to the formation of the New Testament canon of the 4th century.

To do this, we have to move backwards and examine the understanding of canonicity in antiquity. We shall see that the modern notion of canonicity within literary studies and embodied by the current Danish canon debate, although different from ancient conceptions, does have some intersections with the understanding that was prevalent in pre-Christian antiquity (Rutherford 1998, 3). In addition, this will lead us to an understanding of canonicity congruent with the reflections on textual authority and, ultimately, endorsing the viewpoint that canon formation is an excessive form of semiotic closure.

Ancient understandings of canonicity

If the notion of canon that is used in biblical scholarship and its affiliated disciplines is ultimately a Christian concept which is difficult to apply outside its context of origin, it may be helpful to consider the use of the concept in current literary studies. I have already referred to the fact that scholars of literature tend to use the term canon in the sense of a selected list of writers regarded as being prescriptive reading for anybody claiming to be well educated (cf. the now famous canon debate that followed in the wake of Harold Bloom's *The Western Canon* from 1995). Ultimately, this is also the understanding that underlies the recent Danish cultural canon project, in which canons are defined as 'a collection of works which has become accepted and designated as the best or most genuine of its kind.' Such a conception, however, is different from the ancient uses of the term canon.

Although there were ancient lists of the ten Attic orators, of ten historians, ten painters, ten sculptors etc., these lists were never designated as canons. Since the principle underlying such a list was a process of selection (*enkrinein*), the authors (but never the writings) included could be called the selected (*enkrithentes*) or, later, in Roman parlance *classici*, which ultimately referred to those who belonged to the first class (*primae classis*) in political and military language (Pfeiffer 1968, 207). It is, of course, this concept which lies behind the later talk about classics in the Renaissance and onwards, and which has

---

11   The first evidence of the specific Christian use of canon to denote the list of books of the Bible accepted by the Christian church as sacred scripture is found in Athanasius *de decr. syn. Nic.* 18 and his 39th Easter Letter; and the 59th Canon of the Council of Laodicea (cf. Nils Arne Pedersen's contribution to this book). Although Eusebius *H.E.* 4,25, 3 is often said to be the first instance in which the term canon is used in this specific Christian way (for instance, Pfeiffer 1968, 207), it is more likely to refer to a Christian rule of faith contained in various sacred scriptures of the Christian church, see the discussion in McDonald 1995, 51. Another important Christian use of the term canon was in the context of rules for the practice of penance, see Oppel 1937, 71f.

become closely connected with ideas about canonical authorships in modern literary studies. Complete catalogues of writers were developed in connection with endeavours of categorisation conducted at the great locations of learning such as the Library of Alexandria or the Library of Pergamum; but these catalogues were called *pinakes* in Greek or *indices* in Latin and never *canones* (Vardi 2005, 133). Greek and Latin simply did not have a word for the designation of selective lists. The modern usage of canon to denote such lists is, therefore, of a more recent date and goes back to David Ruhnken, who was the first to use the word in this sense in 1768 (Oppel 1937, 47).

Canōn in Greek, which originally meant a carpenter's rule or yardstick, and, therefore, could be used metaphorically to designate a rule, norm or standard of excellence, came to be used in a number of different domains such as philosophy, ethics, rhetoric and grammar (see Oppel 1937, 40-51). Common to all these different uses is the emphasis on a canon as something to be followed or imitated, since it provides an exemplary guideline for thinking, conduct, expression, style etc. What is canonical is also prescriptive for human thinking and acting. In the *Life of Moses*, for instance, Philo emphasises that Abraham, Isaac and Jacob are 'the model (*kanōn*) of the wisdom they have obtained' (1,76). They are clearly representatives of virtues that Philo's audience should endorse and express by their conduct. Similarly, in the realm of rhetoric Dionysius of Halicarnassus can point to Lysias as 'the best model (*kanōn*) for an Attic tongue' (*Lys.* 2). Be that as it may, the common feature that unites these different uses is the attempt to extrapolate a particular element or elements and make it/them determinative for continuous cultural development. They are accorded the role of prescriptive guidelines for the ongoing *semiosis*.

Although in the ancient uses of the term canon we do not find anything entirely equivalent to the modern notions of canon in literary studies, we do find an emphasis on something to be imitated and something ascribed authoritative status, which is held to be prescriptive for the realm to which it refers. Naturally, in this context it is also worth noticing the early Christian use of the term canon in the expression 'canon of truth' (*regula veritatis*) or 'canon of faith' (*regula fidei*) to designate the core of the Christian doctrine and held to be the standard of faith and practice in the early church (see, for instance, Irenaeus *Haer.* 1.9.4).

It is also true, as Amiel D. Vardi has argued, that despite the fact that we do not find the modern literary notion of canon as such:

the concept, or rather, cluster of kindred concepts, was not alien to the classical mentality, and was represented, for example, by the term 'classicus' coined by Aulius Gellius in the second century C.E., by terms such as 'ordo' or 'numerus' used by Quintilian, or by the Greek term *enkrithentes*, 'those judged worthy of inclusion' (2005, 132).

In addition, several such lists of names regarded as 'classical' have been preserved from antiquity, which is a further indication of the prevalence of the phenomenon (tables of such lists are found in Vardi 2005, 151).

It is not difficult to understand the development of the later specific Christian coinage of the term on this background, but if we narrow the understanding of canon and canonicity to this phenomenon only we miss the pervasiveness of the mechanisms that underlie any attempt to impose constraints on the processes of *semiosis*. Although the different lists of selected writers found among Greek and Roman authors were not designated by the term canon, we have ample evidence that they functioned as such – in other words, they were normative catalogues prescribing literary models to be imitated. In a recent article, Loveday Alexander has documented the way in which ancient medical literature similarly pays witness to the existence of a canonical body of writings concentrated around the legendary figure of Hippocrates. The Hippocratic corpus of writings – whatever the exact number of writings was – had the status of authoritative texts which every new generation of theorists and practitioners had to receive and appropriate in order to negotiate it afresh (2007, 151). Like the occurrence of hermeneutical activity prompted by the existence of authoritative writings, the medical tradition also had its example of *deuterosis*. In Late Antiquity Galen became the perceptual lens through which the Hippocratic tradition was received. Be that as it may, the existence of such lists amply proves that what later – in continuity of the Christian tradition – came to be identified with canon formation is something much more prevalent and foundational. It is an attempt – whether deliberate or not – to control the semiotic process by installing semiotic closures that are given the function of determining the subsequent development. This applies to all areas of life, as we have seen from various examples discussed above. Paradoxically, however, the signs contained in a given list or canon will – as long as this list or canon is recognised as authoritative – be reproduced by subsequent interpretations. But a canon cannot prevent the continuous riverrun of *semiosis*.

Conclusion

The aim of this essay has been to examine various gradations and understandings of authoritative writings and formations of canons. I have argued that there is an intrinsic relationship between the formation of canons and the allotment of authority to particular writings. Since textual authority is a notoriously slippery term, it has proved important to distinguish between four different grades of the phenomenon. Textual authority may be situated at the level of content, whereby a particular text disclaims responsibility for its own discursivisation by attributing authorship to the realm of the divinity. It also may be situated at the level of form, whereby a particular writing borrows from the authority attributed to a literary form by adopting a literary form that is accorded cultural significance in a particular social context. To use a genre that is ascribed authority is also to make a strong statement about the status of one's own text. Another important aspect has to do with the social acknowledgement of the authority of a given text by its recipients. Finally, authority may also be related to the artefactual status of writings, as can be seen, for example, in cases where texts are used in the context of divination. These four aspects of authority do not necessarily exclude each other, but they do often mutually enforce each other.

The ascription of authority to particular writings may be seen as an effort to influence the cultural process by extrapolating cultural elements as particularly determinative for the ongoing *semiosis*. This may be seen as a simpler form of canonisation. In accordance with Jonathan Z. Smith's reflections upon canonisation, I have argued that the selection of particular writings as being culturally prescriptive embodies an attempt to install a semiotic closure on the riverrun of semiosis. Whether in the form of a selection of a fixed set of writings or in the form of ascribing authority to one particular text, both phenomena reflect the attempt to control the processes of culture. Although different understandings of canonisation exist, they all share the element of a semiotic privileging and culturally regulating function. This is evident from ancient canons as well as contemporary ones like those which the Ministry of Culture and the Ministry of Education in Denmark have published recently.

Canons as formal selections of fixed sets of writings constitute a further development of authoritative texts. Between these two poles we find the more prevalent feature of open canons like the Graeco-Roman lists or the bibliography prepared by Kasper Bro Larsen, which contain a number of authoritatively recognised texts with regard to a particular segment of culture. Unlike the use of the term canon in the narrow (Christian-coloured) sense, an authoritative body has not officially selected these lists at a particular point in time, and nor have the lists been formally closed; but they mirror the same attempt to install barriers in the semiotic riverrun. The great paradox of ascribing authority to particular texts or selecting a number of writings as especially determinative for subsequent cultural development, however, is that the attempt to close the process of semiosis is bound to fail because new ruptures of interpretation will counter every closure. Hence, we are confronting a very basic cultural mechanism.

Finally, we have seen how the formations of canons and the allotment of authority to particular writings are intrinsically related to the forging of identity. Since authoritative texts and canons are attributed a culturally prescriptive or regulating function, they should determine the identity of those who adhere to them – whether it be a contemporary group of scholars attempting to study the discursive fight over religious texts in antiquity or an ancient community of christ-believers struggling to unfold the impacts of their new faith in various life situations. Canonisation and the allotment of authority to particular writings essentially involves the selection of a given number of signs ascribed a semiotic foundational character for the development of identity in a given culture. But like notation in music, this selection will result in more new instances of semiotic riverrun instead of having a constraining effect.

Bibliography

Alexander, Loveday 2007. 'Canon and Exegesis in the Medical Schools of Antiquity'. In: Philip S. Alexander and Jean-Daniel Kaestli (eds.), *The Canon of Scripture in Jewish and Christian Tradition. Le canon des Écritures dans les traditions juive et chrétienne.* Lausanne: Éditions du Zèbre, 115-153.

Alexander, Philip S. 2007. 'The Formation of the Biblical Canon in Rabbinic Judaism'. In: Philip S. Alexander and Jean-Daniel Kaestli (eds.), *The Canon of Scripture in Jewish and Christian Tradition. Le canon des Écritures dans les traditions juive et chrétienne.* Lausanne: Éditions du Zèbre, 57-80.

Assmann, Jan 2006. *Religion and Cultural Memory. Ten Studies.* (Cultural Memory in the Present). Stanford: Stanford UP.

Bloom, Harold 1995. *The Western Canon: the Book and the School of the Ages.* London: Macmillan.

Brooke, George J. 2005. 'Between Authority and Canon: The Significance of Reworking the Bible for Understanding the Canonical Process'. In: Esther G. Chazon, Devorah Dimant, and Ruth A. Clements (eds.), *Reworking the Bible: Apocryphal and Related Texts at Qumran.* (STDJ 58). Leiden/Boston: Brill, 85-104.

Brooke, George J. 2007. 'Canon in the Light of the Qumran Scrolls'. In: Philip S. Alexander and Jean-Daniel Kaestli (eds.), *The Canon of Scripture in Jewish and Christian Tradition. Le canon des Écritures dans les traditions juive et chrétienne.* Lausanne: Éditions du Zèbre, 81-98.

Cancik, Hubert 2003. 'Standardization and Ranking of Texts in Greek and Roman Institutions'. In: Margalit Finkelberg and Guy G. Stroumsa (eds.), *Homer, the Bible, and Beyond. Literary and Religious Canons in the Ancient World.* (Jerusalem Studies in Religion and Culture 2). Leiden/Boston: Brill, 117-130.

Finkelberg, Margalit 2003. 'Homer as a Foundation Text'. In: Margalit Finkelberg and Guy G. Stroumsa (eds.), *Homer, the Bible, and Beyond. Literary and Religious Canons in the Ancient World.* (Jerusalem Studies in Religion and Culture 2). Leiden/Boston: Brill, 75-96.

Horst, Pieter van der 1978. 'Sortes: Sacred Books as Instant Oracles in Antiquity'. In: Leonard V. Rutgers, Pieter W. van der Horst, Henriëtte W. Havelaar, Lieve Teugels (eds.), *The Use of Sacred Books in the Ancient World.* (Contributions to Biblical Exegesis & Theology 22). Leuven: Peeters, 143-173.

Käsemann, Ernst 1970. *Das Neue Testament als Kanon: Dokumentation und kritische Analyse zur gegenwärtigen Diskussion,* Göttingen: Vandenhoeck & Ruprecht.

Kraft, Robert A. 2007a. 'Para-mania: Beside, Before and Beyond Bible Studies'. *Journal of Biblical Literature,* 126, 5-27.

Kraft, Robert A. 2007b. 'Finding Adequate Terminology for "Pre-Canonical" Literatures'. http://ccat.sas.upenn.edu/rs/rak/SBL2007/canon (seen 06.07.2008).

Lamberton, Robert 1986. *Homer the Theologian. Neoplatonist Allegorical Reading and the Growth of the Epic Tradition.* Berkeley/Los Angeles/London: University of California Press.

Lewis, J.P. 1964. 'What Do We Mean by Jabneh?' *Journal of Bible and Religion,* 32, 125-132.

Markschies, Christoph 2003. 'The Canon of the New Testament in Antiquity. Some New Horizons for Future Research'. In: Margalit Finkelberg and Guy G. Stroumsa (eds.), *Homer, the Bible, and*

Beyond. Literary and Religious Canons in the Ancient World. (Jerusalem Studies in Religion and Culture 2). Leiden/Boston: Brill, 175-194.

Martinéz, Florentino Garzía 2000. 'Temple Scroll'. In: Lawrence H. Schiffman and James C. VanderKam (eds.), *Encyclopedia of the Dead Sea Scrolls.* Oxford: Oxford UP, 927-933.

McDonald, Lee Martin 2007 (1995). *The Biblical Canon. Its Origin, Transmission, and Authority.* Peabody, Massachusets: Hendrickson.

Najman, Hindy 1999. 'Interpretation as Primordial Writing: Jubilees and Its Authority Conferring Strategies'. *Journal for the Study of Judaism*, 30, 379-410.

Oppel, Herbert 1937. *KANΩN. Zur Bedeutungsgeschichte des Wortes und seiner lateinischen Entsprechungen (Regula-Norma).* (Philologus, Supplement vol. 30, no. 4). Leipzig: Dietrich'sche Verlagsbuchhandlung.

Petersen, Anders Klostergaard 2004. '*Philosophical Fragments* in a New Testament Perspective'. In: Nils Jørgen Cappelørn, Hermann Deuser and Jon Stewart together with Christian Tolstrup (eds.), *Kierkegaard Studies Yearbook 2004*, Berlin/New York: De Gruyter, 39-62.

Petersen, Anders Klostergaard 2007. 'Rewritten Bible as a Borderline Phenomenon – Genre, Textual Strategy, or Canonical Anachronism'. In: Anthony Hilhorst, Émile Puech and Eibert Tigchelaar (eds.), *Flores Florentino. Dead Sea Scrolls and Other Early Jewish Studies in Honour of Florentino Garzía Martínez.* (Journal for the Study of Judaism Supplement Series 122). Leiden/Boston: Brill, 285-306.

Petersen, Anders Klostergaard 2008. 'The Naturalness of Rhapsodomantics'. In: Anders Lisdorf and Kirstine Munk (eds.), *Unveiling the Hidden – Contemporary Approaches to the Study of Divination.* (Religion and Society). Berlin/New York: De Gruyter. Forthcoming.

Pfeiffer, Rudolf 1968. *History of Classical Scholarship. From the Beginnings to the End of the Hellenistic Age.* Oxford: Clarendon.

Rutherford, Ian 1998. *Canons of Style in the Antonine Age. Idea-Theory in its Literary Context.* (Oxford Classical Monographs). Oxford: Clarendon.

Smith, Jonathan Z. 1978. 'Sacred Persistence: Towards a Redescription of Canon'. In: William Scott Green (ed.), *Approaches to Ancient Judaism. Theory and Practice.* (Brown Judaic Studies 1). Missoula, Montana: Scholars Press, 11-28.

Snoek, Joannes Augustinus Maria 1998. 'Canonization and Decanonization: An Annotated Bibliography'. In: Arie van der Kooij and Karel van der Toorn (eds.), *Canonization and Decanonization. Papers Presented to the International Conference of the Leiden Institute for the Study of Religions (LISOR), Held at Leiden 9-10 January 1997.* (Numen 82). Leiden/Boston/Köln: Brill, 435-506.

Stern, David 2003. 'On Canonization in Rabbinic Judaism'. In: Margalit Finkelberg and Guy G. Stroumsa (eds.), *Homer, the Bible, and Beyond. Literary and Religious Canons in the Ancient World.* (Jerusalem Studies in Religion and Culture 2). Leiden/Boston: Brill, 227-252.

Stroumsa, Guy 1998. 'The Christian Hermeneutical Revolution and its Double Helix'. In: Leonard V. Rutgers, Pieter W. van der Horst, Henriëtte W. Havelaar, Lieve Teugels (eds.), *The Use of Sacred Books in the Ancient World.* (Contributions to Biblical Exegesis & Theology 22). Leuven: Peeters, 9-28.

Talmon, Shemaryahu 2002. 'The Crystallization of the 'Canon of Hebrew Scriptures' in the Light of Biblical Scrolls from Qumran'. In: Edward D. Herbert and Emanuel Tov (eds.), *The Bible as Book. The Hebrew Bible and the Judaean Desert Discoveries*. London: The British Library & Oak Knoll Press, 5-20.

Ulrich, Eugene 1999. *The Dead Sea Scrolls and the Origins of the Bible*. (Studies in the Dead Sea Scrolls and Related Literature). Grand Rapids, Michigan/Cambridge – Leiden/Boston/Köln: Eerdman – Brill.

Vardi, Amiel D. 2003. 'Canons of Literary Texts at Rome'. In: Margalit Finkelberg and Guy G. Stroumsa (eds.), *Homer, the Bible, and Beyond. Literary and Religious Canons in the Ancient World*. (Jerusalem Studies in Religion and Culture 2). Leiden/Boston: Brill, 131-152.

'An Easy Introduction to the Danish Cultural Heritage'. http://www.kum.dk/sw37439.asp (seen 05.06.2008) 'Rapport fra Udvalget til styrkelse af historie i folkeskolen'. www.uvm.dk/06/documents/historie_000pdf (seen 05.06.2008). '35 milepæle i demokratikanon'. http://www.uvm.dk/08.dk.htm?menuid=6410 (seen 05.06.2008)

NORMATIVITY AND THE DYNAMIC OF MUTUAL AUTHORISATION

THE RELATIONSHIP BETWEEN 'CANONICAL' AND 'NON-CANONICAL' WRITINGS

Jesper Hyldahl

Introduction

In the earliest Christian church two types of written material were mutually dependent on each other. One group consisted of scriptures which could be rewritten only very little or not at all, and which became representatives of textual stability owing to their increasing authoritative status. The other group consisted of texts which could be rewritten, containing less binding common values defining Christian identity. These texts, which were not eventually included in the Christian canon, were characterised by textual fluidity. They were subject to moderation and rewriting, and were adjusted to suit varying situations and new social or theological concerns. So these writings were transmitted in a similar way to oral traditions.

The Christian Bible came into being in the interplay between orality and literacy. What this means with regard to the questions of authority and normativity will be discussed below. But first a few general remarks on orality, literacy and interpretation are appropriate.

Orality and literacy

The alphabet and writing are the most important and far-reaching technological inventions in the history of humankind. As the use of writing became increasingly widespread in the Greek world around the 6th century BC, and the manner of cultural transmission adjusted to accommodate this new technology, there were a number of wide-ranging consequences. Literacy made certain factors appear which were not strongly articulated under the previous purely oral culture. These were: a more efficient way of accumulating knowledge, a stronger concept of history and tradition, and a greater focus on or perhaps even a transformation in human consciousness.[1] Literacy shaped the human mind, so that the listener or reader, especially in the poetic performance – in comparison to the situation in oral cultures – was in a better position critically to distinguish between the self and the things told. This is owing to the fact that language, because of its reification in writing and its visibility, could more easily be used as an object of analysis and critical reflection. This also led to the well-known distinction between

---

1   See e.g. Havelock 1963; Ong 2002.

mythos and logos, or poetical narrative and logical argumentation, between fables and truth, between poetry and philosophy. But it also caused speculation regarding various levels of communication, operating with various distinctions between language and reality, thereby emphasising the necessity of critical interpretation. Hermeneutics as philosophy was born.

From Homeric psyche to Platonic mind

Prior to the written narrative, poets and rhapsodes were bearers of the cultural canon and thus responsible for the ongoing transmission of the Greek *paidaia*. When using the term canon in this context, it appears that canon does not designate a fixed list of texts but instead applies to a set of common values that were important to the coherence of a well-defined society. The Greek canon was communicated orally from generation to generation, often through professional performance in the Greek theatre. Without any writing, Greek poetry existed only potentially in people's memories. According to the conventions of oral communication, the content of this canon was marked by a high degree of elasticity, constantly being adjusted according to the common opinion and the audience's expectations. The audience mirrored themselves in the performing characters. As part of the social convention, the audience often surrendered to the poetic performance and were formed by the story being told, thereby becoming part of a common history.

One consequence of this is that the Homeric psyche was defined by the imitation of poetical experience, being unable to acknowledge the distinction between the tradition and the self. The sense of objectivity was completely absent. The Homeric mind did not possess the tools that made this distinction recognisable.

Mimetic self-identification with tradition in oral culture was the greatest obstacle to a philosopher like Plato. Trying to break with the poet's monopoly, critics like Plato would maintain that the audience was kept hostage in the poetic performance through the power of imitation (*mimesis*), unintentionally assuming that what they heard was the truth. Nothing could be more wrong according to Plato, for whom poetry was just an image of the world of phenomena, instability and perception and thus nothing more than an image of an image of the eternal world of truth and stability. Plato's dialectical method represents a rejection of the legitimacy of the process of mimesis in which the self is abandoned in favour of poetic manipulation making the listener identical to another existence. So Plato expelled the poets from the ideal state. In the early Christian era Plato's position seems to have been echoed in the Church Fathers, according to whom the Christians were not allowed to take part in public performances. As the majority of the Christians were illiterate, the manipulative aspect of the performance could not be controlled.

For Plato poetry could not adequately represent truth – at best it was just a second-degree imitation of the truth. As Havelock has argued, writing was the invention that enabled a change in human consciousness, of which Plato was a manifestation and which enabled Plato to criticise the role of the poets. Given the fundamental impact of the technology of writing on his own mind, it may seem like a paradox that Plato remained critical of written language and for several reasons actually preferred spoken language. As the human mind is liberated from the poetic experience and becomes capable of critical reflection, the concept of logos is reinterpreted pertaining to truth, logic, arguments, concepts and absolute norms, and not to single events in the narrative plot. In pre-literate cultures logos was indistinguishable from mythos. Writing makes language seem like a visible phenomenon, the narrative in its literary form being a stable object that the reader can push back and place at a distance. It can thus be an object for analysis, reflection and critical interpretation. By moving backwards and forwards in the text, it can answer the questions that are being asked.

It was the effects of the technology of writing that prevented its immediate appropriation in the mimetic character of poetic performance. Thus, literacy creates two associated phenomena. On the one hand the shift from pure orality to literacy enabled the human mind to be more conscious and analytical. The human psyche was redefined and conceived as an independent thinking mind. The Muses, who were the ultimate authorisers of the poetical tradition, were then replaced by the human psyche and thinking as the guarantee of truth. On the other hand, from this transition also followed the idea of literary standardisation and the understanding of text and narrative as something referring to the distant past, now also expressing archaeological knowledge without immediate actuality.

Thus, the popularity of writing was the beginning of a process of decisive separation between the cultural canon and the self-understanding of the literate mind. How to deal with this cultural dissonance soon became an urgent problem for philosophers and literate people. It is notable that the alliance between the reflecting mind and the process of textual standardisation equipped philosophers for semiotic theorising and hermeneutic speculation.

Critical interpretation

As long as written narratives were subject to the conventions of oral communication, the need for critical hermeneutic theories was not urgent. Written narratives that were communicated orally were easily changed and adjusted according to the expectation of the audience. When first written down (or transcribed), an equilibrium exists between words and the reader's interpretation of reality because the words in their former oral communication have occasioned a reality-creating process. Reality is in this sense always interpreted reality as it is formed by language. As long as the written text was adjusted according to oral structures, the equilibrium continued to exist.

However, texts with a high cultural and literary impact soon achieved a normative and authoritative status within society that made continuous adjustments equally difficult. Textual fixation became part of the picture, and from now on texts were consciously preserved for posterity intact and unchanged. This consciousness of textual standardisation occurred very early with the epics of Homer (4th century BC) (Lange 2004, 54), much later with the Jewish scriptures (1st-2nd century AD), and even later with the Christian scriptures (late 2nd century).

The implicit appropriation characteristic of oral communication was then replaced by minor moments of irritation, by fractures and inconveniences in the mind. A gap between the narrative and the reader's opinion becomes increasingly conspicuous. Whereas orality by its very nature surmounts such a gap, writing and textual fixation threatened to make poetry obsolete. As all language communication implies interpretation, any meeting between text and reader, between spoken word and audience, involves an interpretative process. In comparison to a poetic mind, it is advantageous to the literate mind to use analysis to make this interpretation critical, intending through conscious hermeneutic strategies to harmonise the tension between word and reality.

Stoic hermeneutics: Problem solving

Stoic philosophers realised that the Homeric epic was an inseparable part of Greek education and culture. It became urgent to justify an ongoing use of old fables and stories, even though from a first-hand impression these stories seemed to contradict Stoic philosophy. But for the Stoics, poetic language was the best means of describing the real concern of Stoic philosophy: "things divine and human". The Stoics developed a theory on language and interpretation, including a triadic semantic distinction between things signified (σημαινόμενα), signifier (σημαίνον) and sound and things existing (τυγχάνον) (Sextus Em. *Adv. Math.* 7,11f.). Things signified are the actual thing indicated, then functioning as the incorporeal link between two physical phenomena, that is, the sound and the existing, actual thing. This theory was apparently inspired by Aristotle, but while Aristotelians argued that words always depend on cultural convention and thus are merely referential, the Stoics could point towards the alliance of perception and the concept of logos, with logos ensuring that impressions imprinted on the soul (καταληπτικά φαντασία) reflect a true conformity between sound, signification and actual things.[2] Ideally, this results in a direct proportion between expression and meaning so that words have a natural connection to their reference.

These linguistic semantics worked well when it came to propositions and proper (κύριος) language, that is, statements that can be judged either true or false. But with non-propositional statements such as poetic language, this natural relationship was replaced in favour of a figurative understanding (κατάχρησις). Poetic language merely involved the imitation of real things, constituting a turn away (τρόπος) from the literal discourse to a literary code in the form of an allegorical composition. Interpreted according to the right philosophical code, it is possible to make poetical statements meaningful.

---

2   See M. Irvine 1987, 40ff, for instance.

Interpreters of Homer such as the Stoic Cornutus and the Stoic-inspired Heraclite, both apparently from the first century CE, were able to make Homer legitimate reading by using Stoic semiotics. Cornutus maintained that poets like Homer had unintentionally used very old etymologies in poems, and Heraclite said that Homer had intended to conceal the truth in poetic language. The de-etymologising or de-allegorising process should make it possible to reach the truth underneath poetic language. The fact that this truth merely confirmed the philosophy of the stoic reader is of no surprise, and the Stoics could thus argue that their philosophy was the oldest and most original of all the competing philosophical systems.

Writing had made problematic the natural connection between sign and thing, between language and its external reference. As long as a message was communicated through purely oral channels, the natural connection was maintained. But when written down, a separation between language and reference was inevitable. This phenomenon pertains not only to the transition from pure orality to the spread of the technology of writing in 8th-6th century BC, but also to the composition of New Testament literature.

Ancient hermeneutics asked for the underlying meaning of the text. Old hermeneutics primarily involved problem solving, intending to harmonising between differing opinions, explaining that under the textual surface the hidden truth or authorial intention corresponded to and confirmed contemporary knowledge. However, when Stoic semiotics started to influence fractions of Jewish and Christian theologians, it took an interesting turn. Sometimes it was just not possible to refer to hidden meanings. Scriptural chestnuts, for instance anthropomorphic and anthropopathic language about God, were then explained by sophistically involving the reader as a fundamental player in the hermeneutical process.

Taking the reader into perspective, Philonic hermeneutics emphasised sociopolitical functionality, maintaining that biblical texts did not always describe reality but demanded ethical decisions from their readers. Later on, Clement of Alexandria and Origen used similar arguments in order to defend the biblical sayings. Some texts cannot claim meaning on their own terms, but can potentially become actualised and create meaning in so far as meaning emerges in the interplay between text and reader.

Authorisation

If texts could not fulfil the audience's expectations and confirm their opinions, they were in danger of becoming irrelevant and forgotten. Most texts actually became redundant and were left behind. Only texts in which the reader could meaningfully mirror his or her own world would survive the historical process of forgetfulness. Texts survive either because of their relevance (by being accommodated to new challenges and sometimes by being placed in libraries) or because of their authority. However, the claim of authority is always questionable and cannot be taken for granted.

Homer, Plato, the Jewish and the Christian Bible represent authoritative traditions for their respective users. With regard to the Christian Bible, we need to address the question of authorisation and ask who is doing the authorising and how the Bible is authorised.

Is formal authorisation by church leaders (i.e. bishops) sufficient? Or is the Bible authorised by God or the Holy Spirit because of its non-formal, rhetorical claim to be or to represent the word of God (cf. Wolterstorff 2004). It has also been suggested that the Bible is authorised by its common use in the Christian community (cf. Brenneman 1997, 136-147). But speaking of such non-formal circumstances, pointing solely to the communal use of the Bible seems to be unsatisfying. The Bible is just authorised by communal use or by being the voice of God to the extent that we are able to accept it as such. There is another phenomenon of authorisation at play.

For the Bible and other normative texts, Brenneman seems right to point out 'that "the Bible is adaptable for life" remains the key to its ongoing canonical authority' (p. 25). The Bible's normativising function should not be reduced to guidelines for faith and religious practices, but must also have something to do with the formation of a person's whole identity and world of thought. This being the case, one must consider whether the Bible can maintain its authoritative status at all if the Bible's narrated world and the reader's world cannot relate to one another. A balance must exist between this individual appropriation and communal use. In an era largely influenced by oral structures, the common may have had precedence over individual autonomy because of the process of mutual identification. When literacy became widespread, the situation may have changed in favour of individuality.

The dynamic of mutual authorisation

An interpretation may make good sense when analysed from the perspective of text and reader or the perspective of text, reader and author, but may fail completely when analysed in connection with the actual reader's understanding of reality and the world around us. The Bible can be read meaningfully according to text-reader-author approaches. However, if it intends to confirm its authoritative and normative legitimacy, the interpretation needs to relate meaningfully to our understanding of reality. Even though it does not explain everything, it must at least give something to or say something essential about the reader's world. The Bible seems to allow very different readings depending on how one perceives the relationship between meaning and expression. A fundamentalist orientation is able to explain cosmological details, while others in the tradition of dialectical theology would argue that the Bible is very useful, and indeed almost indispensable, when a person hopes to achieve an authentic existence.

Maintaining the binding religious authority of the Bible, believing that the text communicates God's will, creates a tension between the Bible's narrated world and secular belief systems, i.e. the prevailing cultural opinion. The fact that the Bible's actual words are believed to represent God's will makes the Jewish and Christian Bible different from the Greek cultural canon. The tension can be equally outspoken in both environments, but in comparison to the Greek canon the Bible will often try to restrict or revise secular thinking. Believing that the Bible does not just represent but actually *is* the word of God, the fundamentalist camp expresses the revising argument against secular thinking in its highest degree, whereas other groups act more openly.

In any case, their acceptance of the text's authoritative status means that Christian readers will always try hard to harmonise not only contradictory statements within the Bible but also the textual expression of the Bible to match their own understanding. From that perspective, the Bible works differently from other kinds of literature. However, this harmonising tendency occurs not because readers make the Bible's world into their own, but because of a dialectical exchange of imagery and knowledge. For that matter, reading involves interpretation both of the textual expression and of the reader's understanding and prejudgements which the reader is prepared to risk, eventually resulting in a successful "fusion of horizons", to speak in Gadamerian terms. Without success, the normative status would be questionable. Or in other words: we anticipate that because they are normative the texts will correspond to our horizon of understanding, that is, to our prejudgements or intertextual framework, not least if the texts have already helped to form our horizon. If they fail to correspond, the interpretation continues to and fro, ideally until a kind of equilibrium has been reached.

Sometimes readers felt the need to comment on their reading experiences and publish their interpretations. These interpretations were made manifest in commentaries on authoritative writings, in handbooks, and in alternative quasi-liturgical writings such as apocryphal texts, martyr literature and new poetry. Unexplained elements or 'gaps' in the narrative provided a resource for literary creativity. For instance, later readers wanted to know what Jesus told his disciples when he met them after his resurrection. Especially Gnostic Christians, to maintain a higher spiritual teaching of Jesus, used this unexplained element over and over again. Another question was where Jesus' so-called brothers came from, granted that Mary had continued to be a virgin. Owing to their less authoritative (or perhaps unauthoritative) status, 'non-canonical' writings, which were the result of such gaps, could more easily be subjected to continuous adjustment and rewriting. Such textual production helped other readers in the community to put into perspective texts composed in a historical situation different from their own, thereby minimising the cultural dissonance between the text's world and the reader's. Setting the Lutheran principle of *sola scriptura* aside, these alternative texts, in combination with authoritative writings and other factors, helped to form the audience or reader. Rewritings and apocrypha belonged to the frame of intertextuality – a reservoir that is hermeneutically activated through reading or listening. So religious thoughts are not only based on the biblical canon but also depend on the existence and use of other writing belonging to tradition. One can try to give it a fresh start, as the reformers did in order to obliterate the impact of the Roman Catholic dogma by emphasising the principles of *sola scriptura* (Luther), the discernment of mind (Erasmus), or the fact that God spoke directly in scripture (Calvin). However, this seems just to create new traditions making the ongoing assertion of these principles virtually impossible.

For the same reason, the practical usage of alternative text forms contributes to the ongoing normative status of formally authoritative texts. As such, alternative, more fluent texts also have some authority because they are controlled by the texts they interpret or to which they are related. However, the question is whether these texts also have normative status. Given their undeniable impact on the beliefs of the community, one is tempted to allow these texts some normativity, perhaps to a lesser degree. But seen from the perspective of the religious community, the users probably did not regard these texts as normative because textual stability only applies to the group of texts being interpreted – not to interpretations or rewritten texts.

Inspired by George G. Brooke (2007), who has recently discussed the canonical processes, this kind of relationship between canonical writing and the various phenomena of interpretation can be categorised as a dynamic of mutual authorisation:

The study of canonical processes is never solely about how the beautifully leather-bound Bible came to sit on the church lectern, but about how text and interpretation inform one another, providing a dynamic of mutual authorisation in which the interpretative techniques used to relate each to the other are the key to permitting both the ongoing life of a text composed long ago and the open-endedness of the interpretation.

This mutual authorisation pertains particularly to textually fixed narratives. In the former purely oral culture, in which listeners often tended to identify themselves with the characters in the performance, listeners did not know of any critical interpretation. For an illiterate (Homeric) mind, internal irregularities within the narrative or even contradictions would not be acknowledged or regarded as a problem. The story was meant to accommodate the audience's expectations, and was not really a challenge. An outstanding disproportion between performance and audience would be seen as a disaster excluding the required identification process.

But with textual standardisation the tension between the text's world and the reader's world creates a dilemma with regard to authority. This dilemma cannot be solved solely by the claim of authority (the voice of God, use by the community or the authority of the church leaders), but must also include personal interpretation and appropriation and thus reach a harmonious status when it comes to the reader's intertextual framework.

The idea of mutual authorisation implies that interpretations are also authorised. As in the case of the Bible, the same questions about on authorisation can be posed. Is an interpretation formally authorised by the biblical text being interpreted, by divine inspiration, by faith, or by communal agreement? Or how much depends on our environment, that is, the convention of the Christian community? And who controls this?

As far as interpretation is concerned, it is also necessary to consider the extent to which the ongoing authorisation of an interpretation depends on its ability to relate meaningfully to the life of the individual reader or listener.

Closedness and open-endedness

It is the open-endedness of interpretation that makes it reasonable for a canon to consist of a closed list of specific writings. Scriptural diversity means that scriptural meaning is never restricted to just one interpretation. Instead, it is always open-ended and able to adapt to a variety of different life situations and opinions. It is 'a prism through which light from the different aspects of the Christian life is refracted' (Child 1992, 672).

However, is the divine message in fact open-ended? It was probably never intended to be so. The Bible is diverse and its interpretation open-ended only from a literary perspective. Composed according to oral structures and transmitted orally, diversity was never a problem. Open-endedness is an unintended consequence of the fact that the biblical canon consists of texts that are generally speaking the products of a history of orality. Only a mind of literacy acknowledges that biblical texts represent a variety of discursive manifestations of the Christ event or of God's acting upon humankind. Only the literate mind would see the problem of unity, arguing that the New Testament texts are all diverse discursive examples pointing to a single common thing: God incarnated and faith in Jesus Christ.

Be that as it may, even though diversity was never intended it turned out to be advantageous for the Bible's ongoing claim to authority (though some would regard diversity as a weakness). In antiquity Clement of Alexandria took the advantage of the open-endedness of biblical writings to its extreme. According to Clement, the qualitative difference between human discourse and divine ineffability prevents a straightforward description of the ultimate truth. The Christian truth could only be expressed indirectly or metaphorically in many different discourses, not just in specific Christian texts but also, owing to divine inspiration, in other kinds of textual production such as Greek poetry, philosophy and other sorts of pagan literature.

Conclusion: Other aspects of the advantage of open-endedness and self-contradiction

When the texts of the Bible were first written and in their early transmission history, they were probably regarded as literally true in terms of the reader's understanding. For most people, the text encompassed just one level of meaning. In its early orally inspired transmission history there were no self-contradictory statements in the Christian Bible. Or at least, they were not recognised or regarded as a problem. Contradictions and diversity are results of literacy. Another reason for scriptural diversity must be found in the process of canonisation itself. The New Testament canon was not composed for anti-heretical theological concerns, but because of the texts' widespread and recognised liturgical use. Adolph von Harnack's influential hypothesis that the New Testament canon is compiled with the aim of outmanoeuvring the heresies is doubtful. The question of universality carried greater weight than the problem of theological diversity.

Scriptural diversity is an obstacle to the literate mind. For instance, as soon as the New Testament texts achieved a formal authoritative status some time in the middle of the second century, internal contradictions became a problem. All the stories in the Christian Bible could not be equally true as the voice of God. Marcion was among the first theologians to emphasise that the Jewish Bible radically contradicts the new Gospel and Paul's letters. Tatian acknowledged the problem of differing versions of the Gospel narrative, making his Gospel harmony, *Diatesseron*. Such activities pertain only to a literate mind.

However, without scriptural diversity the history of Christianity would probably have been very different. Accommodation to differing historical circumstances and secular thinking seems to depend on the literary nature of the Christian Bible.

Contradictory statements in the Bible and many truth claims are perhaps the greatest advantage of the Bible. They make it easier for us to relate to a diverse divine history, because we ourselves are not coherent stories but consist of bits and pieces. The narratives mirror the existential complexity of our lives and perhaps of cultural diversity.

Contradictory statements also make the Bible anti-fundamentalist and anti-ideological by its literary nature. As Brenneman (139) has put it: 'Any canon that does not contain within it the seeds of its own deconstruction will become a tool of ideological and political brutality.' The literary characteristic erects a barrier against any kind of fundamentalism, either political or religious, not regarding modernity and secularism as paradigms contradicting Christian thoughts. Since the first Gnostics there are examples of how secularism and the Bible have worked together, whereas other ancient Christians were apparently more reluctant to accept the connection. This stance seems to depend on the degree of authority in question, and on whether this authority is legitimised verbatim on the textual surface or with reference to a hidden meaning. But even with hidden meanings, the Bible seems to contradict the idea that the text must be univocally meaningful. Its equivocal literary level (the textual surface) always makes doubtful the hermeneutically constructed meaning underneath the actual words. As a result, the rejection of other possible interpretations of reality continues to be problematic from a biblical point of view. If this is regarded as a negative implication of the open-endedness of the biblical canon, the positive aspect of the open-endedness is that it allows new interpretations and ongoing actualising adjustments.

Bibliography

Brenneman, James E. 1997. *Canons in Conflicts. Negotiating Texts in True and False Prophecy*. Oxford: Oxford University Press.

Brooke, George. J. 2007. 'Canonisation Processes of the Jewish Bible in the Light of the Qumran Material'. Paper presented in Aarhus 2007. Will be published in a future volume of the series *Early Christianity in the Context of Antiquity*.

Child, Brevard S. 1992. *Biblical Theology of the Old and New Testament*. London: SCM Press.

Havelock, Eric A. 1963. *Preface to Plato*. Oxford: Basil Blackwell.

Irvine, Martin 1987. 'Interpretation and the semiotics of allegory in Clement of Alexandria, Origen, and Augustine'. *Semiotica*, 63(1/2), 33-71.

Lange, Armin 2004. 'From Literature to Scripture: The Unity and Plurality of the Hebrew Scriptures in Light of the Qumran Library. In: C. Helmer and C. Landmesser (eds.), *One Scripture or Many?* Oxford: Oxford University Press, 51-107.

Ong, Walter J. 2002. *Orality and Literacy*. London: Routledge.

Wolterstorff, Nicholas 2004. 'The Unity Behind the Canon'. In: C. Helmer and C. Landmesser (eds.), *One Scripture or Many?* Oxford: Oxford University Press, 217-232.

NORMATIVITY, IDEOLOGY, AND RECEPTION IN PAGAN AND CHRISTIAN ANTIQUITY: SOME OBSERVATIONS

Karla Pollmann

Conceptual frameworks[1]

Normativity can be defined as the claim to form an absolute standard, a 'rule' (*norma*) with overall validity. It does not refer in a descriptive way to reality as it is, but in a prescriptive way to reality as it ought to be. Thus, it comprises statements with a prescriptive aim of how to act correctly, in the form of precepts, prohibitions, and duties. Such norms are not absolute, but depend on cultural and historical contexts; thus they change during history, although the norms themselves claim absolute, 'transcendent' validity. A useful distinction can be made between meta-ethics, which asks questions like 'what do ethical words and statements mean?', or 'how can ethical claims be justified?'; and normative ethics, which is interested in 'what state-of-affairs is good or desirable?' and 'is a certain kind of action morally right?' Analogously, meta-theology investigates, for instance, 'how does religious language function?' or 'how are theological claims to be justified?', whereas normative theology focuses on questions like 'Does God exist?', 'What is God's nature?', or 'What is the role of Jesus?'

As long ago as antiquity there were attempts to give reasons for the timeless and obliging relevance of certain values or norms. A prominent example would be Plato's theory of forms (Schäfer 2007, 160f.), or the Classical Roman legal theorists of the 2nd and 3rd centuries CE who intended to justify law philosophically as the binding transmission of what is good and right (Ulpian, referring to Celsus, *Digestae* 1,1,1 pr. *ius est ars boni et aequi*; see also Cicero, *De legibus* 2,61 *naturam, quae norma legis est*). Nevertheless, there is a necessary tension between norms and historical change. In a certain given group, norms are seen as the reason and justification to act, to believe and to feel in a certain way. Typical areas where normativity features prominently are ethics as a theoretically founded prescription of how to act rightly (Broadie 1991; Cicero, *Pro Murena* 2 about Cato *vitam ad certam rationis normam dirigenti*; at Sidonius Apollinaris, *Epistulae* 6,1,4 the addressee is praised as *norma morum*), law and legislation as a complex of acknowledged norms comprising reality as a whole (Cicero, *De oratore* 2,178 *iuris norma*; Rainer 1993), language (Coseriu 1970), and religion (Young 1997).

1   I researched some of the material mentioned here in connection with my co-editorship and contributions to an interdisciplinary project directed by Oda Wischmeyer, Erlangen, which will result in a *Begriffslexikon der Hermeneutik* (Berlin 2009), to which various theological sub-disciplines, Classics, literary theory and linguistics will contribute. Moreover, this research is also an aspect of the international and interdisciplinary project under my direction on the reception of Augustine from 430 to 2000, which is being generously funded by the Leverhulme Trust (see www.st-and.ac.uk/classics/after-augustine).

Sometimes *regula* can be used as a synonym for *norma*, for instance at Pliny, *Epistula* 9,26,8 Demosthenes is called a *norma oratoris et regula*, and then particularly in Christianity the important notion of the *regula fidei* (first at Tertullian, *De praescriptione haereticorum* 13.1; Pollmann 1996, 33-38) as the norm for all exegetical endeavour and dogmatic speculation. The other, even more important norm for Christianity is Jesus Christ both as an ethical model for or teacher of a good life and, soteriologically, as the true human end (Phil 2:5-8; Rom 6:3-11; Kotva 1996, especially 78-90), because he is the son of God (Matth 3:13-17). The eschatological structure of the Christian faith turns any of its moral norms (for instance Luke 6:36, which says that we should be ourselves as merciful as God, or the Golden Rule in Matth 7:12) into an interim ethics which is binding at present but is also aware of its ultimate dissolution.

In contrast with a philosophical proposition, which, based on its relation to reality, can be descriptively right or wrong, the practical truth of a prescriptive norm is grounded on its relation to the right desire (*orthe orexis*, Aristotle, *Nicomachean Ethics* 6,1139 a 21-32; Broadie 1991, 219-224). Stoicism claimed that the rational understanding of nature was the crucial norm for a happy life (Cicero, *De finibus* 4,6,14f., Seneca, *Epistula* 5,4 *secundum naturam vivere*). In ancient Greece of the 7th and 6th century BCE, legislation as a normative act was often transferred to individuals like Dracon and Solon of Athens, or Lycurgus of Sparta (Lewis 2007). In Rome, the normativity of tradition, consisting of customs and ancestral role models, was regarded as the foundation of a stable society (Cicero, *De re publica* book 5, mentioned in Augustine, *City of God* 2,21 as quoting *moribus antiquis res stat Romana virisque*, a hexameter taken from the 3rd century poet Ennius, *Annals* fr. 156 Skutsch 1985; Braun et al. 2000). Whereas the Greeks had a greater tendency towards theoretical speculation about ethics and normativity, for the Romans this was very much a matter of daily practical realisation on behalf of and for the community. This different approach to normativity can also be observed in the different concepts of a hero in Greek and Roman epic poetry. Whereas in the *Iliad* and the *Odyssey* in particular the heroes act as individuals with all their weaknesses and strengths, thus representing various facets of human nature within the world, the Roman epic, especially Vergil's *Aeneid*, but also for instance Silius Italicus' *Punica*, presents a hero whose actions are guided and driven by responsibility for a group of dependents like family, friends, soldiers or even the entire state, thus representing the human person as a socially responsible being. This socially oriented practical ethics is also reflected in the typically Roman values or norms of *virtus* ('moral excellence'), *pietas* ('dutiful behaviour') and *fides* ('trust, faithfulness'), which are to be performed in relation to the various 'social' circles of family, state and gods (Braun et al., 2000; Pollmann, 2008).

At least as early as the Pre-Socratics, there was an awareness that language, although perhaps natural in origin, was a conventional, normative system of phonetic signs, depending on the agreement of a specific group (Heraclitus, Diels-Kranz 1951-1952, 22 B 32, 48; Xenophon, *Memorabilia* 3,14,2; Augustine, *De doctrina christiana* 2,2,3,3). Thus, the relation between objects of reality and their expression through language, as well as the issue of the possibility of expressing any reality truthfully through language, became prominent philosophical issues, especially in Plato's *Cratylus* and with the Stoics (Coseriu 1970). In Christian times, where the focus was very much on the Word of God which was perceived as normative, these issues gained renewed relevance. Whereas *canonisation* is occupied with the assembling of writings that are deemed normative (as in law and religion, for instance), *normativity* focuses on the authoritative function of those writings within the group on whose behalf they are collected (Lybaek 2002, 62). During this process, diverging positions can be observed which meant that the final canon of the Christian Bible was only fixed in the early 5th century. Moreover, there existed and continues to exist a tension between oral and written traditions. In Early Christianity the Hebrew Bible and orally transmitted Jesus logia were considered normative, while later the established canon was confronted and complemented with an oral and written tradition of exegesis. This reflects the linguistic acknowledgement that only in the actual reception of a text is one of its meanings constituted. The normative hermeneutical horizon for an appropriate interpretation of Scripture includes human reason (Augustine, *De doctrina christiana*, prol.), a dogmatic rule of faith (Origen, *De principiis*, prol.; Tertullian, *De praescriptione haereticorum* 13,1-6) and institutionalised exegetical patterns (Young 1997, especially 285-299). From case to case, these individual elements may have different prominence. Although Scripture was recognised early both in the Jewish and the Christian tradition as a mixture of descriptive and prescriptive texts, exegesis generally attempted to establish the prescriptive normativity of the entire Bible, both concerning the present ethical conduct and the soteriological-eschatological future. Modern biblical scholarship has emphasised that in biblical texts the descriptive and the prescriptive aspects cannot always be clearly separated (Schwienhorst-Schönberger 2006, 117f.)

Such an understanding of the Bible potentially supports a view of Christianity, as well as of other religions, as an ideology, that is, as a plan of action based on human reason to shape society, to interpret history, or to legitimise power: both ideology and religion demand absolute loyalty of their followers, and claim to present absolute truth and general validity. From the Pre-Socratics onwards, religion has been criticised as a false ideology (for instance Xenophanes of Colophon, Diels-Kranz 1951-1952, 21 B 11, 14, 15, 16, and Critias, Diels-Kranz 1951-1952, 88 B 25). The difference between political philosophy and ideologies of power is sometimes fluid: attempts to legitimise certain forms of power are to be found, for instance, in Xenophon's *Cyropaedia*, Isocrates (*Oratio ad Philippum* 114-116; *Nicocles* 5,29-35), and in Cicero's *De re publica* (Kloft 1979). Ideology can also manifest itself in cultural practices (Wlosok 1978) and political values (see also above p. 52). For instance, Athens presented itself in tragedies in the fifth century BC as the refuge of the needy and the protectress of panhellenic law (Bernek 2004). It created a sharp ideological contrast to its political enemy, Thebes, which was characterised in its myths by incest, fratricide and other sacrileges. However, when Rome adopted the Theban myth as a matrix for its identity, the 'Thebes' which for Athens represented the other now represented for Rome its negative self, as at the beginning of Rome there had also been fratricide. Thus, a myth that supported a positive, official state identity could suddenly turn into an instrument of ideological criticism (Pollmann 2004, 30). Such ideologies are particularly pertinent in times of crisis or political change like the transition from the Roman Republic to the Early Principate (Dettenhofer 2000), for instance, or when dominion over a different culture had to be justified (Herklotz 2007). The justification of Roman Imperialism based on the claim that it brought peace and civilisation to other peoples (Vergil, *Aeneid* 6.851-853) was also popular in later times, for instance in a Christianised version in Eusebius, *Historia ecclesiastica* 1,2,17-27 and *Laus Constantini* 16,4. On the other hand, the imperial structure of Rome's history has been criticised at least from Polybius until Augustine (Fuchs 1938).

Generally speaking, Christianity defines itself as a religion that is hostile towards ideology. In 2 Cor 10:4-5 ('For the weapons of our warfare are not carnal, but mighty through God to the pulling down of strongholds: casting down imaginations and every high thing that exalts itself against the knowledge of God, and bringing into captivity every thought to the obedience of Christ') there is an explicit warning to be immune against such temptations and indeed fight against them. While it is to be noted that Augustine hardly ever quotes these verses and does not comment on them at all (although he is of course aware of the problem of ideology as such), his opponent Pelagius comments between 405 and 410 on 2 Cor 10:4-5, defining the battle of the soldiers of Christ as a spiritual battle against three types of enemies: first, the external enemy that physically threatens with carnal weapons against which Christians can successfully defend themselves with words under the power of God (Souter 1931, 2,285 '*plus verbo valemus quam alii homines armis carnalibus possunt*'); secondly, against false doctors, i.e. heresies, which disguise their perverse teaching with astute arguments and which Paul, with the help of God's grace ('*virtute gratiae spiritalis*') blinded with his word (Souter 1931, 2,285), with which Pelagius refers to Acts 13:6-11, where Paul literally blinded a false prophet on Paphos; and finally, Pelagius includes the enemy from within that has to be destroyed, that is, hypocritical fellow-Christians who wish to monopolise Christian understanding (Souter 1931, 2,286 '*qui sub nomine obsequii Christi omnem intellectum sibi cupiunt captivare*').

The so-called Ambrosiaster, an anonymous exegete and very probably a cleric who had sometimes wrongly been identified with Ambrose and who wrote in Rome 366 and 384 (Hunter 1989, 284f.), following the Antiochene tradition of literal exegesis, commented relatively extensively on 2 Cor 10:4-5: he emphasises that this means that as his servants we have to defend the profession and teaching of the one God (CSEL 81/2, 273) and that the spiritual arms signify the faith of an unspoiled proclamation (ibid. '*arma spiritalia fides est incorruptae praedicationis*'). The truth of the faith destroys all other thoughts that avert us from obedience under Christ and God's law. These arms, or this truthful proclamation 'captivates the intellect by conquering it *with reason* when it contradicts, and leads it, now humble and meek, to the faith of Christ, against which [or: whom] it had previously fought' (CSEL 81/2, 274 '*captivat intellectum, dum contradicentem* <u>ratione</u> *vincit, et ad fidem Christi, cui prius repugnaverat, humilem et mansuetum inducit'*). Modern commentaries still go along with this interpretation (e.g. Bultmann 1985, 184-186; Harris 2005, 676-684).

A specific example

Ambrosiaster clearly emphasises the monopoly of the true faith, and expressions like *'per servos suos'* and *'incorruptam praedicationem'* lead one to suspect that a privileged and exclusive class are its guardians, especially the clergy. His claim is that those who dare to contradict Christ are to be fought against with the law of God, which scatters their counsels (CSEL 81/2, 274 *'contra quos pugnat dei lex dissipans consilia eorum'*). We will have a look at one specific example to test how Ambrosiaster practises what he preaches in his own exegesis, by looking at his investigation of the position of the two genders within Christianity.

As a starting point we use his exegesis of Gal 3:28 ('There is not male and female'), on which Ambrosiaster commented in his commentary of Galatians (Pollmann 2009). He emphasises (CSEL 81/3, 42) that there is no difference between the faithful (*'nullam distantiam credentium'*), in order that it will not be counted against anyone what they were before they came to the Christian faith (*'ut nulli praeiudicetur quid fuerit antequam crederet'*). For all people the same promise has been given by God, in whom there is no difference in regarding different types of persons (*'nulla discretio personarum'*), except with respect to their moral conduct (*'nisi morum ac vitae'*). This means that in God's eyes human beings of the one faith are differentiated according to their merits and not according to their personal attributes (*'ut homines unius fidei meritis distinguantur, non personis'*). While the Neo-platonic philosopher and Christian Marius Victorinus, who also wrote a commentary on Galatians a few years earlier than Ambrosiaster, uses the same notion of *persona* (Cooper 2005, 299 n. 19; 300 n. 21), it is only Ambrosiaster who adds the meritocratic element. In his commentary on Colossians 3:11 (Souter 1931, 2,466), Pelagius has a similar phrase (*'aput deum non praeiudicat sexus vel genus vel patria vel condicio, sed conversatio sola: nam carnalis est ista diversitas'*), likewise emphasising the meritocratic element, which in view of his overall theology is hardly surprising. Both he and Ambrosiaster write here against an ideology that presumes that some people are more equal than others.

It is noteworthy that Gal 3:28 is the most egalitarian statement about the quality of the sexes in the New Testament letters. Its transgender claim is mirrored in the theoretical thinking of Judith Butler, who claims that in this world there is already no male and female prior to the cultural engenderings of those two categories of identity. The idea that sexual identity is natural, that there are two genders or even sexes in nature, is a cultural construct. (Butler 1990, 9-11). While some exegetes notice the potential tension between Gal 3:28 and other Pauline statements, others, including Ambrosiaster, choose to highlight other passages at the expense of Gal 3:28 (cf. in modern times Schlier 1965, 175 n. 4), taking a lead especially from the misogynistic and exegetically not unassailable interpretation of the Fall of Man in 1 Tim 2:13f., which claims that the woman is subordinate to the man because she brought sin into the world (cf. Ambrosiaster, *Commentarius in epistulam ad Timotheum primam* 2,151, CSEL 81/3, 264). An interestingly oscillating interpretation is offered by Ambrosiaster, *Commentarius in epistulam ad Colossenses* 3,11,4-6 (CSEL 81/3, 196f.): there are two different images of God in human beings, one of which consists in the recognition of the Saviour, in which the woman also partakes, by attempting a virtuous life in obedience to God. The other image of God pertains only to the man and reflects the pre-lapsarian creation of the sexes already in hierarchy. While the extra-Trinitarian relationship between God and his creation is equivalent to Adam alone being the image of God, the intra-Trinitarian relationship between the Father and the Son is mirrored in the hierarchical image of man and woman, consisting in the derivation of Eve from Adam (Hunter 1992, 449; similarly Ambrosiaster, *Quaestiones Veteris et Novi Testamenti* 24; 45; 106; 127). For the male human being this results in a double image, namely his likeness with the extra-Trinitarian unity of God in man alone and, together with the subordinated woman, in the similitude of the mystery of the Father and the Son (CSEL 81/3, 197).

Ambrosiaster is careful to emphasise the distinction between the non-hierarchical relationship of Father and Son and the hierarchical relationship between the sexes due to the inferior nature of human beings, who cannot produce like from like (Hunter 1992, 448f.). As Hunter (1992, 451-454) rightly highlights, Ambrosiaster validates his misogynistic exegesis by invoking political and legal practices of his time (fewer legal rights for women) and contemporary church customs (no females in the clergy). Thus he sacralises political and ecclesiastical order and ideologises in a circular argument contemporary practice with his exegesis, which confirms the present social order. This is his conservative reaction to other contemporary exegetes, like Jerome in particular, who advocated asceticism for men and women as a revivification of a pre-sexual, pre-lapsarian paradise of equality of the sexes, against traditional Roman secular practice and at the expense of the clergy. In his attempt to nip these ideas in the bud, Ambrosiaster goes further than all other exegetes of Genesis 1-3 by claiming a pre-lapsarian hierarchy of the sexes and by declaring the commandment of Gen 3:16 (woman dominated by husband) to be a restoration of the pre-lapsarian condition of a patriarchal paradise which had been disrupted by the Fall.

He admits that women are the same as men in substance and nature, and that they have access to salvation through a virtuous life. At the same time, however, he consolidates the contemporary gender hierarchy by justifying it with the woman's pre-lapsarian subordinate status: the new order of the New Testament will not invalidate her subordination in this life. Ambrosiaster's claim that the fact that woman is made of man speaks for her derivative inferiority is not something which pagan philosophy would necessarily support. For instance, Aristotle (*De generatione et corruptione* 1,7, 324a25-b13) highlights that agents, by acting on other things, can themselves be affected in respect of the active power in question. Moreover, this statement is by no means necessarily justified by the text: Genesis describes in a rising sequence the creation of increasingly higher creatures. Consequently, the woman can be seen as the ultimate climax of creation. To the creation of both man and woman an equal number of words is accorded in the Hebrew text. Moreover, she is the only creature not made of earth: even man is God-inspired earth, whereas woman is God-inspired man.

Conclusions

Drescher (1962, 6-13) lists a number of very helpful criteria that distinguish between an ideology and a religion (he has predominantly the Christian religion in mind): whereas an ideology promises its direct and un-ambivalent application, the comprehensiveness of its thought system and security, the total explanation of the world and of the human being through the environment and matter, Christian religion moves in a more open thought system where there is some ambivalence, where the sense of the world and of individual events can only be finally determined at the very end of time, where there is no objective evidence, where there is room both for speculation and for uncertainty, as Jesus questions people about their convictions and denies the one-dimensionality of ideology or even of the Bible (Matth 4:1-11 and Luke 4:1-13). Drescher (1962, 16) quite rightly stresses the danger of religion becoming an ideology by turning into a sect, by being dominated by arguments that rather belong to the realms of science, by dogmatisation and by clericalisation. Connected to our material, the least that can be said about Ambrosiaster as an exegete is that he creates a circular argument between the justification of his own exegesis and the justification of contemporary social order for some Biblical verses; whereas others (like Gal 3:28) are eschatologically postponed into an unknowable future. Thus, Ambrosiaster not only turns existing practices he approves of into the norm for the interpretation of Scripture, but also (vice versa) turns his exegetical results into the fixated ideology which confirms these habits as normative. Thus the freedom, richness and potential challenge of the Christian message and the biblical text are abandoned.

Bibliography

Bekker, Immanuel 1831-1870. *Aristotelis Opera*. Berlin: Preussische Akademie der Wissenschaften.

Bernek, Rüdiger 2004. *Dramaturgie und Ideologie. Der politische Mythos in den Hikesiedramen des Aischylos, Sophokles und Euripides*. Munich: Saur.

Braun, Maximilian et al. (eds.) 2000. *Moribus Antiquis Res Stat Romana. Römische Werte und römische Literatur im 3. und 2. Jahrhundert vor Christus*. Munich: Saur.

Broadie, Sarah 1991. *Ethics with Aristotle*. Oxford: Oxford University Press.

Bultmann, Rudolf 1985. *The Second Letter to the Corinthians*. Minneapolis: Augsburg Publishing House (German original 1976).

Butler, Judith 1990. *Gender Trouble: Feminism and the Subversion of Identity*. London/New York: Routledge.

Cooper, Stephen A. 2005. *Marius Victorinus' Commentary on Galatians. Introduction, Translation, and Notes*. Oxford: Oxford University Press.

Coseriu, Eugenio 1970. *Die Geschichte der Sprachphilosophie von der Antike bis zur Gegenwart 1.* Tübingen: A. Francke Verlag.

Dettenhofer, Maria H. 2000. *Herrschaft und Widerstand im augusteischen Prinzipat.* Stuttgart: Steiner.

Diels, Hermann / Kranz, Walther 1951-1952 (and reprints). *Die Fragmente der Vorsokratiker: Griechisch und Deutsch*, 3 volumes. Berlin: Weidmannsche Verlagsbuchhandlung.

Drescher, Hans-Georg 1962. *Ideologie und christlicher Glaube.* Wuppertal/Barmen: Jugenddienst-Verlag.

Fuchs, Harald 1938. *Der geistige Widerstand gegen Rom in der antiken Welt.* Berlin: Walter de Gruyter.

Harris, Murray J. 2005. *The Second Epistle to the Corinthians. A Commentary on the Greek Text.* Grand Rapids, Michigan: Eerdmans.

Herklotz, Friederike 2007. *Prinzeps und Pharao. Der Kult des Augustus in Ägypten.* Frankfurt am Main: Verlag Antike.

Hunter, David G. 1989. 'On the sin of Adam and Eve: a little known defence of marriage and childbearing by Ambrosiaster'. *Harvard Theological Review*, 82, 283-299.

Hunter, David G. 1992. 'The paradise of patriarchy: Ambrosiaster on woman as (not) God's image'. *Journal of Theological Studies*, 43, 447-469.

Kloft, Hans (ed.) 1979. *Ideologie und Herrschaft in der Antike.* Darmstadt: Wissenschaftliche Buchgesellschaft.

Kotva, Joseph J. 1996. *The Christian Case for Virtue Ethics.* Washington, DC: Georgetown University Press.

Lewis, John D. 2007. *Early Greek Lawgivers.* London: Bristol Classical Press.

Lybaek, Lena 2002. *New and Old in Matthew 11-13. Normativity in the Development of Three Theological Themes.* Göttingen: Vandenhoeck & Ruprecht.

Pollmann, Karla 1996. *Doctrina Christiana. Untersuchungen zu den Anfängen der christlichen Hermeneutik mit besonderer Berücksichtigung von Augustinus, De doctrina.* Fribourg: Universitätsverlag.

Pollmann, Karla 2004. *Statius, Thebaid 12.* Paderborn: Schöningh Verlag.

Pollmann, Karla 2008 (forthcoming). 'Ambivalence and moral *virtus*'. In: M. Vielberg et al. (eds.), *Roman epic.* Stuttgart: Meiner Verlag.

Pollmann, Karla 2009 (forthcoming). 'Non est masculus et femina – Gal 3,28 in Kommentarauslegungen des 4./5. und des 20. Jahrhunderts: Ein nicht eingelöstes Vermächtnis?'. In: Andreas Grote et al. (eds.). Würzburg: Augustinus-Verlag.

Rainer, Michael 1993. 'Recht: Antike'. In: Peter Dinzelbacher (ed.), *Europäische Mentalitätsgeschichte.* Stuttgart: Kröner Verlag 489-512.

Schäfer, Christian 2007. 'Idee'. In: Christian Schäfer (ed.), *Platon-Lexikon.* Darmstadt: Wissenschaftliche Buchgesellschaft 157-165.

Schlier, Heinrich 1965(1949). *Der Brief an die Galater.* (4th edn.). Göttingen: Vandenhoeck & Ruprecht.

Schwienhorst-Schönberger, Ludger 2006. 'Präskriptive Texte'. In: Helmuth Utzschneider and Erhard Blum (eds.), *Lesarten der Bibel. Untersuchungen zu einer Theorie der Exegese des Alten Testaments.* Stuttgart: Kohlhammer 2006, 117-126.

Skutsch, Otto 1985. *The Annals of Ennius, Edited with an Introduction and Commentary*. Oxford: Oxford University Press.

Souter, Alexander 1922-1931. *Expositiones xiii epistularum Pauli*, 3 vols. Cambridge: Cambridge University Press.

Wlosok, Antonie (ed.) 1978. *Römischer Kaiserkult*. Darmstadt: Wissenschaftliche Buchgesellschaft.

Young, Frances 1997. *Biblical Exegesis and the Formation of Christian Culture*. Cambridge: Cambridge University Press.

'THAT IS BELIEVED WITHOUT GOOD REASON WHICH IS BELIEVED WITHOUT KNOWLEDGE OF ITS ORIGIN.'[1]

TERTULLIAN ON THE PROVENANCE[2] OF EARLY CHRISTIAN WRITINGS IN DEBATE WITH HERETICS

Jakob Engberg

For the sake of.... Ancient and modern provenance debates in the service of a wider thesis

I am aware that the Book of Henoch....is not accepted because it is not admitted into the Jewish canon. I suppose it is not accepted because they did not think that a book written before the flood could have survived that catastrophe which destroyed the whole world: if that be their reason, let them remember that Noe was a great-grandson of Henoch and a survivor of the deluge. He would have grown up in a family tradition and the name of Henoch would have been a household word, and he would surely have remembered the grace that his ancestor enjoyed before God and the reputation of all his preaching, especially since Henoch gave the command to his son Mathusala that knowledge of his deeds should be passed on to posterity. Therefore, Noe could surely have succeeded in the trusteeship of his ancestor's preaching because he would not have kept silent about the wonderful providence of God who saved him from the destruction as well as in order to enhance the glory of his own house.[3]

In the first book chapter three of Tertullian's, *The Apparel of Women*, Tertullian thus argues for the authenticity of the (first) book of Henoch. Tertullian suggests that it had been (re)written by Henoch's great-grandson Noe after the deluge, according to family tradition. This passage is useful for a comparison between ancient and modern debate and polemic on the provenance of ancient writings.

Tertullian's suggestion on the provenance of Henoch would not satisfy modern scholarly criteria for the study of provenance or transmittance. But Tertullian wrestles with questions which still confront any scholar who wants to deal with the provenance

---

1   Tertullian, *Adversus Marcionem* 5,1,1. The context: '*nihil interim credam nisi nihil temere credendum, temere porro credi quodcunque sine originis agnitione creditur*' ('For the moment my only belief is that nothing ought to be believed without good reason, and that that is believed without good reason which is believed without knowledge of its origin'). This and any other translation from *Adversus Marcionem* is in the translation of Evans 1972. Quotes from other ancient writings will, unless otherwise stated, be in my own translation.

2   The provenance of an ancient writing is defined as its time and place of origin and its authorship and (intended) audience.

3   This and any other translation from *The Apparel of Women* is in the translation of Quain, i.e. Arbesmann, Daly, Quain 1959.

of any ancient document: How did this document survive centuries of conflagration, and how has it been transmitted to the present day?

Furthermore Tertullian's interest in the book of Henoch was not purely and not even primarily antiquarian. He was rather interested in the book of Henoch because he could use its description of the relationship between fallen angelic powers and women and its description of angels in heaven to argue:

a) Generally for the main point in his writing: that women ought (and need) not dress up in order to attract men.
b) Specifically: That woman in heaven would receive an angelic status equal to man and thus be handsomely rewarded for any abstinence on earth.

Today few scholars would be occupied with the same agenda as Tertullian when studying the provenance of ancient Jewish or Christian writings, but like Tertullian few scholars would study provenance purely or even primarily out of antiquarian interest. On the contrary, such questions would most frequently be studied on the basis of and contributing to a larger thesis like the development of eschatology, church offices, Christology, the relative importance of Jewish and Hellenistic influence in Early Christianity etc.[4] Bluntly stated, this produces a situation where the provenance of an ancient Jewish or Christian writing is first established with reference to a thesis on the development of such phenomena, and where secondly the writing thus dated and attributed is used to corroborate the thesis. Such circular arguments cannot be avoided altogether, as we are here entering the hermeneutical circle. However, scholars should realise the circularity of such argumentation and state it clearly for the benefit of their readers.

When scholars compare a particular writing with other writings in order to arrive at its relative dating, they are often faced with the additional complicating factor that the other ancient writings with which they are comparing the writing they are focusing on are also often dated and fixed using such methods, and even with reference to the writing on which the focus is being placed.[5]

The realisation that such dating and attribution of authorship is based on circular arguments makes scholars grasp at any straws lying outside the circle; and at this point other factors are taken into consideration – political events like the destruction of the Jewish temple or alleged persecutions of Christians on the one hand, and any ancient

---

4   Such examples are so legio that even examples make little sense; but e.g.: relative Jewish instead of Hellenic leanings of Gospel authors and the implications for dating: Barrett 1978, 3-5; 'primitive Christology' and 'primitive ecclesiology' proving an early date of Luke and Acts: Witherington 1998, 61; and the concern with offices in Pastorals and its implications for dating: Prokorný and Heckel 2007, 661-669.
5   Cf. for instance the many attempts at dating different gospels (also but not only canonical) in relation to each other; different Pauline and different Johannine letters in relation to each other; and James and 1 Peter in relation to different Pauline letters.

tradition or debate on the provenance of the ancient writing in question on the other.[6] Questions regarding the provenance of early Christian writings are discussed not only by scholars but also by a more popular debate. The popular debate has often been divided between critics of Christianity on the one hand, trying to argue polemically against the trustworthiness of gospel traditions – and Christians trying apologetically to argue for its reliability on the other. When discussing the provenance of the early Christian writings, scholars and popular debaters ('polemists' and 'apologists' alike) often refer briefly or extensively, disapprovingly or approvingly to what the Church Fathers had to say on this subject.[7]

Ancient provenance debates examined, the purpose of this article

Having pointed out that most modern scholars discussing provenance are not driven by antiquarian interest, I should also state that my interest is not antiquarian – and nor do I seek to arrive at a more appropriate fixing of provenance of any early Christian writing. My interest in studying ancient debates on provenance is to assess or understand how and why such debates were used to ascribe normative status to some texts and remove it from others. Only secondarily might such studies prove to be relevant in assessing and understanding:

a)   The value of ancient statements on the provenance of ancient Jewish and Christian writings, statements that are still being used approvingly or disapprovingly by scholars when they debate the provenance of the very same writings.

b)   What happens when statements and arguments from one polemic context (the ancient debate) are reused in a scholarly context or in a modern polemic context.

Frontlines and battlefields in ancient provenance debates, the material for this article

As seen above, the provenance of ancient Christian writings is debated today on different levels and between different groups. This resembles the debate that went on in antiquity. Debates on the provenance of writings that were important for different ancient groups were conducted so to speak across different frontlines and on different battlefields:

---

6   Dating from alleged references to the destruction of the Jewish temple, e.g. Beare 1981,7; Hengel 2000, 78-79 and 189-195; Witherington 1998, 61. For a critique of attempts at dating early Christian texts on the basis of references to alleged persecutions (with many references to such attempts): Newman 1963 and Engberg 2007, 50, 73, 123, 145, 153-154 and 164-169. Dating from ancient traditions (or a critique of such attempts): Pokorný and Heckel 2007, 374-375, 477-478 and 530-531; Newman 1963, Beare 1981,7; and Witherington 1998, 56.

7   E.g. http://www.apologetik.dk/?p=213#more-213; http://www.jesusneverexisted.com/john.htm; http://www.jesusneverexisted.com/revelation.htm; http://www.facingthechallenge.org/gospels.php; and http://www.biblestudyplanet.com/q44.htm.

a) Internally, i.e. between persons or groups recognising each other as representatives of legitimate but not necessarily correct positions.
b) Sectarian, i.e. between persons and groups deriving from the same religious tradition condemning each other as representatives of illegitimate positions.
c) Externally, i.e. between persons and groups perceiving each other as representatives of distinct and different traditions.

Only examples of the two first kinds of debates will be analysed here. Firstly the debate on the provenance of Revelation between different early Christian authors will be discussed as an example of the first kind of debate. Secondly, as an example of the role of provenance debates in combating alleged heretics, Irenaeus' provenance debate on the origin of the Gospel of John will be compared with Tertullian's debate on the provenance of the 'canonical' gospels in polemic with Marcion. In this article I will only refer briefly to the third kind of debate (the external debate), without analysing it. In debate with a certain Apion, who had criticised Judaism, Josephus firstly argued for the antiquity of Jewish Scripture, i.e. a defence of its authority being questioned by Apion; secondly Josephus' argued for the novelty and spurious authorship of even the oldest of Greek literature, the poems wrongly (according to Josephus) attributed to Homer, i.e. an attack on the authenticity and antiquity and thereby the status of writings dear to Apion's tradition.[8]

Context of ancient debates on provenance

As noted above, ancient (like modern) provenance debates were seldom conducted out of an antiquarian interest. On the contrary – they were part of a vivid debate regarding the right religion, theology, way of living, etc. The provenance debates were (logically) most intimately linked with the part of this debate that based its arguments on writings. The ancient protagonists' debate on writings included the following questions:

a) Which, if any, writings ought to be ascribed normative status, and to which degree in relation to other phenomena carrying authority (such as office, charisma, power, gender, money, status, order etc.)?
b) How are particular writings to be interpreted?
c) Who has the right to interpret particular writings?
d) What is the right interpretation of particular writings?

The provenance debates were an important ingredient in the debate on the first of these questions, since most people would be inclined to believe that a falsified writing of recent origin could not carry any weight (or at least not the same weight) compared

---

8   Josephus, *Contra Apionem* 1,1-23. Cf. Pilhofer 1990, 194-196.

with a writing ascribed to a hero of the distant past (see below). Tertullian's argumentation over the book of Henoch testifies to this.

The authority of antiquity and the preference for the eyewitness

Tertullian's argumentation on the book of Henoch indicates an underlying premise: people in antiquity were generally inclined to respect traditions and admire things that were thought to be older more than things that were thought to be of more recent origin.

In Dio Cassius' history, written around 230 C.E., Dio puts a speech into the mouth of the Roman plutocrat Maecenas. In this speech in 30-29 B.C.E., Maecenas advises the young Octavian (later Augustus) to worship the divine according to ancestral tradition.[9] But this is not enough: Octavian must also encourage and even force everyone else to do the same. Finally, Octavian must punish anyone who introduces new deities or cults. In Suetonius' biography on the emperor Augustus, he writes (93): 'With regard to foreign religious ceremonies (*caerimoniarum*), he was a strict observer of those which had been established by ancient custom; but others he held in no esteem.'

It is not important here to debate whether Maecenas ever held such a speech or whether Augustus practised religion in the way related by Suetonius. What is important here is that Dio's composition or relation of the speech and Suetonius' description of Augustus' religious habits testify:

a)   to the general respect for ancestral and / or ancient tradition (cf. Pilhofer 1990);
b)   that this respect was often proportionally followed by suspicion of anything new;
c)   that these tendencies were especially lucid in relation to religion.

Sometimes linked to this phenomenon, and at other times at odds with it, there was a tendency to respect an eyewitness – a person who could speak from their own experience or from their own studies.[10] When analysing the debates on provenance in antiquity, we will look for both a bias in favour of ancient tradition and a bias in favour of the experiences of eyewitnesses. With such cultural biases it can be assumed that a protagonist in a debate on provenance would attempt to discredit his opponents' writings as being too recent and the authorship of these writings as being spurious; and correspondingly that this protagonist would try to argue for the antiquity of the writing dear to himself and to ascribe it to a respected figure who was supposed to be an authority on the subject in question (Josephus against Apion above).

9   Dio Cassius, *Historia Romana* 52,36,1-3. E.g. also Beard, North, Price 1998, 214.
10   E.g. Marincola 1997. E.g. also Josephus, *Contra Apionem* 1,9 and 1,53; Acts 13:31; 1 John 1:1; Theophilus, *Ad Autolycum* 3,2; Tertullian, *De fuga in persectuione* 9,3 and *De anima* 17,14.

Internal debate on provenance, the provenance of Revelation
discussed in relation to the debate over chiliastic eschatology

Eschatology was debated animatedly in ancient Christianity. Since the interpretation of texts played a role in all these debates, so did debates on the status of texts in general or the status of one text in relation to others – and thus also the debate on the provenance of these texts. Here we will focus on how a debate on the provenance of Revelation played a role in the debate over chiliastic eschatology, i.e. whether there would be one thousand years of earthly rule by Christ before the end of time. The focus will be on the part of this debate that was carried out between Christian groups and individuals who recognised their 'opponents' in this debate as fellow Christians. With the explicit references to a kingdom of Christ lasting for a thousand years in Revelation 20, it is no surprise that this book came to play a pivotal role in this debate.

Justin on the provenance of Revelation in Christian debate on eschatology.
In the *Dialogue with Trypho* the Jew Justin wrote (81,4):

a man among us called John, one of the Apostles of Christ, received a revelation and prophesied that Christ's followers would rest in Jerusalem for a thousand years, and that afterwards the universal and, in short, everlasting resurrection and judgement would take place.

Hereby Justin clearly claims that Revelation was written by John the apostle. It is possible and even likely that Justin here builds on a tradition that was rather well established, since he can make the claim without having to argue for it. However, this is not to say that he did not have a clear interest in claiming this authorship in the context of exactly this debate over the millennium. On the contrary, the interest is clear: for a Christian reader, the name of John would confer status on Revelation and thus underscore the chiliastic eschatology that Justin derives from it. Justin as a character in his own writing makes his claim in dialogue with the Jew Trypho, but of course as the author Justin must have had a wider audience in mind. In relation to the whole dialogue, different scholars have argued for different intended audiences:[11] a) primarily Jews; b) primarily pagans, or c) primarily other Christians. However, even those arguing for primarily external intended audiences would rarely (if ever) deny that other Christians also read and were intended to read the dialogue. This is enough for us, as we can find clear evidence in the context of Justin's claim on Johannine origin that other Christians held other views concerning eschatology, and that Justin probably tried to impress Christians influenced by such views with his argumentation.

Firstly, and as already indicated, a Christian reader was more likely to be impressed by arguments building on a book from the apostle John than any Jewish or pagan

---

11   E.g. Hyldahl 1966, 17-21 and 296 and Skarsaune 1976, 59 arguing for primarily a pagan audience or Engberg 2004, 129-131 arguing for primarily a Christian intended audience including, however, many converts.

reader would have been. Secondly, the entire chapter preceding the quoted passage on the provenance of Revelation is concerned with the questions of the millennium, and here Justin explicitly refers to Christians with alternative views. In chapter 80 Trypho asks Justin whether he thinks that Jerusalem will be rebuilt as a place of congregation for Christ, the Christians, the patriarchs, the prophets, the Jewish saints and their proselytes. Justin answers: 'that I, with many others, feel that such an event will take place.' But Justin then continues with the explanation that 'there are many pure and pious Christians who do not share my opinion'. Here is a positive invitation for such readers to follow Justin's argumentation. Before the end of the chapter, however, those with alternative views are rhetorically reduced to 'so-called Christians' and it is claimed by Justin that:

I and every other completely orthodox Christian feel certain that there will be a resurrection of the flesh followed by a thousand years in the rebuilt, embellished and enlarged city of Jerusalem, as was announced by the Prophets Ezechiel, Isias and the others.

Thus the Christian reader influenced by alternative views first had the option either of following and agreeing with Justin's argumentation (with no blemish attached for the previous error), or of seeing himself or herself being rhetorically excluded from the group of 'completely orthodox' Christians.

We cannot tell whether Justin's rhetoric succeeded in persuading some Christians influenced by non-chiliastic ideas. But we can say:

a)   Firstly, that other important Christian authors of the second and third centuries like Irenaeus and Tertullian shared Justin's views both on eschatology and on the authorship of Revelation. Irenaeus even added a date for its composition towards the end of the emperor Domitian's reign, i.e. 96 AD.[12]

b)   Secondly, that not everyone was convinced, and that on the contrary the alternative position on eschatology was about to find powerful champions who also introduced new ideas on the provenance of Revelation.

---

12   Irenaeus, *Adversus Haereses* 4,20,11; 5,30,3; 5,33,3-4, cf. also Osborn 2001, 139-140. Tertullian, *Adverses Marcionem* 3,14,3; 3,24,4 and 4,5,2, e.g. also Brox 2001, 246-247, note 113. It is sometimes claimed with reference to the last passage (4,5,2) that Marcion rejected Johannine authorship of Revelation, e.g. Aune 1997, li: 'Tertullian reports that Marcion did not regard John as the author of the Apocalypse'; this is in fact not what Tertullian wrote. He merely claimed that Marcion rejected Revelation (outright). As we shall see, Marcion did not base his rejection of any of the writings traditionally ascribed to other apostles than Paul on a claim that they were not written by apostles. On the contrary, it would implicitly appear that he thought them to be of apostolic origin since he based his rejection of them on an argument claiming that the apostles, apart from Paul, had imperfect knowledge and thus proclaimed a judaising gospel and were criticised by Paul (Gal 2) for this (below).

Rejection of Revelation with arguments based on its provenance

Eusebius quotes a Christian author of the early third century, Gaius, who claimed in a work against Montanists that the heretic Cerinthius was the author of Revelation, and that he had falsely published it under the name of 'a great Apostle', with Revelation 1:1 in mind none other than John.[13] Gaius wrote:

But Cerinthus also, by means of revelations which he pretends were written by a great apostle, brings before us marvellous things which he falsely claims were shown him by angels; and he says that after the resurrection the kingdom of Christ will be set up on earth, and that the flesh dwelling in Jerusalem will again be subject to desires and pleasures. And being an enemy of the Scriptures of God, he asserts, with the purpose of deceiving men, that there is to be a period of a thousand years for marriage festivals.

Gaius' non-chiliastic eschatology was thus clearly linked to his rejection of Revelation as a genuine work of John the apostle and his ascription of this work to the heretic, Cerinthus. The need to reject Johannine authorship reveals:

a)   that Gaius thought that many of his readers would otherwise consider John the apostle to be the author of Revelation (not surprisingly, in view of the claims of Justin, Irenaeus and Tertullian).
b)   that many of them, like Justin before them, would interpret the eschatology of Revelation as chiliastic.
c)   that a Johannine authorship would clearly lend too much status to Revelation and thus to the kind of millennarianism that Gaius tried to oppose.

The ascription of the work to the heretic Cerinthus, even hiding his authorship under the false name of John, was clearly intended to have the opposite effect of firstly utterly removing any normative status from Revelation; and secondly removing it as an underpinning of the chiliastic eschatology opposed by Gaius.[14] The link between the provenance debate, the normative function of early Christian texts and theological debate is thus again established. However, once again we are not at liberty to claim from this link that Gaius simply invented the theory of such a heretical origin of Revelation. He may have been influenced by tradition or by his own interpretation that Revelation and Cerinthus' theology were related. In relation to the intended audience for Gaius'

---

13   Quote from Eusebius, *H.E.* 3,28,2. On Cerinthus in general: Irenæus, *Adv. haer.* 1,26,1; Eusebius, *H.E.* 3,28 quoting both Gaius and Dionysius. On Gaius: Eusebius, *H.E.* 2,25,6.
14   One might argue conversely that a claim that Cerinthus published any writing (and therefore also Revelation) under a false name might have the purpose of discrediting the man (as an impostor) rather than the work. For Gaius this would surely have been a welcome side-effect, but I maintain that it could only have been a side-effect. The passage quoted by Eusebius was from a work opposing Montanists, who were highly unlikely to be in tune with Cerinthus on anything else than chiliasm. Gaius presumed that his readers already saw Cerinthus as a heretic, and by associating him with Revelation he could discredit the book. In other words, Gaius went for the 'ball' not the 'man'.

argumentation, the most natural assumption is that Gaius' claim was made with a view to persuading Christians who Gaius thought were influenced by the chiliastic eschatology of Revelation.

Eusebius clearly shared Gaius' hostility towards Cerinthus, as Eusebius continues with a critique of him also based on passages from Irenaeus (Irenaeus *Adv. haer.* 1,26,1 and 3,3,4). We shall now see that Eusebius and Christians more contemporary with Gaius shared Gaius' view on eschatology, but found it more expedient or prudent to come to terms with the apparent chiliasm of Revelation and reduce its apparent apostolic status in less radical ways – still in debate with other Christians.

Dionysius' refutation of chiliasm and his moderate critique of Revelation

In the early third century a bishop of Arisone in Egypt, Nepos, had written a book, *Refutation of the Allegorist*, in which he apparently argued for a chiliastic eschatology, building his argumentation on Revelation and disapproving of allegorical interpretations of this book.[15] When he died chiliastic beliefs were common amongst Christians in the villages of the Arsiniote nome, and Nepos' book with its verbal interpretation of Revelation was allegedly held in high esteem as proof of the correctness of this position. Around the middle of the third century, however, these Christian villagers received an illustrious visitor: none other than the bishop of Alexandria, Dionysius (died 264 C.E.). He was dismayed upon hearing about their views on this subject, and therefore took the time to meet all the villages elders, teachers and deacons with whom he thoroughly but amicably conversed about the subject for several days. Dionysius' non-chiliastic eschatology carried the day. Afterwards Dionysius wrote a treatise, *On the promises*, in which he argued in written form against the chiliast position defended by Nepos.

We know of this incident and debate only because small passages of this otherwise lost work are quoted in Eusebius' Church History.[16] From these passages it is clear that Dionysius matches the allegedly amicable tone of debate in the Arsinoite nome with praise for his (deceased) 'opponent' or rather 'partner' in the written debate, Nepos. Dionysius praises Nepos' faith, zeal, familiarity with Scriptures and poetry, and he is only and specifically critical of Nepos' chiliastic eschatology. It was apparently difficult for Dionysius to interpret Revelation in a way in which he could suppress its chiliastic eschatology, so the most obvious solution was to try to reduce the value of Nepos' evidence, i.e. to reduce the normative status of Revelation. Dionysius (therefore) argues that Revelation could not have been written by the apostle and evangelist John. Dionysius clearly presumes that the Gospel of John and 1 John were written by the apostle, so he can build his argument on a comparison between these two writings on the one hand and Revelation on the other, arguing for:

---

15   For a contemporary critique of allegorical interpretations of early Christian writings, e.g. Irenaeus, *Adv. haer.* 5,35,1.

16   This and the following: Eusebius, *H.E.* 7,24-25. E.g. also Altaner & Stuiber 1966, 210-211; Quasten 1962, vol. 2, 104-105; Lane Fox 1986, 265-266.

a) differences in style and language, with the language of John and 1 John being of superior quality;
b) differences in Christology, the openings of John and 1 John finding no parallel in Revelation,
c) other differences in theology, e.g. being evident through key words and terms (like light, life, truth, grace, joy, the Lord's flesh and blood) used in the Gospel of John and 1 John but not in Revelation;
d) differences in the way the authors designate themselves;
e) the difference that the authors of the first two writings claim to be eyewitnesses of the Lord – a claim which is not made by the author of Revelation.

Once again, Dionysius' views are rather moderate. As we have seen, and as claimed by Dionysius, others before him had argued that Revelation was a heretical work written by Cerinthus and falsely published under the name of John the apostle. Dionysius argues that he does not want to reject Revelation because it is dear to many brothers, an interesting criterion arguing from consensus and reminiscent of the kind of arguments presented by Tertullian, which we will analyse below. Dionysius therefore ascribes Revelation to another John, and suggests:

a) a man named after John;
b) John Mark (cf. Acts 15:37-39);
c) or a John buried like John the apostle in Ephesus.

The last suggestion is preferred by Dionysius, but with no argument. It is of course possible that Dionysius honestly believed in a tradition that ascribed Revelation to this otherwise anonymous John; but it is obvious why he should also *want* to believe this and *make this claim* instead of the rejected ascriptions of authorship to John the apostle and Cerinthus and his own suggestion of John Mark. Of these suggestions, the ascription to Cerinthus would force Dionysius to reject the writing outright (and he clearly did not want to do this), and the ascription to an apostle or even a disciple of an apostle like John Mark would confer too much status on the work, which contained difficult passages for Dionysius' eschatology. With an unknown orthodox John as author, the book would lose normative status but could still be used in less authoritative ways by those who cherished it.

Views on the provenance of Revelation, eschatological views and the use of writings

We have now seen the book of Revelation ascribed first by Justin and Irenaeus to the authoritative figure of John the apostle, then by Gaius to the heretic Cerinthus, and finally by Dionysius to a less authoritative but generally orthodox John. For Justin and Irenaeus on the one hand and Gaius on the other, their respective embracing or rejection of Revelation and their consequent ascribing of authorship was clearly and logically linked to their equally different eschatological views. Dionysius generally shared eschatological views with Gaius. Logically this should have led him to reject Revelation. Two things, however, might have held him back and resulted in his reserved approval of this text and its ascription to a not very prominent but at least orthodox author:

a) The allegorical interpretation which according to Dionysius should be employed could deter people from reading it literally, and could justify its continued reading.[17]

b) The widespread use and approval this text had found amongst Christians respected or even admired by Dionysius. This is an explicitly stated reason for not rejecting the text.

The use of Revelation by people or in writings respected by Dionysius is thus seen to influence crucially his evaluation of this text. A similar phenomenon is also a factor in Tertullian's debate on the provenance of the book of Henoch. Tertullian's last argument in favour of the authoritative status of the book of Henoch was that 'we have a testimony to Henoch in the Epistle of Jude the Apostle'.[18]

Links between the ancient and the modern debate on the provenance of Revelation

In the case of the debates over the provenance of Revelation we find a remarkable overlap between the ancient and the modern debate. This overlap concerns the question of dating, the debate on authorship, and the arguments used in these debates. The modern literature on this subject is naturally so vast that only a few examples can be mentioned here.

Each of the ancient positions on authorship has found its modern champions, but of course with different twists (E.g. also Aune 1997, li-liii). Gaius' claim that the heretic Cerinthus wrote Revelation finds the support of only few scholars, but the more general theory that it was written under the false name of John in an attempt to confer upon it the authority of the apostle is widespread.[19] Other modern scholars follow one or more of Dionysius' (more moderate) suggestions, ascribing Revelation to other Johns, e.g. John Mark, John the Elder etc., suggesting different kinds of relationships or no relationship at all between Revelation and 2 John and 3 John. One example is Martin

---

17   Cf. Hyldahl 2004 and Hyldahl 2007, who has convincingly argued that a change of culture and modes of thinking between the age at which a particular writing was written and the age of a later reader often makes a literal interpretation of the text untenable; but if there is a traditional attachment between the reader or his community and the text, then an allegorical reading of the text can serve the apologetic purpose of preserving this attachment and avoiding any untenable interpretations.

18   Tertullian, *De cultu feminarum* 1,3,3. The reference to Henoch is in Jude 14. Incidentally, it might be noted that Tertullian herby seemingly without controversy claimed apostolic origin for the Book of Jude. For a similar line of argument ascribing authoritative status to Hebrews based on it being used by Clement of Rome, Eusebius, *H.E.* 3,38,1-2.

19   E.g. Strecker 1992, 33-34; Becker 1969, 101 and Dunkerley 1961, 298.

Hengel, who tries to identify Dionysius' 'John buried in Ephesus' with 'John the Elder' referred to, according to the interpretation of Eusebius in his *Church History*, by Papias of Hierapolis (early second century).[20] On the basis of this identification he argues that John the Elder wrote Revelation around 68-70 AD, adding that it might have been edited by his students after his death (Hengel 1989, 127). Finally, some scholars maintain that the work is a (genuine) work of the apostle John, and these scholars again have different theories concerning the relation or the lack of relation between Revelation, the Gospel of John and the three Johannine letters.[21]

Concerning the date, it is actually quite astonishing that Irenaeus' dating to approximately 95 AD is accepted by so many modern scholars. In his commentary on Revelation, Aune describes this dating as the 'prevailing opinion' until 'the nineteenth century, and again…in the twentieth century' and according to a translator of Irenaeus' *Adversus Haereses*, Brox, Irenaeus' dating is the 'bis heute dominierende Ansicht zur Entstehungszeit dieser neutestamentlichen Schrift.'[22]

Finally, all Dionysius' arguments for claiming that John and 1 John were written by another author than Revelation are repeated approvingly, disapprovingly, or without due reference in modern scholarship.[23]

Sectarian debate on the provenance of the Gospels

Irenaeus, the late dating of the Gospel of John, and the Gospel as an anti-heretical gospel
The literature on the four-gospel canon of Irenaeus and his elaborate argumentation for its mystical significance is vast, so vast indeed that we will not here (in vain) attempt to contribute anything new to this overall debate.[24] Here we will only focus on a small aspect of Irenaeus' argumentation and ask why Irenaeus claims that the *Gospel of John* was the youngest. After claiming that Matthew wrote his gospel and that Mark and Luke were the authors of their Gospels, respectively influenced by Peter and Paul, Irenaeus continues (*Adv. haer.* 3,1,1): 'Thereafter John, the disciple of the Lord, who had rested on his breast, also gave forth his own gospel, while he was living in Ephesus in Asia.'

For Irenaeus, the Gospel of John is clearly held in high esteem. It is clearly attributed to the apostle, and modern scholarship has not failed to notice that language and

---

20   Eusebius, *H.E.* 3,39, where one could add that Eusebius' interpretation of Papias serves the purpose of ascribing Revelation to another author than John the apostle. This ascribing must have been most welcome to Eusebius because he, like Dionysius, was opposed to chiliastic eschatology. In his *Chronology* (Olymp. 220) where chiliasm and the authorship of Revelation is not on the agenda, Eusebius maintains, like Irenaeus (*Adv. Haer.* 5,33,4), that Papias was a hearer of John.

21   E.g. Hembold 1962, 77-79; Barrett 1978, 132-136 and Smalley 1994, 37-39.

22   Aune 1997, lvii and Brox 2001, vol. 5, 228, note 106.

23   E.g.: Disapprovingly: Stott 1988, 20-38. Approvingly: Schmithals 1992, 9-10. Without reference: Westcott 1886, xxx-xxxi and xxxix-xliii and Beasley-Murray 1987, lxviii-lxx.

24   Irenaeus, *Adv. haer.* 3,1,7-9. For a claim on the importance and vast scholarly literature on this subject, Skeat 1992, 194: 'Every study of the Canon of the Four Gospels begins, and rightly begins, with the famous passage in which Irenaeus,…, seeks to defend the Canon by finding a mystical significance in the number four.'

thought from the Gospel of John and the Johannine corpus permeate the writings of Irenaeus.[25]

With this in mind, and with the cultural bias attaching higher esteem to older writings than younger, why should Irenaeus be interested in emphasising the late origin of the Gospel of John? Of course he might genuinely believe it to be recent, but this is only half an explanation since:

a) Irenaeus himself argues from the cultural bias that ancient is better than recent in his argumentation against heretics, and in a passage closely connected to the quoted passage on John (3,4,3).
b) it can be shown that his dating of John's gospel as the most recent also served a purpose in his argumentation (below).

In the quoted passage, John and the Gospel of John are mentioned in order to establish that the churches founded and/or led by apostles, as well as important churches in Asia, are attributed by Irenaeus to John (3,3,2-4,1), and were carriers of the tradition on truth (3,1-5). This tradition was based not only on writings but also on a link with the apostles, a link cherished even by converted and illiterate barbarians (3,4,2). John as an apostle had given passive protection against heretics by establishing this tradition, but more actively he had disassociated himself from heretics. Irenaeus relates how John refused even to be in the same public bath as Cerinthus (3,3,4)

In the two main parts of the book (3,6-15 and 3,15-23) Irenaeus uses this twofold basis, writings and successive tradition, to argue for his views on two major themes: the oneness of God and Christology. In both parts Irenaeus returns to the provenance of the Gospel of John, now claiming that it was specifically written in order to refute the heretical views of Cerinthus and others concerning these two major themes (3,11,1-4 and 3,16,8). The exegesis is rather thorough, and Irenaeus mentions and quotes various passages, also from other Johannine writings, in which he claims that it is evident that John fought the same heretical positions that Irenaeus is now fighting.[26] In chapter 16 Irenaeus additionally introduces the idea that Jesus prophetically fought and warned against the same heretics that his apostle John fought in practice in his writings.

In *Against the Heretics*, Irenaeus frequently argues that heretics were late in origin and owed their origin to specific people influenced by Satan. In other words, a bias in favour of antiquity is used against the heretics. According to Irenaeus, heretical ideas never originated as general ideas at grassroots level in congregations; they were always a result of individuals preying like wolves amongst sheep upon the flock of the Lord, with their origin in the original heresy of Simon Magus[27] In order to maintain

---

25   Mutschler 2004 and Osborn 2001, 186-189 (but in the last instance only Irenaeus' use of the Gospel of John).
26   E.g. John 1:1-5; John 1:10-11; John 1:14 (both passages); John 1:6-7; 2 John 7-8; 1 John 4:1-3 and 1 John 5:1.
27   E.g. Irenaeus, *Adv. haer.* 1,23,1; 1,23,5; 1,24,1; 1,24,4; 1,26,1; 1,29,4; 2, pref.,1; 2,9,2 and 2,32,3-5. Tertullian argued similarly, e.g. *Praescrptio haereticorum* 3. Cf. also Gregory 2003, 206.

this view, and in order to have none other than the apostle John himself fighting these late wolves in person and in his writings, Irenaeus has to date the activities and the authorship of John as being late as well.

Tertullian's rhetorical tactic in refuting Marcion: turning his own evidence against him

We will now turn to Tertullian, who as we shall see followed Irenaeus in many things, but crucially not in regard to the relative dating of the four gospels. Tertullian did not use the motive that the apostle John personally and in writing fought heretics, a claim that Tertullian might have thought only emerged years after the death of any apostle. But this was not because Tertullian could not see the 'beauty' in having an apostle fight the heresies for him. On the contrary, he explicitly claims in his *Refutations of all heresies* (33) that it was very easy for him to fight the heresies which existed in the days of the apostles because Paul himself had fought them in his writings. But Tertullian really did not need the apostles to live after the time of certain heretics to enable these apostles to fight these heretics in their writings. Instead, Tertullian expanded the thesis of prophetic fighting of heretics in writings to include the apostles. The apostles had foreseen heresies, and could therefore write against them even before any specific heresy emerged (1 and 4-7). But let us now turn to Tertullian's views on the provenance of gospels presented in opposition to Marcion.

In chapters four to five of book four of Tertullian's work against Marcion, Tertullian discusses the provenance of the Gospel of Matthew, John, Mark and Luke. We will analyse his views and arguments on this subject, also discussing their possible relations to Irenaeus' view or other early Christian traditions on the same subject. Finally, we will try to establish how Tertullian's views and arguments suited his overall purpose of combating Marcion.

From the outset of book 4 (4,1,1, compare also 4,4,3 and 4,6,1-2), Tertullian claims that in his refutation of Marcion he will use Marcion's own writings, his *Antitheses* and his (according to both Tertullian and Irenaeus) altered edition of the Gospel of Luke (e.g. Irenaeus, *Adv. haer.* 3,11,7). The procedure described by Tertullian is modelled on a court procedure whereby a defendant accepts that the case should only be tested on evidence supplied by the plaintiff arguing that it had been wrongly and maliciously produced and/or interpreted. This earns for the defendant the right to act as the complainant, and this is exactly the position which Tertullian rhetorically assumes. To be able thus to switch between the rhetoric available to a defendant and the rhetoric available to an accuser is evidently beloved by Tertullian, since this rhetorical change of role is already found in his *Apologeticum*, where he originally presents himself as a kind of counsel for the defence (1,1) only to switch tactics and accuse the magistrates of perverting justice and acting against the laws (1,4).

Marcion's critique of the Gospels which were not his own

When analysing what Tertullian had to say on the provenance of different gospels and why the first answer to the last question is that he discussed these matters in this context because the subject was brought up by his opponent Marcion in his *Antitheses*, Tertullian wrote (4,3,3):

Marcion strives hard to overthrow the credit of those gospels which are the apostles' own and are published under their name, or even the names of apostolic men (apostolicorum), with the intention no doubt of conferring on his own gospel the repute which he takes away from those others.

It would appear from this and from Tertullian's reply, failing for instance to argue that Marcion was deriding gospels that Tertullian would likewise not approve of (see below), that Marcion was debating the same four gospels that Tertullian was debating (the Gospels of Matthew, John, Mark and Luke) and drawing their authority into question. If this inference from context is correct, Marcion's debate is an early testimony to the development of an implicit four-gospel canon.[28] This interpretation, however, rests on the traditional position of Harnack and others that Tertullian actually based his critique of Marcion on Marcion's so-called *Antitheses*.[29]

However, this interpretation has been challenged – for instance by Andrew Gregory, arguing that Tertullian is not basing his critique on the *Antitheses* but only on a series of anachronistic assumptions and conclusions:[30] a) Tertullian knew and respected four gospels, b) Marcion used only one, c) this gospel resembles the gospel known to Tertullian as Luke's, d) thus Tertullian simply assumes without any evidence that Marcion has discarded three gospels and perverted the fourth. Gregory concludes:

All that is known to Tertullian is the fact that Marcion did use a *Gospel* which Tertullian recognises as a shorter form of *Luke* than that to which he himself is accustomed, and this empirical evidence alone is sufficient to make it necessary for Tertullian to explain as to why Marcion used only one Gospel whereas the church used four.

Gregory also claims it to be a likely possibility that Marcion's gospel was not based on the gospel of Luke but rather on an earlier (now lost) gospel that was a source for both Marcion and Luke. However, the challenge to the traditional view can easily be demolished when the passage is read carefully and in context:

---

28   Cf. Harnack 1924, 40-42 and less explicitly Zahn 1904, 38; but against this Campenhausen 1968, 174-175. Compare Irenaeus, *Adv. haer.* 3,11,7: Different heretics prefer different gospels (Matthew, Luke, Mark or John). Hans von Campenhausen has argued that Irenaeus' argumentation for the four-fold gospel canon was original (Campenhausen 1968, 230-234). T.C. Skeat has argued convincingly that Irenaeus depended on an earlier tradition for his argumentation (Skeat 1992, also Hengel 2000, 215, note 215.). Cf. also Hengel 2000, 20 and 221-222, note 83, where he analyses Justin, *Tryphon* 103 and argues convincingly for the probability that Justin recognised an implicit canon of Matthew, John, Mark and Luke around 160 AD.

29   Harnack 1924, 74-92, 43*-56* (parts of Beilage III), 256*-314* (Beilage V) and 328*-344* (parts of Beilage VI)

30   This and the following: Gregory, 2003, 208-209 (quote: 209).

a) Firstly, Tertullian does not say that Marcion omits to mention or use the gospels of apostles or apostolic men. Rather more actively, Tertullian says that Marcion 'strives hard' to discredit them.

b) Secondly, Tertullian also indicates how Marcion argued his case: namely by using the Pauline censorship of other apostles in the epistle to the Galatians (below) to claim that other apostles were mistaken and that their gospels were mistaken too. It is actually a rather clever argument, and here and elsewhere Tertullian invests considerable energy in its refutation.[31] One might reasonably ask why Tertullian should have invented and ascribed a good argument to his opponent, an argument which actually forces Tertullian to criticise the apostles for doing something under certain circumstances which they censor under others, something which Tertullian is clearly uneasy about doing.

c) Thirdly, Tertullian distinguishes carefully between what Marcion actually did, namely strive 'hard to overthrow the credit of those gospels which are the apostles' own and are published under their name, or even the names of apostolic men'; and what Tertullian presumes to be Marcion's motive in doing so: 'with the intention no doubt of conferring on his own gospel the repute which he takes away from those others.' In other words, acting in tune with his self-representation as a barrister refuting his opponents on the grounds of the evidence produced by these opponents (below and 4,1,1), Tertullian distinguishes clearly between the evidence submitted by his opponent (Marcion's critique of the gospels in his *Antitheses*) and what Tertullian can only presume to be his motives for submitting this evidence.

d) Fourthly, later in his work Tertullian adds that in his *Antithesis* Marcion claims to have corrected a gospel (cf. Harnack 1924, 250*) which had 'been falsified (*interpolatum*) by the upholders of Judaism with a view to its being so combined in one body with the law and the prophets that they might also pretend that Christ had that origin'(4,4,5).

e) Fifthly, all the available evidence points to a clear, substantial and close affinity between the Gospel of Luke and Marcion's gospel.[32] Since both these writings are attested in the same time and place, and since one of them was probably used by Christians in Rome, Christians with whom Marcion had been and was in contact (positively and negatively), the simplest and most 'economical' way of explaining this affinity is to argue that one was dependent on the other. It is an unsound method to explain the similarity by introducing a purely hypothetical third gospel of which there is absolutely no other trace.

The traditional interpretation is thus vindicated: Marcion knew and challenged the gospels of Matthew and John, Mark and Luke. To the traditional view it can be added that

---

31 Tertullian, *Adversus Marcionem* 4,4,3-4,5,1 and *Præscripto hæreticorum* 23-24, see also Irenaeus, *Adv. haer.* 3,13,1.
32 Cf. Hengel 2000, 12; 31-33; 217, note 42; 232, note 151.

Marcion's challenge against the authority of these four gospels apparently (b above and a below) did not include any claim that they were not written by apostles or apostolic men (contrary to Harnack 1924, 41). Marcion clearly intended to discredit the gospels, and he clearly could have done so by referring to a tradition or an argument that could have supported a claim that one or more of these gospels had been attributed wrongly to an apostle or an associate of an apostle. His apparent and implicit acceptance of the claimed authorships would indicate that he knew of no such tradition or argument that might draw the authorship into question. This is no argument from silence:

a) Firstly: Tertullian explicitly mentions that Marcion used Paul's rebuke of the apostles for perverting the gospel of Christ referring to Paul's Letter to the Galatians (chapter 2); and that it was (4,2.2-3): *on this ground* (statum) that Marcion strived *to overthrow the credit of those gospels which are the apostles' own and are published under their names, or even the names of apostolic men.* Marcion thus finds his argument against the status of the gospels not in any claim that they were not written by the ascribed apostolic authors, but rather by trusting that they were written by apostles and then finding a passage showing that Paul rebukes these apostles.

b) Secondly: Marcion based his theology on a radical interpretation (and Tertullian would say mutilation) of Paul. Marcion's trust in the traditional attribution of the Gospel of Luke to the associate of Paul, Luke, would have made it logical for him to choose this gospel as the one to be reworked. Martin Hengel comments on what he regards as an old tradition for the relationship between Paul and Luke and the Gospel of Luke, and continues: *Marcion presupposes basically the same scheme and can therefore declare the purged Luke to be the Gospel preached by Paul.*[33] Taken on its own, this cannot have been the most logical choice with its genealogy and its narrations on the nativity, all of which Marcion had to remove as judaising.[34]

It can thus be concluded that Marcion's critique of other early Christian groups did include a polemic against their writings, but that Marcion did not challenge the provenance ascribed to these writings by other Christians.

Tertullian's skirmish, his debate with Marcionites over the provenance of the gospels

'...from among the apostles the faith is introduced to us by John and by Matthew, while from among apostolic men Luke and Mark give it renewal' (*Adv. Marc.* 4,2,2). Here as elsewhere, Tertullian makes it clear that he operates with four gospels. This is

---

33 Hengel 2000, 232, note 151 for the quote, and 99-104 for the tradition on the relationship between Paul and Luke.
34 Harnack 1924, 253*-254*; Evans 1972, xx; Hengel 2000, 230, note 134. Cf. Irenaeus, *Adv. haer.* 3,14,1-4.

not extensively argued, a fact indicating that Tertullian presumed that such an implicit four-gospel canon would be uncontroversial among his readers.

It is, however, interesting that Tertullian clearly distinguishes between gospels deriving from apostles (ex apostolis) and gospels deriving from authors associated with apostles (ex apostolicis). In this context Tertullian argues that both the gospels deriving from the apostles (Matthew and John) and the gospels deriving from the apostolic men (Luke and Mark) are written on the authority of Christ and are all with their differences in detail and arrangement proven to be in harmony with each other on the essentials of faith (capite fidei), i.e. the one and only God, the creator; his Christ, born of a virgin and the fulfilment of the law and the prophets. Nevertheless, Tertullian's distinction is introduced in order to facilitate a distinction in authority between the four gospels. Tertullian writes (4,2,4): 'Now Luke was not an apostle but an apostolic man, not a master but a disciple, in any case less than his master, and assuredly even more of lesser account as being the follower of a later apostle, Paul'. Firstly then, the authoritative status of the gospels of Luke and Mark is less than the status of the gospels of John and Matthew. Secondly, Tertullian describes Luke as a follower of Paul (compare 4,5,4) and Paul as a later apostle, thereby relegating the Gospel of Luke to a tertiary status. Tertullian does not qualify or explain his statement, so clearly he presumes that his reader is fully aware of which older apostle Mark was following in a manner that could be compared to the way in which Luke followed Paul. On the basis of this passage alone, we would be unable to determine who Tertullian was comparing Paul with. Turning to a later passage in Tertullian's work against Marcion and to Irenaeus, whose writings Tertullian knew,[35] the identity of this older apostle and his link to Mark, as yet unmentioned in the work of Tertullian but nevertheless presumably known by Tertullian's ancient reader, can be established. Both Tertullian and Irenaeus claim that Mark wrote his gospel according to the tradition handed on by Peter (4,5,4). On the basis of the passage from *Adversus Marcionem* 4,2,4, where Tertullian presumes that his reader knows both the identity of this unmentioned apostle and his link with Mark (without having to mention him by name or describe it), we can conclude that the tradition linking Peter and Mark and thus explaining the provenance of the Gospel of Mark was widely known.[36]

It is quite obvious why Tertullian should want to relegate the Gospel of Luke to a tertiary status below the status of the gospels of Matthew and John in the fist place and the Gospel of Mark in the second: Marcion and the Marcionites recognised only one gospel, an altered edition of the Gospel of Luke[37] – in Tertullian's words (4,2,4): 'For

---

35 E.g. Evans 1972, xviii and Gregory 2003, 209.

36 In writings prior to Tertullian's *Adversus Marcionem* (207-208 C.E., cf. 1,15), this tradition is attested by Papias (app. 120 C.E.; Eusebius, *H.E.* 2,15,2 and 3,39,15); Irenaeus, *Adv. haer.* 3,1,2 and 3,10,6 and Clemens of Alexandria (app. 200 C.E., Eusebius, *H.E.* 2,15,2 and 6,14,6-7). Finally, if the traditional dating (app. 170) of the so-called Muratorian Canon is accepted, Metzger 1989, 305, note 1 might be right in suggesting that the beginning of the fragment could indicate that the lost opening of the text had included a tradition about a link between Peter and Mark. Cf also Hengel 2000, 78-80.

37 Cf. Tertullian, *Adversus Marcionem* 4,1,1; Evans 1972, 643-644; Harnack 1924, 39-44.

out of those authors whom we possess, Marcion is seen to have chosen Luke as the one to mutilate'. With a forensic metaphor, so loved by Tertullian, it is then claimed by Tertullian that his opponent is not using the best of the available evidence in his case between him and Tertullian, between impiety and truth (4,1,1 and 4,5,3-4). Following this line of argument, Tertullian next argues that the Gospel of Luke is the youngest of the four gospels, and that since Marcion claims to have corrected the Gospel of Luke, this corrected (or according to Tertullian's vivid rhetoric 'mutilated') version must be even younger (4,5,6). Explicitly, Tertullian dates Marcion's act of sacrilege (*sacrilegium Marcionis*) in relation to the Gospel of Luke to the time of Antoninus Pius, and in contrast to this he claims that the true gospel tradition is unaltered since the time of Tiberius (4,4,5). With the last part of the argument, Tertullian can no longer build his case on any written gospel, but must claim a tradition in churches established by the apostles and contrast this with the newness of all Marcionite churches (4,4,4- 4,5,7). Like Irenaeus, Tertullian claims an unbroken tradition from Jesus via the apostles to his day. The tradition passed on from apostles to the days of Tertullian followed three routes which supported each other: firstly through churches founded by the apostles, still preserving their word and being in contact with other churches (including Tertullian's own); secondly through disciples of apostles and a succession of bishops to the bishops of Tertullian's day and age; and thirdly through the writings of the apostles (compare Irenaeus above).

Both in relation to written gospels and in relation to tradition in churches, Tertullian employs the so-called proof from antiquity: an argumentation building on the premise that authority (*auctoritatem*) belongs to that which is older, prejudging as corrupt that which is seen to have come later (4,1,1). Tertullian states that he claims the support of the 'succession of times...against the late emergence of falsifiers,...: because the truth...of necessity precedes the false, and proceeds from those from whom its tradition began' (4,5,7).[38]

Ending the proof from antiquity, Tertullian employed a military metaphor and informed his readers that such a tactic was only employed by him when he was lightly armed and skirmishing with the enemy, indicating that now he was fully armed he was preparing himself for the main clash (4,5,7). The main and stated purpose of books four and five of Tertullian's work against Marcion is, as we have seen, to prove Marcion wrong even on the limited evidence provided by Marcion himself (4,1,1; 4,4,3 and 4,6,1-2), i.e. his falsified version of the Gospel of Luke. For Tertullian what we might call the skirmish regarding the provenance of different religious writings was over. The battle for the right interpretation of one of these writings, the altered Gospel of Luke, was about to begin. The progress and outcome of this battle is another story which cannot be told here.

---

38   Cf. Gregory 2003, 209 and Pilhofer 1990, 289-292.

Conclusion

For our purpose of course the skirmish was in focus. The purpose of a skirmish is often to establish your own position in a favourable location and to acquire information on your enemy's. The position established by Tertullian in his skirmish with the Marcionites and analysed above can be summed up by the figure below. By claiming that the Gospel of Luke was younger than the other three gospels, which could also all claim superior status because they were based on more direct contact between Jesus and their author, Tertullian's skirmishing earned him a vantage point from which he could attack the Marcionite position based as it was on an altered version of the Gospel of Luke. It might be that Tertullian honestly believed the Gospel of Luke to be the youngest; it might even be that he was right;[39] this is not for us to decide or even debate here. For us it is firstly important to observe that Tertullian's position on the provenance of the gospels contrasts with Irenaeus' position, thus proving that Tertullian was independent of (but probably not unfamiliar with) Irenaeus' position. Secondly, it is equally important to note that both their positions (true or not, honestly assumed or not) were admirably suited to serve their particular aims.

As we have seen, accounts by eyewitnesses and personal experience written shortly after the events described were given special significance and credence in the ancient world, and early Christian authors, who were comfortable with this culture, of course shared its bias (e.g. 1 John 1:1; Tertullian, *De fuga in persecutione* 9,3 and *De anima* 17,14). With this in mind, we presumed that this bias would also figure prominently in the provenance debates both when the writings of opponents were discredited and when defending one's own favourite writings. This thesis was amply corroborated. For instance, such strategies were obvious in Josephus' Contra Apionem (see above). But we also found that matters were sometimes more complicated than that. Superficially it might seem that Irenaeus and Tertullian, like modern apologists, would have wanted to argue that the gospels were written quite early and by eyewitnesses. But as we have seen, this was not the case – they both found it convenient to argue for a late composition of at least one of the four gospels that they found normative. On closer inspection however, even these lines of argument were linked to the bias for antiquity and first-hand experience. By claiming a late date for the Gospel of John, Irenaeus could make John write his gospel against heretical views that were current around the turn of the first century; and by claiming a later date for the Gospel of Luke and a less glorious authorship (by one who was not an eyewitness to the Lord and not even a companion of an eyewitness), Tertullian could diminish the status of the writing used (mutilated) by his enemy, Marcion.

From the examples discussed in detail above, and also from the example only briefly mentioned, i.e. the debate between Josephus and Apion, it is evident that the argumentation of a protagonist could be both offensive, i.e. discrediting the writings

---

39   Only a minority of modern scholars would argue that the Gospel of Luke is the youngest, but although such a thesis cannot be proved, neither can it be disproved on our available evidence.

important to another person or group by drawing its provenance into question, and defensive, i.e. arguing for a provenance of writings important to one's own position or tradition presumed to confer status on these writings. Both the defensive and the offensive approach were thus used in debates over the three different 'frontlines', between protagonists:

a)   disagreeing on an issue but recognising and respecting each other;
b)   from the same tradition but condemning each other as representing heretical or schismatic positions;
c)   perceiving each other as representing distinct and different traditions.

I will conclude this article by quoting Tertullian one last time: 'Controversy over the Scriptures has no other effect than to upset the stomach or the brain' (Tertullian, *Praescriptio hæreticorum* 16). As we have seen, this view did not make Tertullian spare his readers from extensive debates on the provenance of these scriptures. It is my hope that I have avoided causing my readers any discomfort in those departments by analysing parts of the debates of Tertullian and other authors.

FIGURE: Tertullian's 'ranking' of available 'evidence' in his 'case' against Marcion: The further up the figure you go, the higher the status and the older the age. Lines mark tradition. Paul is here placed lower than Matthew, John and Peter, since Tertullian stressed that Paul was not a disciple of Jesus and only received his gospel through a revelation. Only names in bold typeface represent written evidence (gospels) available to Tertullian and Marcion. Tertullian thus blames Marcion for having based his falsified gospel on the available written evidence with the lowest status and least claim to have an authoritative and direct tradition back to Jesus.

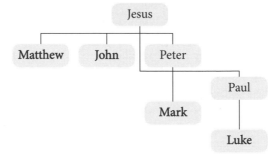

Bibliography

Altaner, Berthold, Alfred Stuiber 1966. *Patrologie. Leben, Schriften und Lehre der Kirchenväter*, Freiburg: Herder.

Arbesmann, R., E.J. Daly, E.A. Quain 1959. *Tertullian: Disciplinary, Moral and Ascetical Works.* (The Fathers of the Church. A new translation). Washington: The Catholic University of America Press.

Aune, David E. 1997. *Revelations 1-5.* (World Biblical Commentary 52). Dallas: Word Books, Publisher.

Barrett, C.K. 1978 (1955). *The Gospel according to St John.* London: SPCK.

Beard, Mary; John North; Simon Price 1998. *Religions of Rome,* vol.1: *A history.* Cambridge: Cambridge University Press.

Beare, Francis Wright, 1981. *The Gospel according to Matthew. A Commentary.* Oxford: Blackwell.

Beasley-Murray, George R. 1981. *John.* (World Biblical Commentary 36). Dallas: Word Books.

Becker, J. 1969. 'Erwägungen zu Fragen der neutestamentlichen Exegese.' *BZ* 13, 99-102.

Brox, Norbert 2001. *Irenäus von Lyon, Adversus Haereses, Gegen die Häresien, 1-5.* Freiburg: Herder.

Campenhausen, Hans von 1968. *Die Entstehung der christlichen Bibel.* Tübingen: Mohr Siebeck.

Dunkerley, R. 1961. 'The Five Johns'. *LQHR* 30, 292-298.

Engberg, Jakob 2007. *Impulsore Chresto. Opposition to Christianity in the Roman Empire c.50-250 AD.* (Early Christianity in the Context of Antiquity 2). Frankfurt: Peter Lang.

Engberg, Jakob 2004. *Reaktioner på kristendommen i Romerriget. Omvendelse og modstand ca. år 50-250.* Dissertation. Odense: Institute of History and Civilization, University of Southern Denmark, 2004. Unpublished but available with an English summary at http://www.humaniora. sdu.dk/phd/afhandlinger.html

Evans, Ernest 1972. *Tertullian Adversus Marcionem. Edited and Translated.* Oxford: Oxford University Press.

Falkenberg, René and Anders-Christian Jacobsen (eds.) 2004. *Perspektiver på Origenes' Contra Celsum.* (Antikken og Kristendommen 1). Copenhagen: Anis.

Gregory, Andrew 2003. *The reception of Luke and Acts in the period before Irenaeus: looking for Luke in the second century.* Tübingen: Mohr Siebeck.

Harnack, Adolf von, 1924 (1921). *Marcion: das Evangelium vom fremden Gott; eine Monographie zur Geschichte der Grundlegung der katholischen Kirche.* Leipzig.

Hembold, A. 1962. 'A Note on the Authorship of the Apocalypse.' *New Testament Studies* 8, 77-79.

Hengel, Martin, 1989. *The Johannine Question.* Harrisburg: Trinity Press.

Hengel, Martin, 2000. *The Four Gospels and the One Gospel of Jesus Christ. An Investigation of the Collection and Origin of the Canonical Gospels.* Harrisburg: Trinity Press.

Hyldahl, Jesper, 2004. 'Origenes og Bibelen: Den fortalte historie og den skjulte betydning. Allegori som apologetisk argument i Origenes' Contra Celsum'. In: René Falkenberg and Anders-Christian Jacobsen (eds.), *Perspektiver på Origenes' Contra Celsum.* (Antikken og Kristendommen 1). Copenhagen: Anis, 117-128.

Hyldahl, Jesper, 2007. 'Allegori i apologetisk perspektiv i alexandrinsk jødedom.' In: Anders Klostergaard Petersen, Jesper Hyldahl, Kåre Fuglseth (eds.), *Perspektiver på jødisk apologetik.* (Antikken og Kristendommen 4). Copenhagen: Anis, 181-206.

Hyldahl, Niels, 1966. *Philosophie und Christentum. Eine Interpretation der Einleitung zum Dialog Justins.* Copenhagen: Munksgaard.

Lane Fox, Robin, 1986. *Pagans and Christians in the Mediterranean world from the second century AD to the conversion of Constantine.* London.

Marincola, John 1997. *Authority and Tradition in Ancient Historiography*. Cambridge: Cambridge University Press.

Metzger, Bruce M. 1989. *The canon of the New Testament: its origin, development, and significance*. Oxford: Clarendon Press.

Mutschler, Bernhard 2004. *Irenäus als johanneischer Theologe: Studien zur Schriftauslegung bei Irenäus von Lyon*. Tübingen: Mohr Siebeck.

Newman, Barclay 1963. 'The Fallacy of the Domitian Hypothesis. Critique of the Irenaeus Source as a Witness for the Contemporary-Historical Approach to the Interpretation of the Apocalypse.' *New Testament Studies* 10, 133-139.

Osborn, Eric 2001. *Irenaeus of Lyons*. Cambridge: Cambridge University Press.

Petersen, Anders Klostergaard, Jesper Hyldahl, Kåre Fuglseth (eds.), *Perspektiver på jødisk apologetik*. (Antikken og Kristendommen 4). Copenhagen: Anis.

Pilhofer, Peter 1990. *Presbyteron kreitton: der Altersbeweis der jüdischen und christlichen Apologeten und seine Vorgeschichte*. Tübingen: Mohr Siebeck.

Pokorný, Petr and Ulrich Heckel 2007. *Einleitung in das Neue Testament. Seine Literatur und Theologie im Überblick*. Tübingen: Mohr Siebeck.

Quasten, Johannes 1962 (1953). *Patrology*, 1-2. Utrecht.

Schmithals, Walter 1992. *Johannesevangelium und Johannesbriefe. Forschungsgeschichte und Analyse*. Berlin: de Gruyter.

Skarsaune, Oskar, 1976. 'The Conversion of Justin Martyr'. *Studia Theologica* 30, 1976.

Skeat, T.C. 1992. 'Irenaeus and the Four-Gospel Canon. *Novum Testamentum* 34, 194-199.

Smalley, S.S. 1994. *Thunder and Love: John's Revelation and John's Community*. Milton Keynes.

Stott, John R.W. 1988 (1964). *The Letters of John*. Leicester.

Strecker, K.D. 1992. 'Chiliasmus und Doketismus in der johanneischen Schule'. *KD* 38, 30-46.

Wescott, Brooke Foss 1886. *The Epistles of John: The Greek Text with Notes and Essays*. Cambridge: Cambridge University Press.

Witherington, Ben 1998. *The Acts of the Apostles. A Socio-Rhetorical Commentary*. Cambridge.

Zahn, Theodor 1904 (1901). *Grundriss der Geschichte des neutestamentlichen Kanons: eine Ergänzung zu der Einleitung in das Neue Testament*. Leipzig: Deichert.

NORMATIVITY AND MEMORY IN THE MAKING:
THE SEVEN HILLS OF THE 'OLD' AND 'NEW' ROME

Gitte Lønstrup

There is a myth concerning Constantinople according to which the Christian Emperor Constantine the Great (306-337) founded his city, Κωνσταντινούπολις, on seven hills:

Le cerimonie inaugurali di Costantinopoli rivelano dunque il sigillo di quella stretta connessione con Roma che il fondatore impresse sulla 'città carissima': un sigillo di cui la città di Costantino portava tante testimonianze: nell'orografia **dei sette colli** (Follieri 1981-83, 230).

La nouvelle Rome, à qui un décret, gravé au Strategion sur la colonne impériale, confère tous les droits de l'ancienne, aura ses **sept collines** historiques au rôle bien défini: ... (Janin 1950, 4).

New Rome (Constantinople) was built on **seven hills** like the antique Rome by the emperor Constantine the Great.[1]

However, Byzantine historians from the fourth and fifth centuries – Eusebius, Socrates, Sozomen, Philostorgius, and Zosimus – who played a crucial role in shaping Constantinople's early historical memory, make no mention of these legendary seven hills in their accounts of the city's foundation.[2] In this paper I shall present the foundation histories told by these authors in order to review what was and – just as importantly – what was not said about Constantine's foundation of his new capital on the Bosporus, especially the various constructions of memory at play in these records regarding Constantinople's much-vaunted creation in the image of Rome. How did the ancient writers portray Constantine's city? And what did they say about the new capital's relationship to the 'old Rome' in their accounts? Finally, I shall attempt to give some

---

1   http://www.istanbulguide.net/insolite/english/seven_hills.htm. For an extensive description of the hills, see Janin 1950, 4; Gylles 1561.

2   Accounts of the foundation of Constantinople: Socrates *H.E.* (*Historia Ecclesiastica 5th c*) 1,16; Sozomen *H.E.* 2,3 (5th c); Philostorgius *H.E.* 2,9 (5th c); Hesykius (6th c). *Patria* (*Patria kata Hesychion Illustrion*, Codex Palatinus 398, 10th c). Ed. Preger, Th. *Scriptores Originum Constantinopolitanarum*, § 42. New York. Arno Press 1975; Malalas, J. (6th c). *Chronographia*, 13,7. *The Chronicle of John Malalas*. English translation by Elizabeth & Michael Jeffreys & Roger Scott. Melbourne 1986; Zosimus (5-6th c). *Historia Nea* 2,3. Greek text: Ed. Paschoud, F. Paris. Belles Lettres, 1971-1989. English translation, *New History*. London. Green and Chaplin 1814; Theophanes (9th c). *Chronographia*, AM 5821. English translation: *Chronicle of Theophanes Confessor: Byzantine and Near Eastern history, A.D. 284-813*. Translation, introduction and commentary by Mango, C. & Scott, R. with the assistance of Greatrex, G. Oxford. Clarendon Press 1997; *Chronicon Pascale* (7th c) 9,233. In: Mommsen, Th. (ed), *Chronica minora saec. IV. V. VI. VII. Monumenta Germaniae Historica, Auctorum Antiquissimorum,* 9, Berlin. Apud Weidmannos 1961. The rites concerning the *Natalis* of the city are not documented until the sixth century. For a description of the foundation see Dagron 1974, 13ff.

indications on when the myth about Constantinople's supposed 'seven hills' may have arisen and why it was subsequently connected to the foundation of Constantinople by Constantine in the fourth century.

'Constructions of memory', or 'memory constructions', is used here as a methodological term, referring to the different monuments, festivals and texts that were erected, performed and composed to shape the social and cultural memory of late Roman people following the re-foundation of a minor Greco-Roman polis, Βυζάντιον renamed Κωνσταντινούπολις as an imperial residence and capital of the Eastern Roman empire.[3] Every such act represents a 'memory-manifestation', an act that inscribes a fact for collective recollection as 'public history', for example, the heavily stage-managed annual celebration of Constantinople's *dies natalis* in the city's hippodrome, which self-consciously mirrored the same celebration that had taken place for centuries in Rome's Circus Maximus.[4] By their very nature, monuments such as the hippodrome and the sculptures decorating it were conscious constructions of memory, as was the public calendar designed to record the feasts to be celebrated and the rituals to be enacted within the hippodrome's memory-laden monumental frame. It is worth considering that even the etymological root of the English 'monument' derives from the Latin verb *moenere*,'to remember'. To a certain extent the architecture, the feasts and the rituals inaugurated in Constantinople confirm that Constantine's city was built as the reflection of Rome. Indeed, Constantinople was the 'new Rome', Νέα 'Ρώμη.

It was only natural that Constantinople as an imperial residence mirrored Rome's basic architectural formula (consisting of a palace, a hippodrome and an imperial mausoleum), as the imperial residences of Constantine's predecessors in Antioch, Thessalonica, Nicomedia, and Sirmium had done.[5] But none of these previous imperial residences ever had the impact on the empire's mother city that Constantinople was to have when it appropriated the idea of Rome. Through the manner of this appropriation, Constantinople simply became Rome, as I shall argue later in this paper. In the process of becoming 'Rome', Constantinople's leaders created a distinctive social and cultural memory that not only likened 'new Rome' to the 'old Rome', but also surpassed and superseded the Rome on the Tiber. For this reason it is necessary not only to consider the likenesses between the 'old' and the 'new Rome', but also the differences between the 'mother' and the 'daughter' – one of these being the undeniable fact that 'New Rome' was not originally founded on seven hills.[6]

---

3   The primary exponents of memory theory used in this study are Jan Assmann (2006) and Paul Connerton (1989).

4   Note in the Roman *Fasti Philocaliani*: 'Natalis Urbis. Circenses missus XXIIII' (*Corpus Inscriptionum Latinarum* 1,2, 1871). The first edition of this calendar was begun in 336 and finished in 354. See also Salzman 1990, 122 table 2. During the fourth century, Rome's foundation day was still celebrated with games in the circus. This continued until 444.

5   Mango 1985, 24. Chantraine 1989, 88-89.

6   Mango 1966. The metaphor of the 'mother' and the 'daughter' was first used in the ekphrasis written by Paul the Silentiary at the re-inauguration of Hagia Sofia in 562.

Founding Constantinople and 'New Rome' 'equal to Rome': the shaping of cultural memory

After the Synod the emperor (i.e. Constantine the Great) spent some time in recreation, and after the public celebration of the twentieth anniversary of his accession, he immediately devoted himself to the reparation of the churches. This he carried into effect in other cities as well as in the city named after him, which being previously called Byzantium, he enlarged, surrounded with massive walls, and having rendered it equal (ἴση) to imperial Rome (βασιλεύουσα Ῥώμη), he named it *Constantinople,* establishing by law that it should be designated *new Rome* (δευτέρα Ῥώμη) (i.e. second Rome).This law was engraved on a pillar of stone erected in public view in the Strategion near the emperor's equestrian statue. He built also in the same city two churches, one of which he named *Irene,* and the other *The Apostles.* … he brought forth their (the pagans') images into public view to ornament the city of Constantinople, and set up the Delphic tripods publicly in the Hippodrome. It may indeed seem now superfluous to mention these things, since they are seen before they are heard of (Socrates, *H.E.* 1.16).

This is the account on the foundation of Constantinople written by the fifth century church historian Socrates Scholasticus, born in the city around 380, fifty years after its official inauguration in 330. In a previous chapter (*H.E.* 1,4) Socrates describes how the founder of the city, Constantine the Great, had besieged his last co-emperor Licinius (308-311) at the battle of Chrysopolis (modern Üsküdar) on September 18th, 324. In the aftermath of this event Constantine took over Βυζάντιον and renamed it after himself on November 8th, 324. Six years later, on the inauguration day, May 11th, 330, the emperor was aspiring not only to make Κωνσταντινούπολις into yet another imperial residence or thanks-giving gesture to his Christian God and protector in memory of the victory in 324, but also to make it the 'second Rome', δευτέρα Ῥώμη, as testified by the law in-scribed in stone and erected in the Strategion.[7]

Inscriptions are unquestionably *aides-memoire par excellence,* employing both figurative and verbal elements to ensure the remembrance of the person or the event they commemorate. The memory which the particular inscription in the Strategion of Constantinople was supposed to manifest was the new cultural memory of the citizens of Constantinople: officially they were no longer citizens of Byzantium, but Constanti-nopolitans. If indeed Socrates' testimony can be trusted, and if such an inscription was in fact erected by Constantine, it was doubtless read aloud and heard by the citizens during the celebrations in 330.[8] However, by that stage this new cultural memory had

---

7   The inscription no longer exists, and the law is not to be found in the *Codex Theodosianus (Theodosiani leges novellae Libri XVI.* Ed. Mommsen, Th. & Meyer, P. M. Berlin 1905. English translation by Pharr, C. 1952. *The Theodosian Code and Novels and the Sirmondian Constitutions,* Princeton), which does not mention the days on which the *dies natales* of Rome and Constantinople were to be celebrated, only that they were to be celebrated (2,8,19). For comments on this inscription, see Mazzarino 1974, 128; Chantraine 1989, 90. Clinton 1845-1853, 104: The name 'Constantinople' appears in a law of November 29th, 330 and December 1st, 334.

8   The inscription mentioned by Socrates has provoked much debate. It is contested whether Constantine ever used the epithet 'new Rome' or whether it was an invention of his son Constantius II (337-61), which both the documentation of the use of the term and the iconographic evidence on the coins seems to indicate (Fig. 1-2), as mentioned briefly below. For a critical approach, see Dölger 1937.

The coins struck for the inauguration of Constantinople, May 11th, 330, did not contain representations of the 'new' and 'old Rome', but only the personification of the *Tyche* of Constantinople modelled on a typically Greek scheme (Toynbee 1947). The earliest dated mint representations of the two cities are from 343, struck for the *Vicennalia* of Constantius II, and again ten years later for his *Tricennalia*. This bronze medallion (*contorniate*) shows Rome (wearing a helmet) and Constantinople (wearing a mural crown like the Greek *Tyche*) holding a shield between them. It dates from the mid fourth century. The legend 'CONSTANTI AVGVSTI' refers to either Constans (337-350) or Constantius II (337-50). With permission from Bibliothèque Nationale Paris, Cabinet des Médailles (AF 17337).

already been made visibly manifest to the people of Constantinople, who were witnessing their city being transformed into an imperial residence thriving with monumental constructions of churches, city walls, a hippodrome and statuary such as the emperor's equestrian statue. These monuments inevitably manifested the fact that Constantinople was becoming 'new Rome' before the remembrance of this process was put into words, carved in stone and read aloud in the Strategion. In Socrates' play with the senses of hearing and seeing – 'It may indeed seem now superfluous to mention these things, since they are seen before they are heard of'– one might see a parallel to the way in which memory is visualised and anchored in monuments before it is verbalised – not only in official inscriptions and decrees, but also in historical accounts.

The portrait of Constantinople drawn by Socrates is dominated by the idea that the city was 'rendered equal to imperial Rome'. However, he is not particularly specific about the form or the nature of this equality. Might it be that he found these likenesses too obvious to mention? In any case, he omits that Constantine inaugurated the hippodrome begun by Septimius Severus (193-211), and built a palace and an imperial mausoleum. Nor does he mention any topographical or urbanistic details such as the hills or the fourteen regions into which the city was divided. Moreover, given the fact that the Romans carefully selected, documented and commemorated their feast days, it is surprising that the dates of the city's foundation or inauguration are not mentioned. Nor is any explanation given as to why exactly May 11th was chosen as the city's *dies natalis*. Apart from mentioning the expansion of the polis by means of new city walls, Socrates limits his accounts to the overall fact that by rendering the city equal to 'imperial Rome', Constantine decreed that it should be designated as the 'second Rome'.

An iconography similar to that in fig. 1 is found on a series of non-dated gold medallions from the reign of Constantius II, possibly struck for the eleven-hundredth anniversary of the foundation of Rome. As Toynbee writes (1947, 141): 'In 348, we may believe, Constantius II, augured on these gold medallions, with their twin-cities and new Constantinopolis types, a rebirth of Rome on the Tiber in Rome on the Bosporus, hinting at the destiny of the then still junior partner to succeed and supersede her senior.' The medallion shown here comes from Thessalonica and dates to the reign of Constantius II. With permission from bpk/ Münzkabinett Staatliche Museen zu Berlin.

The fact that the concept of 'new Rome' did become part of the cultural memory of the Late Roman Empire is evident in medallions and coins as well as the variations of the theme made by poets, orators, historians, and theologians from the fourth century onwards.[9] In fact, the making of Constantinople in the image of Rome made the comparison between Rome and Constantinople, the 'old' and the 'new Rome', a popular literary *topos* for centuries. Among the earliest writers to allude to this theme was Porphyry Optazianus, Constantine's court poet, who speaks of Constantinople as *altera Roma,* the 'other Rome', in a poem dating from 326 (*carmina* 4,6; 18,34). The earliest documented use of the expression 'new Rome' is to be found in a speech held by the prominent court orator Themistius, living in the city in the second half of the fourth century. In this speech, held in 357 in honour of Constantius II (337-61), in whose reign the iconography of the two Romes also began to emerge (cf. fig. 1-2), Themistius juxtaposes Νέα 'Ρώμη, the 'new Rome', and ἀρχαία 'Ρώμη, the 'old Rome'.[10] Fourteen years later, in 381, the renowned theologian Gregory of Nazianzus describes Constantinople as 'the young Rome', ὁπλοτέρη 'Ρώμη in one of his poems.[11] But more importantly, and in the same year, Gregory was patriarch of Constantinople, where the Church Council took place, the famous third canon of which stated that: 'Because it is

9   Like ancient Rome, the representation of 'new Rome' took shape as a female genius, *Tyche,* not as a representation of seven hills. For representations of the 'old' and 'new Rome', see Bühl 1995; Alföldi 1947; Toynbee 1947. On the concept of 'new Rome', see Dölger 1937, 84-85 (who does not think Constantine called his city 'new Rome' but only named it after himself: Constantinoupolis); Irmscher 1981-83, 236.
10 Oration 3,42. See Heather & Moncur 2001, 127; Salvo 2002-4, 131-152; Chantraine 1989, 90.
11 *PG* 37, 1027. Chantraine 1989, 90. Irmscher 1981-83, 238.

new Rome, the bishop of Constantinople is to enjoy the privileges of honour after the
bishop of Rome'.[12] Some decades after Gregory, Socrates, as quoted above, emphasises
that Constantinople was made the 'second Rome' and the equal of 'imperial Rome'.
Other historians such as Eutropius, active around 350-70, and the Arian historian
Philostorgius, writing between 400 and 450, present the relationship between Constantinople and Rome as being based on 'rivalry' rather than on 'equality':

He (Constantine) was the first that endeavoured to raise the city named after him to such a
height as to make it a rival to Rome (*ut Romae aemulam faceret*) (Eutropius, *Breviarium historiae
Romanae* 10,8).

Constantine, after having built the city, called it 'alma Roma', which means in the Latin tongue,
'glorious'. … the emperor … adorned the city in other particulars with such sumptuous mag-
nificence that it became a rival (αντίπαλος) to ancient Rome (προτέρα 'Ρώμη) in splendour
(Philostorgius, *H.E.* 2,9).

Whether an 'equal' (ὁμώνυμος / ἴση) or a 'rival' (*aemula* / αντίπαλος) – why was it
so important to create a relationship between Rome and Constantinople, making the
latter a 'new Rome'? In going to the trouble of making a new capital, why bother to
imitate the old one? Obviously, the very idea of Rome was a powerful construction
(Dölger 1937, 71). 'Innovation' was not a prestigious value in Late Antiquity, whereas
'tradition' and 'antiquity' carried authority. By adopting the name and making the city
equal – or even rival – to the' old Rome', 'new Rome' acquired a significant authority,
which was needed at a later stage to take over the position as capital of the Empire.
This also explains why the comparison between the two cities became such a popular
topos – at least in Constantinople. It is quite significant indeed that historians such as
Ammianus Marcellinus and Claudian almost completely pass over Constantinople in
silence, while Eunapius and Eutropius (although he lived there) show rather negative
attitudes towards the city (Kelly 2003).

The common denominator of the authors mentioned above is that they employ the
new cultural, collective, and living memory of fourth century Constantinople, which
was in the process of becoming 'new Rome', as an overall expression without explaining how it was rendered equal to 'imperial Rome'. From Socrates' contemporary, the
church historian Sozomen († about 448-50), we get some more information.

Sozomen's account of the foundation of Constantinople (*H.E.* 2,3), which I shall
paraphrase below, is more extensive than that of Socrates, and contains more detailed
information on social politics and welfare, constructions of cultural and social memory,

---

12   *Conciliorum Oecumenicorum Decreta*, ed. J. Alberigo, H. Jedin, 1972. Bologna: Istituto per le scienze religiose,
      canon 3,32. This status was further negotiated at the Council of Chalcedon, the 28th canon of which stated that
      the See of Constantinople was equal to that of Rome. This statement was not recognised by the Roman See.

as well as the portrayal of the relationship between Rome and Constantinople based on equality. I shall focus upon the latter two.

As for the concept of equality, Sozomen does not limit himself to the statement that Constantine 'did not fail studiously to make the city which bore his name equal in every respect to that of Rome in Italy'; he also describes in what way the 'new Rome' was equal to the 'old Rome'. According to Sozomen, Constantinople was equal to Rome regarding 'celebrity', 'honour', and 'power'. As a consequence of this the two Romes were to share their name, and their status as imperial capitals and as the government of the empire. Therefore, a senate building (*Capitolium*) was – hardly coincidentally, as pointed out by Eugenio La Rocca – erected in the eighth region of Constantinople; the same region in which the *Capitolium* of Rome had been located since the Emperor Augustus (27 BCE – 14 CE) divided the ancient city into fourteen regions.[13] The fact that the senators of Constantine's city were not equal to those of Rome until the Theodosian period, when they rose from being just *vir clari* to *vir clarissimi*, seems, however, to have been overlooked by Sozomen in his eagerness to demonstrate the likenesses and the equality between the 'new' and the 'elder Rome', νέα Ῥώμη καὶ πρεσβυτέρα Ῥώμη.

Sozomen explicitly emphasises 'equality' three times in the text using two different expressions: ἴσα Ῥώμη and τῇ Ῥώμη ὁμότιμος. But in relation to Rome he indirectly seems to be placing Constantinople in a sovereign position – unlike Socrates, to whom Constantinople is the 'second Rome' (δευτέρα Ῥώμη), which one might argue is hardly the same as the 'new Rome', Νέα Ῥώμη (Chantraine 1989). While Socrates describes the 'old Rome' as 'imperial Rome', βασιλεύουσα Ῥώμη, the epithets used by Sozomen are 'the elder Rome', πρεσβυτέρα Ῥώμη, and 'Rome in Italy', Ἰταλοῖς Ῥώμη, which do not seem entirely equal. On the contrary, they seem to indicate how Constantinople by the fifth century was in the process of becoming Rome, while the 'elder Rome' was losing its authority as an imperial city. These epithets are further emphasised in the sixth century, when Constantinople is no longer just the 'new flourishing Rome', but simply 'Rome' in one of the 32 epigrams written in honour of the late-fifth-early-sixth-century charioteer Porphyrius, to whom seven statues were erected on the *spina* in the hippodrome of Constantinople and frescoes were painted in the emperor's lounge – the *Kathisma*.[14] Of these seven bases only two survive.[15] While Constantinople in these epigrams is called Rome (Ῥώμη), 'ancient Rome' is distinguished as the 'old Latin Rome', 'Rome by the Tiber' and 'Rome of Italy' in the contemporary *ekphrasis* composed by Paul the Silentiary for the re-inauguration of Hagia Sophia in 562. The epigrams as well as the *ekphrasis* were composed during the reign of Justinian, when the city founded by Constantine in the image of the 'old Rome' had reached a point in which it had interiorized that image – or in Paul the Silentiary's words: 'the daughter had out-shone the mother'. In the making of Constantinople the ancient virtue of adhering to tradition

---

13   *Notitia Urbis Constantinopolitanae* (ed. Seeck 1876). La Rocca 1992-3, 569.
14   *Antologia Graecae* XV 47 (in: Loeb, *The Greek Anthology* vol. V): 'Thus Porphyrius was born in Africa, but brought up in Rome' (Τοῦτον Πορφύριον Λιβύη τέκε, θρέψε δέ Ῥώμη…).
15   Dölger 1937, 95 note 35. Vasiliev 1948, 40.

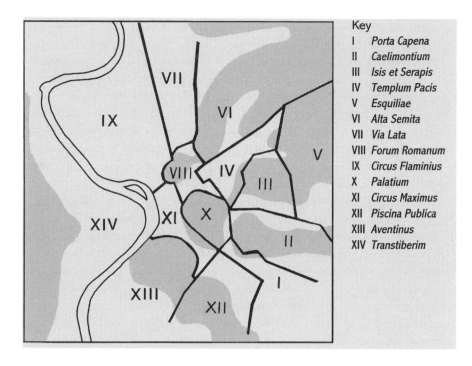

Map of the fourteen regions of Augustan Rome.

Augustus divided Rome into fourteen regions in 7 BCE when he reformed the municipal administration, as mentioned in the *Roman History* of Cassius Dio (55,8). See also Platner 1929. From Amanda Claridge et al.: *An Oxford Archaeological Guide,* Oxford University Press, 1998.

seems to have been combined with an increasing need to break with it. This ultimately gave way to a radical change, that, roughly speaking, inversed the respective roles of the two cities: Constantinople became Rome.[16] The inferiority of 'Rome by the Tiber' to 'Rome' (i.e. Constantinople) arguably brought about the byzantinisation of the very heart of the 'old Rome'; a development testified by the construction of the churches Ss. Cosmas and Damian, S. Theodore and S. Maria in Antiqua in and around the Forum Romanum.

The foundation history told by Sozomen is introduced by an account of Constantine's first choice of a capital – being not a 'new Rome', but rather a 'new Troy', thus creating an alliance with a heritage preceding that of Rome, the legendary forefather of which came from Troy (Aeneas).[17] However, this antiquarian strategy was apparently

16   Dagron 1987. For a critical approach to this thought, see Brown 1982, 171-2. This point will be further elaborated in my PhD dissertation due in May 2010, Aarhus University.

17   This is not the place to go into the social aspects of Constantine's foundation that are put forward by Sozomen, such as the food supply, the peopling of the city and the summoning of aristocratic families to Constantinople. See Brown 1971, 88.

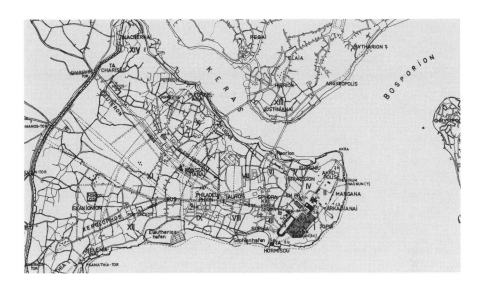

Map of the fourteen regions of Constantinople.

    Like Rome, Constantinople was divided into fourteen regions, and as seen on the maps on figs. 3-4 the Capitolium in both cities was found in the eighth region. From Wolfgang Müller-Wiener: *Bildlexicon zur Topographie Istanbuls: Byzantion, Konstantinupolis, Istanbul bis zum Beginn des 17. Jahrhunderts* Tübingen, 1977.

not approved of by divine providence: in a vision, Constantine is advised to proceed and abandon the building of the 'new Troy'. Following his divine intuition the emperor is led to Byzantium, where he settled 'in obedience to the words of God', enlarging the city with walls and adorning it with the most beautiful temples to God, luxurious houses, a hippodrome, fountains, *porticos* etc. This architectural programme mirrors fourth-century Rome, and as such it can be understood as a construction of cultural memory. Missing in the architectural portrait of Constantinople drawn up by Sozomen, however, is the imperial mausoleum, begun by Constantine in the 'new Rome' – as well as in the 'old Rome'.[18] The building of this mausoleum and the church of the apostles, the erection of churches and memorials in honour of the martyrs, was indeed what mostly captured the interest of the emperor's biographer, Eusebius Pamphilius,

18   There is consensus about the fact that the imperial mausoleum at the Via Casilina, the old Via Labicana, where the emperor's mother, Helen, was buried, was originally destined to Constantine, who, as is well-known, was buried in the Holy Apostles in Constantinople.

who probably died around 339.[19] Despite the fact that he was a living testimony to the building of the city (which he supposedly visited around 336-37), he makes no effort to describe the foundation of the emperor's own city, 'consecrated to the martyrs' God'.

Although Socrates, Eusebius, and Sozomen all fail to mention the actual foundation and inauguration date of the city, the latter two provide interesting – but not entirely corresponding – comments on the calendar. According to Eusebius (*Vita Constantini* 3,48), no demon festivals or superstitious ceremonies were observed in Constantinople, while Sozomen testifies to the transferral of the same 'festal days as those customary to the other Romans'. When consulting the *Fasti Philocaliani* (336-354), a traditional non-Christian Roman festival such as the *Lupercalia* was still remembered in the Late Roman calendar.[20] Unfortunately, a fourth-century Constantinopolitan calendar equivalent of the *Fasti Philocaliani* does not exist. It would have allowed us to get a fuller understanding not only of exactly how many Roman festal days were actually transferred to the 'new Rome', but also of the social memory established in Constantinople – the rituals, ceremonies and feasts being crucial elements in the creation of the new social memory of the city.[21] Nevertheless, it has been argued that the *Lupercalia* were celebrated in the 'new Rome' as well, and non-Christian ceremonies and rituals were most likely part of the foundation and inauguration rites of Constantine's city in 324, 328 and 330.[22] John Lydus (490-550) describes the inauguration ritual in Constantinople as having been performed by (Vettius Agorius) Praetextatus. Whether the master of the ceremony was in fact this famous Roman senator, who was to become guardian of the traditionalist 'pagan party' in Rome, not to mention pontifex of Vesta, Augur and the Father of Mysteries, is not certain but probable, according to Lelia Cracco Ruggini.[23] However, while Lydus gets the date of the *Natalis* of Rome (April 21st, XL MAIAS) right, he seems to have placed the inauguration ritual – performed

---

19   Eusebius, *Vita Constantini* (*V.C.*) 3,48-49: 'And being fully resolved to distinguish the city which bore his name with especial honour, he embellished it with numerous sacred edifices, both memorials of martyrs on the largest scale, and other buildings of the most splendid kind, not only within the city itself, but in its vicinity: and thus at the same time he rendered honour to the memory of the martyrs, and consecrated his city to the martyrs' God. Being filled, too, with Divine wisdom, he determined to purge the city which was to be distinguished by his own name from idolatry of every kind, that henceforth no statues might be worshipped there in the temples of those falsely reputed to be gods, nor any altars defiled by the pollution of blood: that there might be no sacrifices consumed by fire, no demon festivals, nor any of the other ceremonies usually observed by the superstitious.' See *V.C.* 4,58-60: on the church of the Holy Apostles.

20   Although the *Fasti Philocaliani* (*Corpus Inscriptionum Latinarum* 1,2) was not an official calendar, but a private commission made by a man called Valentinus, it is most likely to have reflected the official calendar. See Greswell 1854, 387-390; Salzman 1990. From Constantinople we only have the *Consularia Constantinopolitana* from 395 for the years 245-468 (*Chronica minora saec. IV. V. VI. VII. Monumenta Germaniae Historica, Auctorum Antiquissimorum*, 9, Th Mommsen (ed.). Berlin. Apud Weidmannos 1961, 205-247). But these are annual chronicles that do not include lists of public feasts like Roman calendars such as the *Fasti Philocaliani*.

21   For the importance of rituals and bodily gestures in the shaping of social memory, see Connerton 1989.

22   As for the *Lupercalia* of Constantinople, they are attested in the *Book of Ceremonies* 2.82 (73). See Duval 1977, who traces it back to Constantine. I thank Dr. Neil McLynn for this reference. On pagan rituals at the inauguration of Constantinople and Alan Cameron's critical view on this aspect (*IX Annual Byzantine Studies Conference*, 1983, 84), see La Rocca 1992-93, 562ff.

23   Cracco Ruggini 1980, 610. The inscription erected in honour of Praetextatus contains a series of his honorific titles (*Corpus Inscriptionum Latinarum* 6,31929) as does Praetextatus' funerary inscription (*Corpus Inscriptionum Latinarum* 6,1779).

by these two prominent figures – in the chapter on the month of January rather than in the one on May.[24]

In any case, the 'new Rome' was not identical to the 'old Rome', and certainly not all the festal days customary to the other Romans were literally transferred to Constantinople. The legendary *dies natalis* on the eleventh day before the *kalends* of May (April 21st) was simply neither transferable nor sharable. On the contrary, it was such an ingrown part of Roman heritage that not even the Christian Emperors Theodosius I, Arcadius, and Valentinian II dared to abolish it when they annulled a great number of conventional Roman holidays in 389.[25]

While Rome was celebrated eleven days before the *kalends* of May, Constantinople was celebrated eleven days after the *kalends* of May; a day which in the ancient Roman calendar was the festival of the *Lemuria* that served to appease the spirits of the dead (Greswell 1854, 304-311). Not only was the 'new Rome' given another *dies natalis* than that of the 'old Rome', but the feast itself also differed from that held in Rome, although both birthdays were celebrated with *ludi et circenses* in the respective hippodromes of the two Romes. In Rome, the *Natalis Urbis* was a feast held in honour of the city, while its founding father was celebrated on a separate occasion: the *Quirinalia* on February 17th. In Constantinople, however, May 11th seems to have been a celebration not only of the city but also of its founder, if indeed the testimony of John Malalas (13,8) can be trusted. In his *Chronicle* he describes how the statue of Constantine was carried into the hippodrome in a candlelight procession and was venerated by the emperor and the people. Furthermore, on May 11th the local martyr Mokios was presumably also commemorated, unlike the *Natalis* of Rome, which was kept free of Christian commemorations of saints.[26] Other distinct Christian rituals – as well as the commemoration of Saint Mokios – are described in the eighth-century *Parastaseis*, which mentions the repetition of the 'Kyrie Eleison' and the singing of solemn psalms in the Forum of Constantine, where a chapel supposedly stood beneath the porphyry column.[27] The later *Menologion* of Constantinople suggests a reading from the Evangelist John on the eleventh day of May, the birthday of the city, while the tenth-century *Typikon* of the

---

24   Lydus (5-6th c). *Peri Menon (De Mensibus)*. Ed. N. Schowii, B. Hasii, F. Creuzeri, G. Roether. Lipsiae, Darmstadt 1827, 13; 149. Lydus also mentions another participant in the ceremony, Sopater. He is also mentioned by Eunapius of Sardis (*Vitae sophistarum. Patrologia Graeca* 113, 34), whose approach to Constantinople is rather critical.

25   The birthday of Rome, April 21st, is registered in the Republican calendar *Fasti Antiates Maiores* (84-55 BCE) and in such Julian-Augustan calendars as the *Fasti Caeretani* (12 BCE) and the *Fasti Esquilini* (post 7 CE), as well as the *Fasti Philocaliani* (354 CE) and the *Fasti Polemii Silvii* (449 BCE). All are published in *Corpus Inscriptionum Latinarum* 1. Amongst the ancient writers referring to the foundation day on April 21st are Varro (116-27 BCE), quoted by Solinus *De Mirabilibus Mundi*. Mommsen 1st edition 1864, 1; Plutarch. *Vitae Romuli. The Loeb Classical Library*. London & New York 1914, 12,1; Ovid *Fasti*. Frazer, J.G. (standard English edition), London 1929, 4,806. For the annulment of holidays in 389, see *Codex Theodosianus* 2,8,19-22. See also Salzman 1990, 155; Lim 1999, 279; Lønstrup 2008.

26   *Le Typikon de la Grande Église. Ms. Sainte-Croix no 40, X siècle*. Introduction, commentary and translation by Mateos, J. *Orientalia Christiana Analecta*. Rome 1962. Ponteficium Institutum Orientalium Studiorum, 291. Morcelli 1788: *Menologium deo auspice evangeliorum in dies festos totius anni*. See also Dagron 1974, 395; Janin 1953, 367-371.

27   Krautheimer 1983, 62; Alföldi 1947, 10-16; Dagron 1974, 39-40; Baldovin 1987, 169.

Great Church describes a procession from Hagia Sophia to the Forum (of Constantine), where prayers were said, psalms were sung and lectures were read: Luke 1:46; Acts; 18:1-11 and John 15:9-16.[28]

Remembering territory and topography

As seen above, the accounts of three of the most renowned church historians of the fourth and fifth centuries, Eusebius, Socrates and Sozomen, do not provide information of the inauguration feast, although it seems to have consisted of several Christian elements. Nor do they provide topographical or urbanistic indications of the hills of the city or the fourteen regions into which it was divided as a reflection of the fourteen Augustan regions of Rome (cf. Fig. 4).[29] However, the fourteen regions of Constantinople are known from the Theodosian catalogue, *Notitia Urbis Constantinopolitanae* dating from around 425. This source contains a list of private and public buildings and sites in the city, but only twice is the word hill mentioned, *collis* in the Latin version, λόφος in the Greek: in the entry for the fourth and eleventh regions. However, in the eleventh region the comment is that there are no hills in that region since the landscape is flat (*Regio undecima spatio diffusa liberiore, nulla parte mari sociatur; est vero eius extensio tam plana, quam etiam collibus inaequalis*). In the fourth region, however, it says that there are hills on either side, one of them most likely being the old Acropolis of Byzantium (*Regio quarta a miliario aureo, collibus dextra laevaque surgentibus ad planitiem usque valle ducente perducitur*).[30] The Acropolis was contained within the second region, but in the entry for this region there is no mention of any of the seven legendary hills. It would seem obvious to place such a comment in the short introductory paragraph at the beginning of each region in which notes on the landscape are already extant – or simply in the actual list as seen in the fourth-century Regionary Catalogue, in which – under the heading *Quae sint romae* – one finds the entry *Montes Septem*.[31]

The *Notitia Urbis Constantinopolitanae* was most likely a promotional document showing the richness of Constantinople. If this is so, why would the seven hills on which the city was supposedly constructed be omitted in the list, when they provided the city with remarkable scenery and – more importantly – a powerful analogy to Rome? Obviously, such a parallel to the seven legendary hills of Rome would seem to be a memory construction *par excellence*: making the very topography of the new capital match that of the old. As scholars have rightly pointed out, the so-called fifth and sixth

---

28   *Parastaseis* 1 and 56 (Cameron & Herrin, 131); Dagron 1984, 29ff.

29   Mango 1985, 8; Müller-Wiener 1977, 21 abb. 2.

30   *Notitia Urbis Constantinopolitanae,* see Seeck 1876 and Berger 1988.

31   Mommsen, *Chronica Minora* 9, 545-6; Platner 1906, 70. The hills mentioned in this list are: *Caelius, Aventinus, Tarpeius, Palatinus, Exquilinus, Vaticanus et Ianiculensis.* While the Viminal and Quirinal hills are omitted, *Tarpeius* was often used as another name for the Capitoline hill. However, *Vaticanus* and *Ianiculensis* were not among the original seven hills. As explained by Platner, these areas became increasingly important as the city grew. Further down the list the names of the hills change, and this time only *Caelius* is missing. This list also contains information on 'campi, pontes, termarum, fora, basilicae, aquae, obilisci, circi, theatre, columnae, anfiteatra, ludi, portae, vici, etc.'

hills were not to be found within the precinct of the Constantinian walls, but were only included in the city by the immense walls erected by Theodosius II (401-450). Since the 425 catalogue and the impressive walls both date from the reign of Theodosius II, the inclusion of the fifth and sixth hills may well have fostered the legend of the seven hills as a Theodosian construction of the memory of the re-foundation of Constantinople as a result of this emperor's considerable extension of the city. If the 425 list was written as a promotional document, it may well have served the purpose of spreading this legend of the city's (re-)foundation on seven hills. This, however, is not the case.

In his description of the city's foundation, which includes a passage on the emperor's marking off of the territory, the Arian church historian Philostorgius does not mention the seven hills either. Philostorgius' history is conserved in a ninth-century compilation by Photius, patriarch of Constantinople in 853, who epitomises Philostorgius' passage as follows:

He says that in the 28th year of his reign, Constantine turned Byzantium into the city of Constantinople; and that, when he went to mark out the circuit of the city, he walked round it with a spear in his hand; and that when his attendants thought that he was measuring out too large a space, one of them came up to him and asked him, "How far Prince?" and that the emperor answered, "Until he who goes before me comes to a stop"; by this answer clearly manifesting that some heavenly power was leading him on, and teaching him what he ought to do.[32]

While Philostorgius (or Photius!) concentrates on Constantine's God-inspired marking out of the territory, the fifth century non-Christian historian Zosimus, who lived in Constantinople during the reign of the emperor Anastasius I (491-518), provides us with the most detailed topographical description of the site. In his *New History (Historia Nea)* we find the first mention of a hill, λόφος (Zosimus *Historia Nea*, 2,30). But before going into that, I would like to comment briefly on the city portrait drawn by Zosimus.

Several aspects of his account reveal how Constantinople reflected Rome. This is clear in a statement on the palace being only 'little inferior to that of Rome'. The same thing could be – but is not – said about the hippodrome, which was 200 metres shorter than Rome's Circus Maximus.[33] Instead, Zosimus has an interesting comment on the temple and the statues of Castor and Pollux, which were located in the hippodrome. What he does not mention, though, is that these twins had been the guardians of the city of Rome for centuries (Pietri 1961, 316; Trout 2003, 521-23). Further down it is stated that Constantine built a temple where he 'placed the statue of the Fortune of Rome'. Giving these traditional protectors of the 'old Rome' a home in the 'new Rome', Zosimos seems to belie the point put forward by the Christian authors: that the city was under the protection of the Christian God.

---

32   Philostorgius *H.E.* 2,9. He was born in Cappadocia but lived in Constantinople.
33   While the hippodrome in Rome measured 650 metres, the one in Constantinople was only 450 metres according to Dr. Bryan Ward-Perkins. Lecture: 'Rome and Constantinople compared', Edinburgh, May 11th, 2007 (Colloquium: *Constantinople in Late Antiquity*). See also Ward-Perkins 2000.

The foundation of the city is introduced by a series of Constantine's failures: the murder of his son Crispus, his wife Fausta and the flight from Rome after refusing to partake in the sacrifice on the Capitoline hill during the celebrations of his *Vicennalia* in 326.[34] According to Zosimus, these events drove Constantine to found his own city that initially seemed to take shape as a 'new Troy', as in Sozomen's account. But 'changing his purpose', Constantine sets off to Byzantium, where 'he admired the situation of the place'. Contrary to Eusebius, Socrates, Sozomen and Philostorgius, Zosimus actually describes the extent of the city: 'The city stands on a rising ground' (κεῖται ἡ πόλις ἐπὶ λόφου) enclosed by sea on either side. At this point one would expect him to mention the seven hills, rather than the more neutral expression 'a rising ground'– that is, if the myth of Constantine founding his city on seven hills existed in the late fifth and early sixth centuries. Zosimus, who is one of the best sources on the origins of Constantinople according to Cyril Mango, continues his description of the layout of the city by indicating that the previous Severan Wall extended from the west of 'the hill' (λόφος) towards the sea; from the north of 'the hill' (ὁ βορεῖος λόφος) to the dock and to the shore. Zosimus does not mention the name of this hill in order to distinguish it from other hills, but he is presumably talking about the Acropolis crowned with temples, one of them being the temple of Aphrodite/Venus referred to in his account.

Clearly, the argument in this essay is not whether Constantinople was founded on hills or on flat territory, but rather whether the myth of Constantine founding his city on seven hills is ancient or modern. Like any typical Greek settlement, Byzantium was undeniably founded on an Acropolis, but apart from that hill, what were the names of the other six hills? When consulting the topographical descriptions from Pietro Gylles († 1555) to Raymond Janin († 1972), the seven hills are distinguished by numbers (Janin 1950, 4; Gylles 1561). Only two of them are characterised by names: the so-called seventh hill 'Xerolophos' (i.e. the 'dry hill') and the so-called fourth hill 'Mesolophos' (i.e. 'the central hill').[35] The Greek word λόφος, meaning hill, is obviously present in both of these toponyms. But while 'Mesolophos' was and still is clearly a distinct hill crowned by the monumental *Fatih Camii*, occupying the former site of the church of the Holy Apostles, the hilled nature of 'Xerolophos' is less evident. In fact, when this toponym occurs subsequently in the eighth and tenth century *Parastaseis* and *Book of Ceremonies*, it is not in its character of a hill, but rather as one of the monumental *fora* of the city. This is evident when considering the contexts in which 'Xerolophos' figures: in the *Book of Ceremonies* it is the Forum of Arcadius, one out of several stations in the large squares of the city: 'The Forum (of Constantine), Tauros, Philadelphion, Bouef and Exakionion'. In another instance it says 'in the middle of Xerolophos' and 'under the vault of Xerolophos', like the eighth-century *Parastaseis* (20), in which it says that:

---

34 Krautheimer 1983, 131 note 30. Constantine had already refused to sacrifice in 312 when celebrating the defeat of Maxentius.

35 Janin 1950, 20, 37, 391. 'Philadelphion, carrefour situé au Mesolophos ou Mesomphalos, qui est le centre de la ville à l'époque théodisienne'. Note, however, that the use of this toponym dates from the tenth century. I shall return to this shortly.

'Formerly, some people used to call the Xerolophos a spectacle (θέαμα). For in it were 16 spiral columns …'.[36]

Certainly, when compared to the foundation histories of ancient Rome, the names of the seven hills (Capitoline, Palatine, Aventine, Esquiline, Viminal, Caelian and Quirinal), and their function as distinct landmarks establishing the layout of the city, are essential as in the first book of Livy's *Ab Urbe Condita*. According to Remo Gelsomino, the names of the seven hills of Rome were defined around 44 BCE by Varro in his *De Lingua Latina* (5,7-8.41-54), which became famous through the work of Livy.[37] Indeed, in the first book of *Breviarium historiae Romanae*, Eutropius, living and working in fourth-century Constantinople as *magister memoriae*, does not fail to mention the seven Roman hills in his description of the foundation of Rome, which undoubtedly owes much to Livy. As for the foundation of Constantinople, Eutropius has very little to say in his critical account of Constantine, which has already been quoted above in relation to the new Rome being a rival to the 'old Rome'. There is certainly no mention of the seven hills of Constantinople that might form a parallel to his description of the seven hills of Rome. Although it cannot be excluded that the seven Constantinopolitan hills were included in the concepts of 'equality' and 'rivalry', it seems that although the actual Roman topography gave rise to the legends of Rome, it was rather later legends of Constantinople that were superimposed on the topography of this city.

Seven hills or not, Constantinople was undoubtedly founded in the memory of Rome, as various other examples and expressions used in these sources reflect, from the palace to the hippodrome, from the fountains to the porticoes, and from the senate to celebrity, power and people. Despite the absence of the myth in these ancient sources, scholars of the 19th and 20th centuries frequently repeat that the 'new Rome', like the 'old Rome', was built by Constantine on seven hills. To my knowledge, this point is rarely if ever supported by references to Late Antique sources, but is sometimes followed by a comment that there were not seven hills within the Constantinian walls, but only five.[38] The seven hills referred to by modern scholars were not enclosed within the precinct of the city until the monumental walls of Theodosius II were completed. Thus, when the *Notitia Urbis Constantinopolitanae* was written around 425 the walls had been standing for more than ten years, and yet the seven hills are not to be found in the list. The fact that the ancient sources are not drawn into the discussion endows

36   Cameron & Herrin 1984, 83. Transmitted in an eleventh-century manuscript, but can be dated to the eighth century (cf. Cameron & Herrin 1984,1).

37   Livy 1.33: The Palatine, Capitoline, Aventine and Caelian hills were included by King Tullus; 1,44: The Viminal, Esquiline and Quirinal hills were included by King Servius. A similar example can be found in Vergil (*The Aeneid* 6,783), whose mention of the seven hills of Rome is quoted in Servius' fourth-century commentary (See Platner 1906, 70-74). Gelsomino 1975, 82, 99. In my PhD dissertation I shall elaborate on the comparison of Late Antique descriptions of the seven hills of Rome and Constantinople from both eastern and western viewpoints.

38   Baldovin 1987, 168. 'Although the city was given seven hills and fourteen regions to match the old Rome, there were actually only two main hills, neither of them exceeding fifty meters in height.' See also Mango 1966; La Rocca 1992-93, 571, who only refers to Janin 1950, 4. Fenster (1968, 114, 144, 250, 252, 298) does have references to the concept of ἑπτάλοφος but not in fourth-sixth century sources. I shall return to this concept shortly.

Map of the seven hills of Constantinople showing the numbering of the hills, as well as indications of both Late Antique and Ottoman names of buildings and sites characteristic of the areas around the seven hills.

the myth with a normative character. But when did this normative construction arise and develop?

Perspective & conclusion: the rise of the myth of the seven hills

The French memory specialist Maurice Halbwachs claimed that it is the distance to the past that makes room for the construction of history (Halbwachs 1950, 37, 70, 73). Eusebius, Constantine's own contemporary biographer, certainly made little effort to document the foundation and inauguration of the Emperor's city; whereas the further away one gets from this event, the more is written about it. Although Sozomen provides a more elaborate description than Eusebius and Socrates, he still does not describe the

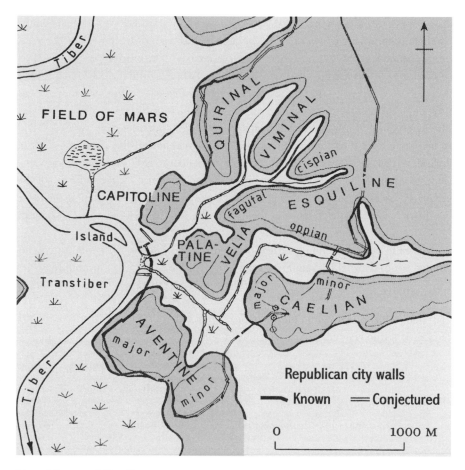

Map of the seven hills of Rome.

In the course of history there has been some confusion about the names of the hills of Rome, since the seven hills of the city were not the same before and after the Servian Walls, and later on *Ianiculus* and the *Vaticanus* were frequently included at the cost of some of the other hills. But despite this confusion, the idea of the seven hills of Rome has always been present in descriptions of the city, which does not appear to be the case in Constantinople, the seven hills of which only seem to be distinguished by numbers from the fifteenth century onwards. From Amanda Claridge et al.: *An Oxford Archaeological Guide*, Oxford University Press, 1998

inauguration date or the ceremony. Suddenly, in the sixth century, the *Chronicle* of John Malalas and the contemporary *Patria* of Hesychios Illoustrios provide information on the date, but not on the seven hills.[39] These sixth-century descriptions of the

---

39   John Malalas 13,7; Hesychios Illustrios, *Patria kata Hesychion Illustrion*, Codex Palatinus 398. In: Preger, Th. (ed), *Scriptores Originum Constantinopolitanarum*. New York. Arno Press 1975, § 42. See also Dagron 1984, 23-29.

date and the ritual celebrated on that occasion are further developed in the seventh-century *Chronicon Paschale* (630).[40] The tendency continues in the era of the great patriographical accounts: the eighth-century *Parastaseis* and the tenth-century *Book of Ceremonies*.[41] Although these descriptions contain an abundance of topographical indications of regions, quarters, milestones and routes within the city, they do not provide information relating to the names or the idea of the seven hills except for the 'Xerolophos'. And as mentioned earlier, where this toponym does occur, it is not in its character of a hill, but rather as one of the great *fora* of the city, the Forum of Arcadius. Had these sources contained such information, they would have indicated that the myth of the seven hills was firmly rooted in the collective memory of the people of Constantinople, as in the case of the people of Rome, who kept using these landmarks as points of reference in the city, as did also the visitors, whose itineraries are documented in the twelfth-century *Mirabilia Urbis*.[42]

Nevertheless, the myth of the seven-hilled Constantinople, the ἑπτάλοφος, actually does seem to be taking shape some time between the eighth and the tenth centuries within the rather obscure context of Byzantine apocalyptic literature.[43] When consulting

---

40   *Chronicon Paschale* (Mommsen, *Chronica Minora* 9, 233) from Whitbys' translation (Liverpool University Press. 1989): '330 Indiction 3, year 25, consulship of Gallicanus and Symmachus. In year 301 from the Ascension to Heaven of the Lord and year 25 of his reign, Constantine the most pious, the father of Constantine II Augustus and of Constantius and Constans Caesars, after building a very great, illustrious, and blessed city, and honouring it with a senate, named it Constantinople, on day five before Ides of May (May 11th), on the second day of the week, in the third indiction, and he proclaimed that the city, formerly named Byzantium, be called second Rome. He was first to celebrate a chariot-racing contest, wearing for the first time a diadem of pearls and other precious stones. And he made a great festival, and commanded by his sacred decree that the anniversary of his city be celebrated on the same day, and that on the 11th of the same month Artemisius (May) the public bath Zeuxippon be opened, which was near the Hippodrome and the Regia of the Palace. He made for himself another gilded monument of wood, bearing in its right hand a Tyche of the same city, itself also gilded, and commanded that on the same day of the anniversary chariot races, the same monument of wood should enter, escorted by the troops in mantles and slippers, all holding white candles; the carriage should proceed around the further turning-post and come to the arena opposite the imperial box; and the emperor of the day should rise and do obeisance to the monument of the same emperor Constantine and this Tyche of the city. The same most sacred emperor Constantine continued as emperor in Constantinople; he separated it from the province of Europe, that is, from its metropolis Heracleia, and appointed for the same Constantinople a praetorian prefect and city prefect and the other major officials. There are from the foundation of Rome until Constantinople was inaugurated 1,080 years.' See also the eighth-century *Parastaseis* chapter 5, 38 and 55-56; the tenth-century *Book of Ceremonies*, 2,79 (70); Berger 1988. For other medieval calendars, see Delehaye 1902 and Morcelli 1788.

41   *Constantine VII Porphyrogenitus, 913-959.* On the tenth-century collections, see Magdalino 2007, 11-15.

42   The idea of the seven hills of Rome was undoubtedly still alive in Late Antique and Medieval Rome, despite the confusion about the original names of the hills. See Platner 1906, 71; *Mirabilia Urbis Romae*, chapter 4 (ed. Accame and Emy (eds.), Rome 2004.

43   A recent study on the concept of ἑπτάλοφος has been made by Brandes (2003), who traces the first sporadic instance of a metaphorical use of the expression ἑπτάλοφος back to the 670s; a use, however, that had nothing to do with the actual topography of Constantinople, but which instead was an assimilation of an apocalyptic and critical expression often used in relation to Rome: the seven-hilled Babylon. I only became aware of this article after the present paper had already been submitted for publication. Although Brandes arrives at the same conclusion, his article differs significantly from the present one in terms of the weight it attaches to the sources. While the present paper unfolds the testimonies of the fourth- and fifth-century historians in order to make it clear what is and what is not being said about the foundation of Constantinople, Brandes refrains from analysing these sources in depth, and focuses instead upon the actual rise of the myth from the seventh and especially from the tenth century onwards, something which the present paper only briefly touches upon.

the *Thesaurus Linguae Graecae*, the first relevant entry after the entries relating to Rome[44] is the eighth-century *Visio Danielis,* falsely attributed to John Chrysostom.[45] This apocalyptic text does in fact describe the foundation of Constantinople, but nowhere does it say that Constantine founded the city on seven hills. Constantine is not even mentioned; only Byzas, the legendary founder of Βυζάντιον, figures in the text. However, ἑπτάλοφος is undeniably used as a metaphorical epithet for the city of Constantinople, indirectly comparing it to Rome and Babylon, or in Fenster's words: 'Denn ursprünglich ist Rom Babylon und die Siebenhügelige und wie früher Rom, so hält nun Konstantinopel den Antichristen auf, der erst nach dessen Untergang erscheinen wird.'[46]

Outside the sphere of the apocalyptic texts, the concept remains almost invisible during the eighth, ninth and tenth centuries except for a few sporadic examples such as the tenth-century *Ekphrasis* written by Constantine of Rhodes and the *Patria Konstantinupoleos* (989/90), transmitted by Georgius Codinus, who lived towards the end of the fifteenth century: 'Mesolophos is in the middle of the seven hills of the city. There are three on the one side and three on the other. The inhabitants call it Mesomphalos.'[47] In the twelfth century Theodoros Prodromos refers to the seven hills, while Niketas Chroniates does so in the thirteenth.[48] But not until the sixteenth century does an actual description of the hills emerge. The fact that a painstakingly detailed description of the seven hills of Constantinople was written by the French ambassador Pietro Gylles († 1555) is hardly coincidental. Gylles undertook the first topographical investigation of Constantinople in the 1540s, by which time the city had become Ottoman Istanbul. However, as reflected in several passages in the book *De Constantinopoleos Topographia,* published *post mortem* in 1561, this enterprise does not seem to have been entirely straightforward:

It was no great difficulty to distinguish the Roman hills, because they were entirely disjoined by valleys, but it is not so easy to distinguish those of Constantinople, because they are conjoined at the top, and besides, the backs of them do not project in so mountainous a manner as they

44   Similar information can be found in the *Greek Lexicon of the Roman and Byzantine Periods from 146 BC to 1100 AD* under the entry ἑπτάλοφος: 'Septicollis; seven-hilled; epithet of Rome. Plutarch, *Vitae Romuli* 2,280; Cicero (*Att.* 6,5,2); *Oracula Sibyllina* (2,18).'
45   Vassiliev 1893, 33ff (esp. 37, 46). The dating of the text does not seem to be absolute, although it is certainly between the eighth and ninth centuries.
46   Fenster 1968, 113-14. In another apocalyptic text, *Anonymi Byzantini,* from the tenth century, ἑπτάλοφος is used to designate a special purgatory for clerics. It is not referring to Constantinople though, but rather to Babylonian Rome. See Radermacher 1898, 4.
47   Hesychios Illustrius (6th c.), '*Patria (Patria kata Hesychion Illustrion, Codex Palatinus* 398, 10th c.). In: Th. Preger (ed.) 1975 (1907), *Scriptores Originum Constantinopolitanarum.* New York: Arno, 219: τὸ καλούμενον Μεσόλοφον μέσον ἐστὶ τῶν ἑπτὰ λόφων. ἤγουν ἡ μία μοῖρα τῆς πόλεως ἔχει τρεῖς λόφους καὶ ἡ ἑτέρα τρεῖς λόφους, καὶ μεσον ἐστι τοῦτο: οἱ δὲ ἰδιῶται Μεσόμφαλον καλοῦσιν αὐτό.
48   Nicetas Choniates, *Historia.* (entry from *Thesaurus Linguae Graecae*).

do in the front, so I cannot better describe them than by calling them a continued ridge of hills, divided each of them by valleys.[49]

Gylles was not the only 'child' of the spirit of the late Renaissance who was fascinated with 'ancient Rome' and the 'new Constantinople': Istanbul. Such fascination also led the King of Denmark to commission a series of portraits of the city and its people by Melchior Lorch, whose famous 11,5-metre long panorama of the hilly cityscape from 1559 displays Istanbul in profile.[50] The seven hills do not play a significant role in this panorama, though.

The aim of this essay was to question whether the idea of the seven hills of Constantinople was a construction of cultural memory established some time between the fourth and fifth centuries, or whether it arose as a later invention. Judging from the evidence presented here, the sources from the first centuries after the foundation of the city provide no indication of the existence of this myth. It seems probable that the myth of Constantine founding his city on seven hills did not originate in the Constantinian period, nor in the Theodosian or Justinianic periods, but some time in the early Medieval period closely related to Byzantine apocalyptic literature; at first assimilated as a metaphorical expression previously designating Rome, and only later fused with the topography of the city. It cannot be excluded that the myth of the seven hills was not an ancient and ingrown part of oral memory and public history too obvious to mention in the 425 catalogue and in the historical accounts. This seems unlikely, though. When seen in the light of the making of memory in fourth- and fifth-century 'new Rome', the mention of the seven hills in these records would only have served the historian's argument that the city in every respect was made the equal of Rome.

Bibliography

Alföldi, A. 1947. 'On the Foundation of Constantinople: A Few Notes'. *The Journal of Roman Studies*, 37, 1-2, 10-16.

Assmann, J. & Livingstone, R. 2006. *Religion and Cultural Memory: Ten Studies*. Stanford, California: Stanford University Press.

Baldovin, J. 1987. *The Urban Character of Christian Worship. The origins, development, and meaning of stational liturgy, Orientalia Christiana Analecta* 228, Roma: Pontificium Institutum Studiorum Orientalium.

Berger, A. 1988. *Untersuchungen zu den Patria Konstantinupoleos*. Bonn: Dr. Rudolf Habelt GMBH.

---

49   Gylles 1561, 56. Further comments on the difficulty in distinguishing between the seven hills: '... for these hills are joined together in such a manner that they seem to lie upon one level. They are both of them on one plain, which, covering the top of the fourth hill is not above four hundred paces in length ... The northern side of the fifth hill has four small hills jetting out of it.'

50   In my PhD dissertation I shall elaborate on these fifteenth-century ideas reflected in maps, such as the so-called 'Düsseldorf drawing' from 1480 (see Buondelmonti, C. 1414-1420. *Liber Insularum Archipelagi,* 1414-1420. Universitäts- und Landesbibliothek Düsseldorf Ms. G 13 Faksimile, Wiesbaden 2005), and in written sources such as the *Synkresis* of Manuel Crisolora.

Brandes, W. 2003. 'Sieben Hügel: Die imaginäre Topographie Konstantinopels zwischen apokalyptischem Denken und moderner Wissenschaft'. *Rechtsgeschichte. Zeitschrift des Max-Planck-Instituts für europäische Rechtsgeschichte* 2, 58-71.

Brown, P. 2006 (1971). *The World of Late Antiquity.* London: Thames & Hudson.

Brown, P. 1982. 'Eastern and Western Christendom in Late Antiquity: A Parting of the Ways'. repr. in P. Brown, *Society and the Holy in Late Antiquity,* London: Faber, 1982, pp. 166-95. (First edition: in *The Orthodox Churches and the West,* ed. D. Baker, *Studies in Church History,* Oxford, 1976), 1-24)

Bühl, G. 1995. *Constantinopolis und Roma. Stadtpersonifikationen der Spätantike.* Berlin: Akanthus.

Cameron, Av. & Herrin, J. 1984. *Constantinople in the early eighth century: The Parastaseis Syntomoi Chronikai.* Leiden: E.J. Brill.

Chantraine, H. 1989. 'Konstantinopel – vom Zweiten Rom zum Neuen Rom'. *Jahres- und Tagungsbericht der Görres-Gesellschaft.* Salzburg.

Clinton, H.F. 1845-1853. *Fasti Romani: the civil and literary chronology of Rome and Constantinople from the death of Augustus to the death of Justin II.* Oxford: Oxford University Press.

Connerton, P. 1989. *How Societies Remember.* Cambridge: Cambridge University Press.

Cracco Ruggini, L. 1980. 'Vettio Agorio Pretestato e la fondazione sacra di Costantinopoli'. In: *Philias charin: miscellanea di studi classici in onore di Eugenio Manni.* Roma: G. Bretschneider, 593-610.

Dagron, G. 1974. *Naissance d'une capitale: Constantinople et ses institutions de 330 à 451.* Paris: Presses universitaires de France.

Dagron, G. 1984. *Constantinople imaginaire: études sur le recueil des Patria.* Paris: Presses universitaires de France.

Dagron, G. 1987. 'Manuel Crisoloras: Constantinople ou Rome'. *Byzantinische Forschungen,* 12, 279-88.

Delehaye, H. 1902. *Synaxarium Ecclesiae Constantinopolitanae e codice Sirmondiano nunc berolinensi – propylaeum ad acta sanctorum novembris,* Brussels: Apud Socios Bollandianos, 1902.

Duval, Y-M. 1977. 'Des Lupercales de Constantinople aux Lupercale de Rome'. *Revue des études latines,* 55, 243-251.

Dölger, F. 1937 (1953, 1964). 'Rom in der Gedankenwelt der Byzantiner'. *Zeitschrift für Kirchengeschicte,* 56, 1-42.

Fenster, E. 1968. *Laudes Constantinopolitanae. Miscellanea Byzantina Monacensia* 9. München: Institut für Byzantinistik und Neugriechische Philologie der Universität München.

Follieri, E. 1981-83. 'La Fondazione di Constantinopoli: riti pagani e christiani'. *Roma, Costantinopoli, Mosca.* Seminario internazionale di studi storici 21 aprile *Da Roma alla terza Roma* (1, 1981, Roma). Napoli: Edizioni Scientifiche Italiane.

Gelsomino, R. 1975. *Varrone e i sette colli di Roma.* Roma, Arezzo: Herder.

Greswell, E. 1854. *Origines Kalendariae Italicae* (4). Oxford: Oxford University Press.

Gylles, P. 1561. *De Constantinopoleos Topographia.* English translation: *The antiquities of Constantinople.* London 1729.

Halbwachs, M. 1950. *La mémoire collective.* Ouvrage posthume publié par Jeanne Alexandre, née Halbwachs. Paris: Presses universitaires de France.

Heather, P. & Moncur, D. 2001. *Politics, Philosophy, and Empire in the Fourth Century. Select Orations of Themistius.* Liverpool: Liverpool University Press.

Irmscher, J. 1981-83. "'Nouva Roma" o "Seconda Roma". *Renovatio o Traslatio?'*. *Roma, Costantinopoli, Mosca*. Seminario internazionale di studi storici 21 aprile 'Da Roma alla terza Roma' (1, 1981, Roma). Napoli: Edizioni Scientifiche Italiane.

Janin, R. 1964 (1950). *Constantinople Byzantine: développement urbain et répertoire topographique*. Paris: Institut français d'études byzantines.

Janin, R. 1953. *La géographie ecclésiastique de l'Empire byzantine*, v. 3: *Eglises et monastères*. Paris: Institut Français d'Études Byzantines.

Kelly, G. 2003. 'The new Rome and the old: Ammianus Marcellinus' silences on Constantinople'. *Classical Quarterly*, 53.2, 588-607.

Krautheimer, R. 1983. *Three Christian Capitals: Topography and politics*. Berkeley: University of California Press.

La Rocca, E. 1992-93. 'La fondazione di Costantinopoli'. *Costantino il Grande: dall'antichità all'umanesimo*. Colloquio sul Cristianesimo nel mondo antico a Macerata 18-20 dicembre 1990. Bonamente, G. & Fusco, F. Università degli Studi di Macerata. II, 553-583.

Lim, R. 1999. 'People as Power: Games, Munificence and Contested Topography'. Harris, W.V. (ed.). *The Transformations of Urbs Roma in Late Antiquity. Journal of Roman Archaeology*. Supplementary series 33. Portsmouth, Rhode Island, 265-283.

Lønstrup, G. 2008. 'Constructing Myths: The Foundation of *Roma Christiana* on 29 June'. *Analecta Romana Instituti Danici*. Roma: G. Bretschneider.

Magdalino, P. 2007. *Studies on the History and Topography of Byzantine Constantinople*. Aldershot: Ashgate.

Mango, C. 1966. 'Review of Sherrard, P.: *Constantinople: iconography of a sacred city'. Journal of Hellenic Studies*, 86, 306-307.

Mango, C. 1985. *Le développement urbain de Constantinople (IVe-VIIe siècles)*. Paris: Boccard.

Mazzarino, S. 1974: *Il basso impero. Antico, tardoantico ed era Costantiniana* (I). Bari: Dedalo.

Morcelli, A. 1788. *Kalendarium Ecclesiae Constantinopolitanae* (2), Roma: Ex officina Giunchiana maiore sumptibus Venanti(i) Monaldini et Pauli Giunchi.

Müller-Wiener, W. 1977. *Bildlexikon zur Topographie Istanbuls: Byzantion, Konstantinupolis, Istanbul bis zum Beginn d. 17. Jh*. Tübingen: Wasmuth.

Pietri, C. 1961. 'Concordia Apostolorum et Renovatio Urbis. Culte des martyr et propagande pontificale'. *Mélanges de l'École française de Rome* 73, 275-322.

Platner, S.B. 1906. 'The Septimontium and the Seven Hills'. *Classical Philology*. 1, 1, 69-80. Chicago: The University of Chicago Press.

Platner, S.B. 1928 (completed and revised by Ashby, T.). *A Topographical Dictionary of Ancient Rome*. London: Oxford University Press.

Radermacher, L. 1898. *Anonymi Byzantini: De caelo et infernis epistula*. Leipzig: A. Deichert'sche Verlagsbuchhandlung.

Salvo, L. de 2002-2004. 'Temistio e Costantinopoli'. Ed. Febronia, E. *Politica retorica e simbolismo del primato: Roma e Costantinopoli (secoli IV-VII)*. Atti del convegno internazionale (Catania, 4-7 ottobre 2001). Omaggio a Rosario Soraci. Catania CULC, 131-152.

Salzman, R. M. 1990. *On Roman Time. The Codex-Calendar of 354 and the Rhythms of Urban Life in Late Antiquity*. Berkeley, Los Angeles, Oxford: University of California Press.

Seeck, O. 1876. *Notitia Dignitatum. Accedunt Notitia Urbis Constantinopolitanae et Laterculi Provinciarum*. Berlin: Apud Weidmannos.

Sophocles, E.A. 1914. *Greek Lexicon of the Roman and Byzantine Periods from BC 146 to AD 1100*. London, Cambridge Mass.: Oxford University Press.

Toynbee, J.M.C. 1947. 'Roma and Constantinopolis in Late-Antique Art from 312 to 365'. *The Journal of Roman Studies*, 37, 1-2, 135-144.

Trout, D.E. 2003. 'Damasus and the Invention of Early Christian Rome'. *Journal of Medieval and Early Modern Studies*, 33, 517-36.

Vassiliev, A. 1893. *Anecdota Graeco-byzantina*, pars prior. Moskau: Universitatis Caesareae.

Vasiliev, A. A. 1948. 'The Monument of Porphyrius in the Hippodrome at Constantinople'. *Dumbarton Oaks Papers*, 4, 29-49.

Ward-Perkins, B. 2000. 'Constantinople, Imperial Capital of the 5th and 6th centuries'. *Sedes Regiae*, Barcelona 400-800, 2000.

PART II

The discursive fight over biblical and post-biblical texts

COMMUNICATION OF AUTHORITY

THE 'PROPHET' IN THE BOOK OF JEREMIAH

Else Kragelund Holt

The hermeneutical background

Actually, it was not until the mid-1980s that the authority of the Old Testament prophets was seriously challenged in the scholarly world of Old Testament exegesis. Before that, historical critical scholars, no matter how positivistic their scholarly ideal might be, tended to have as their heuristic point of departure, explicitly or implicitly, a Christian (Protestant) faith-based concept of divine revelation, or at least to wrestle with the Protestant understanding of the Bible as first and foremost a pathway to God. Generally speaking, exegetes took as their point of departure the twofold conception that 1) at least a core of genuine prophetic oracles was present in the text, and 2) that this prophetic core message was due to divine inspiration. Genuine prophetic oracles *eo ipso* formed a direct link to the word of God, in other words to revelation. Even in the second half of the twentieth century, commentators did not only assume that the prophetic books gave access to an historical person, the prophet, and to his historical message (e.g. Bright 1965, XVI; Holladay 1986-1989, 1). Many of them also wrote about the prophetic messages as being *de facto* inspired by God.

From the 1980s, however, the scene changed so that nobody any longer could talk unconcernedly about the prophet as an historical person, or about the prophetic oracles as an indisputable word of God. The interest, at least in certain Scandinavian and Anglo-American scholarly circles, changed from textual history (e.g. in redactional- and form-critical studies) towards a concern for the 'final form of the text', or the 'canonical' dimension. This development was due not only to general scepticism regarding the Old Testament as a source of history which led to a late dating of the 'historical' narratives in the Old Testament,[1] or to the influence of theories of literature. There was also a direct impetus for methodological change from the works of exegetes like the Irish Old Testament exegete Robert P. Carroll.[2] From the outset Carroll's interest was highly historical. He contested the conventional trust in the historical information given in the prophetic books, including the apparently self-evident connection between the 'author', mentioned in the incipit of the book, and the oracles (e.g. Carroll 1986, 33-37). This scepticism became a point of no return for Carroll and scholars inspired by him,

---

1   In Denmark historical minimalism or scepticism was represented first and foremost in Niels Peter Lemche's dissertation, *Early Israel*, from 1985 and the works that followed by him and others in the so-called Copenhagen school.

2   Carroll 1981; Carroll 1986; an informative collection of articles representing the change of interest is Davies (ed.) 1996.

and in his later writings Carroll dealt increasingly with biblical writings, especially the Book of Jeremiah, from an ideological critical point of departure (e.g. Carroll 1991; 1999). Carroll challenged the authority of the biblical text from more than one angle.

This challenge was met by other members of the exegetical society with surprisingly passionate anger. It was as if Carroll's talk about 'ideology' in lieu of 'theology' confronted the exegetes with their own tacit religious bias. Only on the surface did the traditional historical critical guild seem to be religiously unbiased; when faith-based (especially North-American) research encountered criticism of the ideas in the (Hebrew) Bible, the reaction was severe opposition.[3] The challenging of historicity became a *de facto* challenge of God's authority.[4]

History and theology

This is not the place to go into details regarding the philosophical hermeneutical question of the authority of the Bible. By and large, on the one hand Lessing's 'garstige Graben' (ugly ditch) between the text and the recipients has been acknowledged as insurmountable within historical critical scholarship since its beginning; on the other hand, the hermeneutical attitude towards the Bible has not been especially coherent or without epistemological self-contradictions, as discussed above. On a more pragmatic level, however, the collapse of some exegetes' ultimate confidence in historical methods and results from the 1980s and onwards, combined with the growth of so-called post-modern methodologies, has turned a lot of research in new directions.

Recent methods, whether they focus on literary or historical questions or employ a combination of both, often take as their point of departure the above-mentioned late dating of the books of the Old Testament to the exilic and post-exilic (or in sum: Temple-less) period. Read from this point of view, the texts open up for new understandings. They are understood as dealing with problems in a vulnerable community of exiles in Babylon and Persia or in post-520 BCE Yehud.[5] This was a society troubled by the conflict between on the one hand ex-exiles (returnees), and on the other hand those who were left behind when the upper- and middle-class population was taken into exile in 597 BCE and 587 BCE. This group of primarily low-ranking peasants found their living threatened by the returnee's demands on the property they had been living on for decades, a conflict mirrored in many of the Old Testament books (Berquist 1995, 60-81).

One of the more influential scholars in this field is Daniel L. Smith-Christopher, whose monograph *A Biblical Theology of Exile* (Smith-Christopher 2002)[6] introduced modern psycho-social and social anthropological methodology to the broader field of

---

3   For Carroll's comments on this, see Carroll 1999a, especially 76-77 with note 8.

4   This, of course, is part of a much larger discussion about the importance of history and historicity for Old Testament and Biblical theology; for an overview, see Perdue 1994, 1-110.

5   From c. 520 BCE Judah should be referred to as the Persian province Yehud. For an introduction to the history of Judah after the Babylonian conquest in the early 6th century BCE, see Berquist 1995; Middlemas 2007.

6   See also the preparatory studies in Smith 1989.

Old Testament exegesis. Smith-Christopher reads the texts on the backdrop of insights from refugee studies and studies in Post Traumatic Stress Disorder, as texts which can be elucidated through a comparison to the material in modern anthropological field reports about inhabitants in refugee camps and in societies traumatised by war, civil war, or natural catastrophes such as earthquakes or famine. What is interesting in Smith-Christopher's work is that he has not only a historical interest in these texts, but a theological interest as well, and he uses historical methodology for the sake of theology. The previous intended scholarly separation of history and theology is deliberately crossed over by a scholar who openly admits to having a definitive, theological interest in the texts he deals with in his scholarly work. Smith-Christopher reclaims theological authority for the Old Testament texts.

The theological consequences of the critical exegesis drawn by Smith-Christopher are very different from Carroll's.[7] But the insistence on the Bible's theological authority, positive or negative, is the same.

Jeremiah the prophet

Just as debatable as the question of authority of Scripture is (and must be) in modern age, just as indisputable this authority seems to have been in exilic and post-exilic Judah and Yehud. This was a society which had to redefine itself within a new sociological and ethnic framework. Such a frustrated society can be viewed within two opposite scenarios. Some scholars emphasise the reconstructive abilities of traumatised societies; others 'the debilitating conditions of not having sufficient stability to maintain identity, culture, and rationality' (Smith-Christopher 2002, 78). Examples of both attitudes can be given, and both attitudes may be effective at the same time. We shall not enter into this discussion here. What is of interest in the present context is the possible ability of a given society to 're-construct, or even maintain, precrisis identities' (*ibid*). This was the issue in exilic and post-exilic Judah: the re-construction of pre-crisis, pre-exilic identity.

In what follows I want to demonstrate how the Book of Jeremiah can be read as one instrument among many in this struggle for societal reconstruction through the authorisation of a prophetic message. I take as a point of departure for my reading strategy the fact that in the Masoretic Book of Jeremiah we find a string of commissioning or representation from God to prophet:

---

7   The conclusion drawn by Smith-Christopher is to reject the supremacy of a so-called 'Constantinian' Christianity (cf. John Howard Yoder), i.e. a Christianity which demands to be 'in charge' of the world, and which has inspired a 'Constantinian' exegesis. Over against 'Constantinianism', Smith-Christopher argues in favour of a reading of the biblical texts which 'presumes the viability of a community in exile, and the ability to engage in resistance, even outside of nationalist aspirations or imperial connivance.' Smith-Christopher proposes that '... such readings may inform a radical Christian theological resistance to our own history of imperial connivances and the theologies that have so long excused and supported them' (Smith-Christopher 2002, 25). This declaration cannot surprise the reader, who is informed in the preface that the author sees himself as 'thinking about biblical theology in the Peace Church tradition...' (Smith-Christopher 2002, xiv). This point of departure is even more obvious in his latest publication, Smith-Christopher 2007.

God → Word → Jeremiah

This string leads to a strong identification between the prophet, his book and his God. The identification makes the literary persona of Jeremiah the prophet almost identical with the divine word and even with the divine being; the prophet becomes a metaphor for God (Holt 2007).

In some parts of the book this identification between God and prophet serves to create a schism between the prophet and his audience. But in other parts solidarity and even identification between prophet and people can be noticed.[8] In other words: Jeremiah the prophet serves partly as a vehicle for the divine message, and partly as a role model for the people. He plays both these roles in different imagery, and both roles serve as a tool for the communication of authority.[9] The two roles lead to two different correlations between the three parties in the book (God, prophet and people), which on the surface level are mutually exclusive.[10] Either Jeremiah conjoins God, and consequently is disjoined from the people, or he conjoins the people and is thus separated from God. This, of course, is conveyed not in terms of a direct dogmatic discourse but indirectly through the two basic genres in prophetic literature: oracles and narratives.

The basis for the identification between God and prophet is created in the opening chapter of the Book of Jeremiah, the expanded poetic narrative of the call of Jeremiah. Here the prophet is adjoined to God *qua* his calling on the one hand; on the other hand he is placed in a position as an invincible opponent to the people, Jer 1:17-19 (cf. Holt 2007, 175-179).[11] Jer 1 can be read as a lecture on the sinfulness of the people, a diatribe without any relief, and part of the theodicé which is an important part of the theology of the book.[12] Read in this way, Jer 1 forms the perfect point of departure with the total annihilation of any current, valid, and operative relationship between the speaker and his audience. Such a relationship once existed – as underlined in Jer 2 – but now it has been terminated by the people.

The conjunction of God and prophet on the one hand and the disjunction of God-prophet and people on the other in Jer 1 form the backdrop of the poetry in the following chapters. They circle around the possibility of restoring the destroyed rela-

---

8   Cf. e.g. Louis Stulman's basic assessment of the relationship between prophet and people, Stulman 1998, 138.

9   The only part this literary-theological persona does not play in the Book of Jeremiah is the part of a *historical* person, the prophet Jeremiah ben Hilkiah from Anatoth, not even in the so-called confessions. On the historicity of Jeremiah and his many roles, see e.g. Stulman 1998, 137-166.

10   A closer analysis of the texts points to a more ambivalent understanding, which unfortunately must be kept out of view in this connection; I have touched on this in my presentation at the SBL Annual Meeting, San Diego November 2007, forthcoming.

11   This reading of the call narrative can be disputed in several ways and should not be seen as the only valid understanding; here it serves as a point of departure for the chosen reading strategy.

12   It was not until the very closing of the Book of Jeremiah, the Oracles Against the Nations and especially the Oracle Against Babylon in chapters 50-51, that the ancient reader would find ultimate consolation in the personal, political, and national distress (Holt 2003).

tionship, oscillating between divine admonition and a call to return, but ending in Jer 6 without any clarification.[13]

Jeremiah 6 is a dialogue between God and prophet and between God-prophet and the people. The dialogue between God and prophet adjoins the two so that during the chapter it becomes increasingly difficult to separate the two voices. The Hebrew text poses several linguistic difficulties. However, according to William McKane Jer 6:9-15 illustrates the tendency for the "'word of Yahweh" to become dialogue between Yahweh and the prophet in the Book of Jeremiah', or if more radical emendations are made, 'the extant text illustrates the tendency to convert reflections of Jeremiah into word of Yahweh' (McKane 1986, 145). So, whether we read the text as it is reflected in the MT or follow the emendations of this corrupted text proposed partly by the Septuagint, partly by later scholars, the impression lasts that God involves the prophet in his project, the annihilation of the people, whose ears are uncircumcised and to whom the word of God is an object of scorn. The prophet's reaction is: 'I am full of the wrath of Yahweh; I am weary of holding it in.' (Jer 6:11). In Jer 6:16-17, then, follows a discussion between the people and Yahweh which unveils the people's stubbornness. This arouses Yahweh to turn to a greater audience, the peoples of the whole world, who must serve as witnesses to the annihilation of the people (Jer 6:18-21).

The following pericope (Jer 6:22-26) again displays a dialogue between God-prophet on the one side and the people on the other. Here, however, we find a unanimous lament for the inescapability of the catastrophe. The three parties are united in their terror of the 'Foe from the North,' the mythological God-sent enemy who threatens Jerusalem and Judah. The passage presents the different voices of God, prophet and people, but the emotions expressed are the same. For the first time since Jer 1, we meet a conjunction between the three parties for a short while. But the harmony does not last long. At the closing of Jer 6 God again sets Jeremiah apart from the people, putting him into the most disloyal role imaginable, that of the tester and refiner of the people. Moreover, from the outset the people are expected to fail the test; the disjunction of God-prophet on the one hand and the people on the other is re-established (Jer 6:27-30).

Other examples of poetry serving the conjunction-disjunction matrix could be mentioned. Here, however, we shall turn to the narratives in the Book of Jeremiah to identify the same pattern. The most important example, of course, is the narrative which opens the story about the fall of Jerusalem, Jer 36. Here, Jeremiah is ordered by God to have his secretary, Baruch the Scribe, write all his oracles in a scroll and read them aloud in the temple. When the king is informed about this, he orders Baruch to read the scroll to him, but during the reading the king destroys the scroll. God, however, hides Jeremiah and Baruch from the king, and Jeremiah dictates all the words from the first scroll again and even adds some new words.

---

13   On chapter 6 as the closing of the first compositional part of the Book of Jeremiah, see Stulman 1998, 39-40.

This, of course, is not an historical source of prophetic book production, but a narrative which serves to authorise the prophetic written book in a society which no longer has live access to the prophet. Nothing and nobody, not even a king, can subdue the word of God; and this word of God is preserved for all time in the written book, dictated by God himself.

In Jer 36 the conjunction of God and prophet is emphasised and broadened through an extension of the line of commissioning or representation mentioned above:

$$God \rightarrow Word \rightarrow Jeremiah \rightarrow Baruch.$$

All the way through the chapter Baruch acts on behalf of Jeremiah, who presents the Word on behalf of God. The emphasis on the scribe adds emphasis to the act of writing, and so the string of representation involves God himself in the preservation of his word. Baruch's writing down of Jeremiah's words of God saves these words for the future and thus re-enacts them. The spoken word is turned into writing, the line of commissioning into a running wheel.

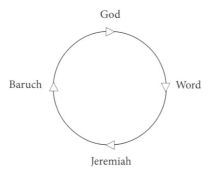

Another aspect helps to underline the authority of the written word of Jeremiah. Jer 36 is often read intertextually together with Jer 26 and 2 Kings 22 (cf. Carroll 1986, 362-368), but the story about the giving of the Law in Ex 32; 34 should also be taken into consideration. The Jeremiah scroll is not the first 'scroll' to be rewritten after a destruction; its predecessor, the Torah, was broken in anger by Moses and was rewritten by him (Ex 32:18-19; 34), and the narrative of the (re-)giving of the Torah adds a surplus of meaning and authority to the scroll narrative in Jeremiah. In both cases there is a re-writing, and in both cases the re-written text is a divine message meant to regulate the life of the people. So the absolute completeness of the written message is stressed in both texts (Ex 34:27; Jer 36:2.32). Furthermore, both re-writings add importance to the first writings. This is most obvious in the Jeremiah narrative, where words are added to the first version (Jer 36:32b); but the emphasis on Moses' shining face in Ex

34:29-35 points to the importance and authority of the re-written tablets instead of the first tablets. All in all, the Moses narrative adds authority to the Jeremiah narrative.[14]

In Jer 36 we find the authorisation motif explicated. In the rest of the story about the fall of Jerusalem (Jer 37-44) it is implicitly represented through the conjunction-disjunction pattern. There, however, the pattern is somehow blurred on the one hand through the position of the prophet over against the people. On the other hand, this blurring serves as the final theological underlining of the people's sinfulness and God's patience and grace to the bitter end. Again, it is the identification of the divine word and the prophet which serves as a marker for the communication of authority, here the authoritative judgement on the pre-587 BCE generations. All the way through the narrative in Jer 36-44 the conjunction, or identification, of God and prophet is at work; all the way through the narrative the prophet speaks and acts on behalf of God and with divine authorisation. And all the way through these chapters God fights for his right to adjoin the people – but in vain.[15]

Concluding remarks – prophetic authority today?

The function of the prophetic text as an authoritative and normative text in its age is indisputable. The overall question remains, however, if the same thing applies in a contemporary context as well. As shown in the introduction to this article, this discussion has never ceased, and it remains of interest within exegesis as well as systematic theology, even today.

In most of the 20th century dialectic theology with its focus on revelation was an inspiration to biblical exegetes, not least in Europe, and the question of the truth of the scriptures posed itself with increasing strength with the constant growth (of the trust) of historical criticism. Exegetes like Wolfhart Pannenberg and Rolf Rendtorff urged the opinion that God's (self)revelation is to be found in history, while e.g. Oswald Loretz found the revelation not in history as such but in one historical event, God's making of the covenant with Israel (Loretz 1964, 41). Loretz treated the making of the covenant as an undeniably historical event. Accordingly, even though the biblical report is written by humans, the event itself contains revelation (Loretz 1964, 51-64).

With the 'collapse of history'(cf. Perdue 1994) this understanding does not seem to be valid any longer. On the contrary, the truth, and accordingly the authority, of the text are not inherent in the text, and can only be acknowledged as an act of faith. We can no longer talk about the authority of a prophetic book on the basis of the book's

---

14   Moses is the most important prophetic figure in Judean religion and Judaism, even though it can be argued that he was created in the image of Jeremiah, see Holt 1989, 118-120. Baruch can be understood as a parallel figure to Moses' brother Aaron, the Levite, who serves as the mouth of Moses, Ex 4:14-17. For a more thorough analysis of intertextuality in Ex 32; 34 and Jer 36, see Holt 2007, 182-186.

15   For a further analysis of the conjunction/disjunction matrix in Jer 37-44, see Holt 'Narrative Normativity in Diasporic Jeremiah', forthcoming.

own (historical!) demand to be authoritative. The authority and thus the normativity of the book depend on the individual reader's choice of faith.

Nevertheless, the authority of the Old Testament prophets is still a matter of debate, not least in North-American biblical scholarship. Three factors, at least, seem to be at work there: First, the situation for liberal Christians in an increasingly conservative environment forces liberal exegetes like Smith-Christopher to take their point of departure in an *a priori* acknowledgment of the text's authoritative status. It is as if a discussion of this and related questions from the outset would prevent more conservative circles from listening to scholarly arguments. Secondly, a widespread conservative exegesis influences universities and theological schools and seminaries in the USA. And finally, the insistence even in post-modern (most often liberal) biblical studies that the meaning of a certain text is ultimately due to the reader's individuality; accordingly, the question of the authority of the text becomes a matter of individual choice.

So the vital question is whether the scholarly debate between American and European exegesis will continue to be possible and continue to develop, or whether the two will each go their own separate ways (the Americans towards orthodoxy of faith, the Europeans towards orthodoxy of secularised reason, to which the question of the normativity of religion becomes only an academic matter). Or will there still be room for a third way, where exegetes are allowed to work with biblical texts as scholarly objects but inspired by a theological or even faith-oriented struggle with the Bible as a normative book?[16]

Bibliography

Berquist, Jon L. 1995. *Judaism in Persia's Shadow: A Social and Historical Approach*. Minneapolis: Fortress.

Bright, John 1965. *Jeremiah*. (The Anchor Bible). Garden City, New York: Doubleday and Company.

Carroll, Robert P. 1981. *From Chaos to Covenant: Uses of Prophecy in the Book of Jeremiah*. London: SCM.

Carroll, Robert P. 1986. *The Book of Jeremiah: A Commentary*. (Old Testament Library). London: SCM.

Carroll, Robert P. 1991. *Wolf in the Sheepfold: The Bible as a Problem for Christianity*. London: SPCK.

Carroll, Robert P. 1999a. 'Halfway through a Dark Wood'. In: A.R. Pete Diamond, Kathleen M. O'Connor and Louis Stulman (eds.), *Troubling Jeremiah*. (JSOT Suppl., 260). Sheffield: Sheffield Academic Press, 73-86.

Carroll, Robert P. 1999b. 'The Book of J: Intertextuality and Ideological Criticism'. In: A.R. Pete Diamond, Kathleen M. O'Connor and Louis Stulman (eds.), *Troubling Jeremiah*. (JSOT Suppl., 260). Sheffield: Sheffield Academic Press, 220-243.

Davies, Philip R. (ed.) 1996. *The Prophets*. (The Biblical Seminar, 42). Sheffield: Sheffield Academic Press.

---

16   For a further discussion, see Holt 2007, 186-189.

Holladay, William L. 1986-1989. *Jeremiah 1: A Commentary on the Book of the Prophet Jeremiah Chapters 1-25*. (Hermeneia). Philadelphia: Fortress Press.

Holt, Else K. 1989. 'The Chicken and the Egg – Or: Was Jeremiah a Member of the Deuteronomist Party?'. *Journal for the Study of the Old Testament*, 44, 109-122.

Holt, Else K. 2003. 'The Meaning of an *Inclusio*: A Theological Interpretation of the Book of Jeremiah MT'. *Scandinavian Journal of the Old Testament*, 17(2), 183-205.

Holt, Else K. 2007. 'Word of Jeremiah – Word of God: Structures of Authority in the Book of Jeremiah'. In: John Goldingay (ed.), *Uprooting and Planting: Essays on Jeremiah for Leslie Allen*. London: Continuum, T&T Clark, 172-189.

Lemche, Niels Peter 1985. *Early Israel: Anthropological and Historical Studies on the Israelite Society Before the Monarchy*. Leiden: Brill.

Loretz, Oswald 1964. *Die Wahrheit der Bibel*. Freiburg, Basel, Wien: Herder.

McKane, William 1986. *'A Critical and Exegetical Commentary on Jeremiah I'*. (International Critical Commentary). Edinburgh: T&T Clark.

Middlemas, Jill 2007. *The Templeless Age: An Introduction to the History, Literature, and Theology of the 'Exile'*. Louisville, London: Westminster John Knox.

Perdue, Leo 1994. *The Collapse of History: Reconstructing Old Testament Theology*. (Overtures to Biblical Theology). Minneapolis: Fortress Press.

Smith, Daniel L. 1989. *The Religion of the Landless: The Social Context of the Babylonian Exile*. Bloomington: Meyer Stone.

Smith-Christopher, Daniel L. 2002. *A Biblical Theology of Exile*. (Overtures to Biblical Theology). Minneapolis: Fortress Press.

Smith-Christopher, Daniel L. 2007. *Jonah, Jesus and other Good Coyotes: Speaking Peace to Power the Bible*. Nashville: Abingdon Press.

Stulman, Louis 1998. *Order Amid Chaos: Jeremiah as a Symbolic Tapestry*. (The Biblical Seminar, 57). Sheffield: Sheffield Academic Press.

THE SALVATION SYSTEM IN THE
SOPHIA OF JESUS CHRIST.
AN EXAMPLE OF TEXTUAL REUSE

René Falkenberg

Introduction

A post-resurrection teaching from Jesus Christ is found in a revelation dialogue entitled the *Sophia of Jesus Christ* (abbreviated *SJC*). The text exists in two Coptic versions: one from *Papyrus Berolinensis Gnosticus* 8502,3 called *SJC-BG*, and one from *Nag Hammadi Codex* (*NHC*) III.4 called *SJC-III*.[1] Two-thirds of *SJC* reuses a description of the heavenly world from the letter of *Eugnostos*.[2] Since *Eugnostos* neither unfolds any clear soteriology nor displays much on the created cosmos, *SJC* was probably composed in order to expand the letter into a more explicit account of the saving teaching and action of Christ in the physical world. All this is exactly what the last third of *SJC* describes, but still, the salvation system is presented in a most sketchy form.

To understand the concise salvation system in *SJC*, we need to establish the structure of the divine hierarchy from the upper heavenly regions down to the created cosmos, since two of the gods in the heavenly realm are closely connected to the soteriology of the lower cosmos. First, the exact number of gods in the pantheon will be determined, since the two versions of *SJC* disagree on that. Second, a god called the immortal Man shows a special soteriological function which needs to be clarified. Third, humankind's salvation history will be described through a three-stage chronology from cosmogonic time until the time of the revelation dialogue. Finally, a specific biblical background will be suggested as inspiration for the salvation system in *SJC*.

The pantheon of the heavenly world

The two versions of *SJC* do not display the same number of hypostases in the upper heavenly world. *SJC-BG* describes a triadic hierarchy, whereas *SJC-III* unfolds a pentadic hierarchy resembling the pantheon of *Eugnostos*, as shown in the following model.[3]

---

1   One fragmentary page in Greek has been recovered from *Oxyrhynchus* (Papyrus 1081).
2   *Eugnostos* is found in *NHC* III,3 and V,1. Since Krause 1964 *communis opinio* has agreed that *SJC* was a rewritten version of *Eugnostos*. Even though disputed among scholars, the letter is possibly a Christian writing, cf. Tardieu 1984, 65f.; Pétrement 1984, 613-627; Barry 1993, 20-22; Pasquier 2007, 582f. For a contrary view, cf. Parrott 1991, 9-16.
3   The difference in numbers is made clear by the use of different prepositions in the two versions: *SJC-BG* has the simple preposition ϩⲛ̄ (*BG* 94,6.9; 102,18); *SJC-III* (and *Eugnostos*) has the direct object preposition ⲛ̄- (III,101,5.7; 106,17). With the verbs (ϣⲱⲡⲉ and ⲟⲩⲱⲛϩ) the ϩⲛ̄ gives a passive translation (e.g., 'X was revealed in (ϩⲛ̄) Y') and the ⲛ̄- gives a transitive translation (e.g., 'X revealed ⲛ̄-)Y') in order to show whether a god is generating either himself anew (passive) or another god apart from himself (transitive).

MODEL 1: The heavenly pantheon in *Eugnostos* and the two versions of *SJC*

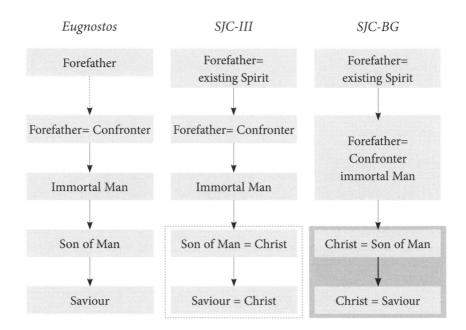

Basically, the hierarchy of *SJC* has been taken from *Eugnostos*. At first sight, the system of *SJC-III* seems to be the original one, since it shows a hierarchy similar to the one from *Eugnostos* and since *SJC-III* is the older of the two *SJC* versions.[4] However, compared with *SJC* as a whole, the triadic hierarchy of *SJC-BG* probably reflects a more coherent form of the intended pantheon. In connection with names and titles of the higher gods, *SJC-BG* on the one hand shows a conscious and independent use that is missing in some detail in *SJC-III*, which on the other hand is almost too influenced by *Eugnostos* because of their juxtaposition in *NHC* III.[5]

As shown in Model 1, *Eugnostos* and *SJC* agree to call the highest god the Forefather. This title serves to distinguish him from the Father, which is the reflected image of the Forefather and therefore called the Confronter (Ἀντωπός, lit. 'One standing face to face').[6] In *Eugnostos* this entity plays a special role: in order to maintain the absolute transcendence of the highest god, the generative process in the heavenly world must be kept away from him and be applied instead to the Confronter, whose

---

4   The *BG* version is from a fifth-century codex; the *Nag Hammadi* version is from a fourth-century codex, cf. Parrott 1991,1.
5   In case of thematic or philological uncertainties within the text of *SJC-III*, the scribe of codex III could have noticed and then incorporated into *SJC-III* the formulations from the previous tractate in the codex (i.e., *Eugnostos*). Then, the relatively clear-cut heavenly account in *SJC* becomes obscure in *SJC-III*, whereas the consistent heavenly system still exists in its more coherent state in *SJC-BG*.
6   *Eugnostos* III 74,20-75,9; *SJC-BG* 90,12-91,13; *SJC-III* 98,19-99,10.

prime function is to serve as the generative starting point (dotted arrow in Model 1).[7] In *SJC*, this sophisticated use of the Confronter is no longer extant: the highest god indeed takes part in the generative process, since the existing Spirit functions as his active aspect and the first begetter (*BG* 87,16-88,18; *SJC-III* 96,21-97,16). Therefore, *SJC* does not need the Confronter as the independent hypostasis shown by *Eugnostos*. Only *SJC-BG* compensates for this by merging the Confronter and the following hypostasis, the immortal Man (*BG* 94,5-11).[8] Thus, *SJC* no longer emphasises the generative function of the Confronter – as in *Eugnostos* – but rather emphasises his function as an anthropological paradigm: in *SJC*, the Confronter now functions as the prototype of a heavenly race called the confronters (ἀντωποί), probably indicating spiritual human beings.[9] We will soon see this parallelled in the function of the immortal Man, who also seems to be a prototype, but this time of earthly human beings.

In both versions of *SJC*, the immortal Man generates the Son of Man, who is also known as 'the First-engenderer, the Son of God' (*BG* 98,7-99,7; *SJC-III* 103,22-104,13).[10] Afterwards, *SJC-III* again disagrees with *SJC-BG*: the former understands the next emanation, the Saviour, as the product of the Son of Man (similar to *Eugnostos*), whereas the latter sees the Saviour as the self-hypostasation of the Son of Man (bold arrow in Model 1) (*BG* 102,15-103,4; *SJC-III* 106,15-21). In *SJC* as a whole, these two hypostases are best understood as one and the same, since the Son of Man has a heavenly as well as an earthly function (like his father the Confronter/the immortal Man). This is said explicitly in *SJC*:

… the Son of Man; he who is called the First-engenderer; he who is called the Saviour; this is the one who appeared (*BG* 108,1-7).

The Son of Man in his revealed form acts as the Saviour ('this is the one who appeared') in the earthly world. There he crushes the authority of the archontic rulers and teaches humankind knowledge.[11] The fact that the Saviour is the self-hypostasation of the Son of Man is also indicated, in that the two versions of *SJC* agree to designate both the Saviour and the Son of Man as Christ.[12]

---

7   The absolute transcendence of God is one of the main characteristics of Middle Platonism. Because of the transcendence of the godhead, it is philosophically problematic to explain the derivation of everything else from him. On the special use of the Confronter figure in *Eugnostos* and related literature, cf. Trakatellis 1991, 91-93; 100-102.

8   In the parallel the Confronter reveals the immortal Man as a new entity (*SJC-III* 101,4-8).

9   Of course, this function of the Confronter as an anthropological paradigm is found in *Eugnostos* as well, but not as his prime function as insisted in *SJC*.

10 In this study the Coptic text of *SJC-BG* is preferred as the basis of the translation for three reasons: (1) The more coherent system is found in *SJC-BG*; (2) the scribe of the *BG* version is more careful than the codex III scribe (e.g. homoioteleuton often occurs in *SJC-III*); (3) four pages are missing in *SJC-III* (109-110; 115-116). All translations are the author's own, based on the critical text found in Parrott 1991.

11 *BG* 102,7-103,9; 104,7-13; III 106,9-24; 107,11-16.

12 In *SJC-III*, the Son of Man is identified with Christ only once (*SJC-III* 104,20-22) whereas this is seen on three occasions in *SJC-BG* (99,7-9.14-16; 101,7-9).

To sum up: A closer look at the triadic structure of *SJC* shows that the names of the three hypostases signify their mutual relationship and specific function in the salvation system. The pentadic system of *Eugnostos* is reduced to a triadic hierarchy in *SJC* (most clearly found in the *BG* version), since two entities are merged with their subsequent hypostases: the Confronter with the immortal Man, the Son of Man with the Saviour. Thereby it is indicated that these gods have differentiated heavenly functions on the one hand and cosmic functions on the other. These functions are closely connected to soteriology.

The immortal Man and the soteriological implications

The special function of the immortal Man in *SJC* has been observed previously by Pheme Perkins (cf. 1971): (1) In *SJC* the immortal Man is a fallen god and plays a significant role in the text. (2) Because of *SJC*'s far too brief descriptions of soteriology, the means of understanding the role of the immortal Man and other earthly matters lie not only in *SJC* itself but also in comparative material such as *Apocryphon of John* (abbreviated *Ap. John*) and the Ophite system.[13] An important supplement – not mentioned by Perkins – is the Writing without Title *On the Origin of the World* (abbreviated *Orig. World*).[14]

We will soon use these three texts to describe the three-stage chronology of the salvation system in *SJC*, but first we must examine the function of the immortal Man. At the end of an anthropogonic account, the Saviour makes a didactic statement about his saving teaching and action:

But I have taught you about the immortal Man and I have untied the fetters of the robbers away from him (*BG* 121,13-17).

Both the teaching and action of the Saviour concern the immortal Man: (1) The teaching about him is closely connected to a specific knowledge ('I have taught you about the immortal Man'). (2) The saving action is primarily concerned with the liberation of the immortal Man from 'the fetters of the robbers', which probably points to his imprisonment by lower cosmic entities, the evil Archons. Since the didactic statement sums up the anthropogony of *SJC*, a third point can be made: (3) As a being in this world, the immortal Man is somehow connected to anthropology.

The immortal Man rarely occurs in the Nag Hammadi texts. He is found only in *Eugnostos*, *SJC*, and *Orig. World*, but the last two differ from the first in their descrip-

---

13   The *Ap. John* is found in *NHC* II1; *SJC-III*1; IV1; and *BG*2; the Ophite system in Irenaeus, *Adv. Haer.* 1,30.
14   *Orig. World* is found in *NHC* II5 and XIII,2.

tion.[15] The aforementioned three points concerning the didactic statement are not found in *Eugnostos*, but parallels exist in *Orig. World*: (1) The immortal Man is described in a similar way in connection with the bringing of knowledge to human beings.[16] (2) Because the light of the immortal Man has been mixed with cosmic substance, he is imprisoned in the sensible world and not able to return to the spiritual world (II 112,10-13). (3) The immortal Man is closely connected to human beings of this world, and in addition his existence enables them to condemn their creators, the evil Archons (II 103,19-22; 112,25-113,11). This condemnation theme is also found in *SJC* when the reason is given for blowing the principle of life into the first human:

... so that this immortal Man might fit well with the robes in this place to condemn the robbers (*BG* 120,16-121,3).

Here, the immortal Man is again contrasted to the archontic 'robbers'. That he 'might fit well with the robes in this place' probably points to his connection with human beings in their bodily existence in the earthly realm. However, the act of blowing into the first human being is primarily associated not with the intimate connection between the immortal Man and human beings, but rather with the judgment on the evil archontic forces. Still, this passage points at the immortal Man's role in the salvation history, which is also implied when the purpose of the self-hypostasation of the Confronter as the immortal Man is given:

... so that through this immortal Man they (i.e. human beings) might attain the salvation and wake up from oblivion through the emitted Interpreter; this is the one who is with you until the end of the poverty of the robbers (*BG* 94,11-19).

The immortal Man here seems to function as an instrument of salvation, but not *the* instrument ('the emitted Interpreter'), which probably points to the knowledge bringer *par excellence*, the Saviour. The immortal Man makes humankind capable of receiving the saving knowledge, but the saving act (the awakening 'from oblivion') is reserved for the Saviour (*BG* 104,14-16; *SJC-III* 107,16-18).

To sum up: In spite of *SJC*'s three concise descriptions of the immortal Man in the earthly realm and especially his connection to the anthropology, we are still given some information: (1) Knowledge of the immortal Man's purpose and placement in the cosmic world is of some importance to the saving teaching. (2) Before the Saviour was sent into the cosmos, the immortal Man was imprisoned there by the archontic forces. (3) The immortal Man has been connected to the bodily existence of humankind

---

15 Two other differences exist: In *Eugnostos*, the Arch-engenderer is a heavenly entity (*SJC-III* 82,18), but he is the earthly ruler in *SJC* (*BG* 119,14-16) and *Orig. World* (II 102,11-12); in *Eugnostos*, πρόνοια is used as a stoic *terminus technicus* (*SJC-III* 70,20-71,3) but functions as both a heavenly and a cosmic being in *SJC* (*BG* 78,5; 106,9-10; 126,8-9; *SJC-III* 91,5; 108,16; 119,2) and *Orig. World* (II 111,32).

16 II 104,2-3; 107,26; 118,10-11; 120,15-17; and especially 123,31-34.

and thus enabled it to condemn the Archons. (4) The immortal Man makes human beings capable of receiving the message of salvation, but alone he is unable to disturb the anthropological hibernation ('oblivion'). In short, the immortal Man is closely connected to the salvation history of humankind and should probably be understood as an anthropological paradigm: The history of the immortal Man equals the history of humankind. To unfold this paradigmatic function it is necessary to study the salvation system from creation to the time of the revelation dialogue.

The *three-stage chronology of the salvation system*
The salvation system occurs in three specific periods of time. Most of the drama is described, although often it is only implicitly hinted at. In order to uncover the implicit descriptions, we need to examine related literature found in *Ap. John*, the Ophite system, and *Orig. World* especially.

The first stage concerns cosmogony, the second concerns anthropogony, and the third the present time of the revelation dialogue, where specific instructions on how to attain salvation are given to the Disciples of Christ.

Cosmogonic time

In the Nag Hammadi scriptures the creation of the physical world is often connected to the so-called fall of Sophia, briefly mentioned only in *SJC-III* (114,14-18). No other explicit references to cosmogony are present in the text. However, an allusion to the fall may be at work when the archontic forces are called robbers.[17] In *Ap. John*, the Ophite system, and *Orig. World* it is not Sophia herself that falls out of the heavenly world, but her divine power which is stolen by Yaldabaoth together with his evil Archons and then used to make the created world.[18] This could explain why the archontic rulers are called robbers in *SJC*. Even though the existence of the Sophia power is only implicitly indicated, it is probably this power that is in need of reintegration into the heavenly world due to its consubstantiality with spiritual essence. Thus, in *SJC* the Sophia power becomes *the primary object of salvation*. Salvation is only fulfilled when her power is taken back from Yaldabaoth and his minions and then restored to its original heavenly existence. In order to liberate Sophia power, anthropogony takes place.

Anthropogonic time

In *SJC*, the creation of human beings is connected with a drop from the heavenly world coming down to the world of chaos (the created cosmos):

---

17   *BG* 94,18; 104,12; 121,3.16; *SJC-III* 101,15; 107,16.
18   *Ap. John* II 1,19-21; 11,9 etc.; *Adv. Haer.* I 30,4.6; *Orig. World* II 99,29-100,10.

A drop from the light and the Spirit came down to the lower regions of the Almighty of the chaos, so that he (the Almighty) could reveal their moulded forms from that drop to judge the Arch-engenderer who is called Yaldabaoth. That drop was revealed[19] in their moulded forms by means of the breath in order to (become) a living soul (*BG* 119,5-120,1).[20]

The heavenly drop is important to the human soul, probably the pre-existent soul itself. The soul-drop enables the Almighty to bring human beings ('their moulded forms') into existence and thereby damn the chief archon, 'the Arch-engenderer/Yaldabaoth'. The soul-drop together with 'the breath' makes the soul of human beings 'a living soul'. Again, *Orig. World* shows important points of contact: (1) The drop has anthropological connotations in *Orig. World* as well (II 113,17-34). (2) In a way similar to the drop of *SJC*, the immortal Man of *Orig. World* is sent as light from the heavenly reign down to the earth (II 108,2-5). (3) Just as the drop in *SJC* enables the moulded forms to judge the archon ruler (Yaldabaoth), the immortal Man in *Orig. World* also enables the moulded forms to judge the Archons (II 107,25-34; 113,7-9). Making a comparison with *Orig. World*, we are in *SJC* probably justified in identifying the drop as the immortal Man.

The connection between the soul-drop and the breath seems to reveal the principle of life because they cause the first human being 'to (become) a living soul'. This is developed further in the text following the previous section:

It (the drop) was cold and slept in the oblivion of the soul, when it became warm by means of the breath from the great light of the Male. And he thought thoughts, so that those in the world of the chaos and everything therein received every name from this immortal one, when the breath was blown into him (*BG* 120,1-13).

Before the soul-drop is connected with the breath, it is cold and sleeps 'in the oblivion of the soul'. Then the breath causes the drop to become warm. Notice that even though the drop is activated by the breath, it is *not* awakened from its oblivion sleep. This function is reserved for the Saviour.

The heating up by the breath gives the first human being both noetic capability ('he thought thoughts') and the ability to rule the inhabitants 'in the world of the chaos' (by the giving of 'every name'). This points to the mental potential of the human race, and thus, the first human being is entitled 'this immortal one', probably echoing the immortal Man and his paradigmatic role.

SJC does not explicitly inform us about the nature of the breath. Again, we need to examine *Ap. John* and the Ophite system to find out that the breath is the fallen Sophia power: In cosmogonic time her power was stolen by Yaldabaoth, but in anthropogonic

---

19   A passive translation of ⲁⲥⲟⲩⲱⲛ︮ϩ ⲛ̄ⲛⲉⲩⲡⲗⲁⲥⲙⲁ ⲉⲃⲱⲗ is preferred here, since the preceding sentence states that the Almighty is probably the active revealer of the moulded forms.

20   Another version of the anthropogony is found in *BG* 103,10-16; *SJC-III* 106,24-107,5.

time he blows this power into the nostrils of Adam unknowingly, thereby making the human race epistemologically stronger than himself and his archontic forces.[21]

In *SJC*, the blowing of the breath represents the taking back of the Sophia power from the robbers. The fact that the Sophia power is called 'the breath from the great light of the *Male*' only indicates the ultimate source of the breath, i.e., the Forefather. The primary function of the soul-drop is to drain the spiritual power (the breath) from the created cosmos. In fact, thanks to the assistance of the Saviour *liberating Sophia power is the raison d'être of the soul-drop.*[22]

Model 2 seeks to sum up the first two stages of the salvation system (creation of the world and humankind). A well-known myth from *Ap. John*, the Ophite system, and *Orig. World* helps to establish the events in *SJC*. What Model 2 shows is probably a special interpretation of the first chapters of Genesis:

MODEL 2: Prehistoric events according to cosmogony and anthropogony

In *SJC*, the Forefather is the highest god in the triadic pantheon. Before the beginning of time he reveals the confronters through a mirror (*BG* 90,15-92,7; *SJC-III* 98,22-99,19). The first of these is called Father/the Confronter/the immortal Man, holding the posi-

---

21   *Ap. John* II 19,23-28; *Adv. Haer.* 1,30,4.6.14. In *Orig. World*, the pre-existent souls are taken captive by the Arch-engenderer (II 114,20-24), but it is Sophia that blows the spiritual power into the first man (II 115,11-14).
22   *BG* 121,6-13. Even with the breath and the soul-drop, humankind is only ψυχικός (*BG* 121,6-9). As we soon will see, the spiritual principle of the Forefather is what human beings are in need of.

tion of a second god in the heavenly hierarchy. The confronters are probably the same as the pre-existent souls of the heavenly human beings called the Race which has no reign over it. The Confronter functions as a paradigm for this spiritual Race; in the form of the fallen immortal Man – as the drop – he also functions as a paradigm for human beings in the created world.

In the divine hierarchy the immortal Man brings forth the Son of Man, who is the third god in the pantheon. The female partner of the Son of Man is called the Mother of the All, the fallen Sophia.[23] She is responsible for the creation of the world called the Seventh (*BG* 109,1-4). In order to separate the heavenly world from the created cosmos, the Forefather creates a pericosmic curtain (*BG* 118,7-11; *SJC-III* 114,21-24).

In cosmogonic time, the Sophia power resulting from the fall is stolen by the robbers. This power is in need of reintegration into the heavenly world, and therefore the drop is sent into the world in anthropogonic time. There, presumably the Almighty creates the moulded forms (human beings) from the soul-drop in order to drain the Sophia power from Yaldabaoth and his Archons. This draining takes place when the breath gives the moulded forms a living soul. The principle of life immanent in every human being activates their spiritual potential, but still the soul-drop is sleeping in the oblivion of the soul. This oblivion sleep points forward to the coming of the Saviour and his awakening of humankind.

Present time

In the time of the revelation dialogue, the teaching of the Saviour is made accessible to everyone and not to a specific Christian group (*BG* 126,3-5; *SJC-III* 118,24-25). The only demand on the disciples is celibacy or ascetic behaviour.[24] Still, *SJC* clearly underlines that salvation comes by the Saviour:

I released that creation! I broke the work of the thieving tomb! I have awakened it (the drop),[25] so that it might bear much fruit through me, namely that drop; this one that was sent through Sophia to be perfected and no longer exist as faulty. No, – it will be fertilised through me; it is I who am the mighty Saviour! (*BG* 104,10-18).

The archontic rule ('the work of the thieving tomb') is broken by the Saviour when he has given humankind his heavenly teaching ('I have awakened' the drop). Notice that Sophia sends the soul-drop into the cosmos in order to right her wrongs, but on her own she cannot fulfil the salvation of human beings. A more specific definition of this fulfilment – or bearing fruit – is found later in *SJC*:

---

23   *BG* 99,9-12; *SJC-III* 104,16-18; 114,14-18. The fall in *SJC-III* has a close literary parallel to *Orig. World* (II 98,13-23).
24   *BG* 82,12-14; 105,17-106,8; *SJC-III* 93,19-21; 108,8-15.
25   The pronominal suffix is in the masculine but the drop is in feminine gender. Nevertheless, the context makes it clear that the drop is the most likely candidate here, cf. Parrott 1991, 133.

Therefore I came here, so that they will be fertilised with that Spirit and the breath and from two become one and the same as (it was) from the beginning, so that you will bear much fruit (*BG* 122,6-13).

The Saviour appeared in the world to impregnate humankind with the spiritual principle from the highest god that he represents. The Saviour himself manifests the invisible Spirit (*BG* 78,11-15; *SJC-III* 91,10-12), which is probably identical with the existing Spirit of the Forefather. When the Saviour gives his saving teaching to the disciples (as representatives of humankind), he enables their immanent Sophia power ('the breath') to be connected to his spiritual being ('that Spirit'). The reintegration of Sophia's fallen power back into the heavenly world can begin, and Spirit and Sophia power will 'become one and the same as (it was) from the beginning' (probably a speculation on Gen 1:27; 2:24). Thus, the disciples fulfil salvation ('bear much fruit').

The following paragraph in *SJC* explicitly states both what the disciples need to know and how they bear spiritual fruit in order to reach heavenly existence. Four criteria, each beginning with the formula 'he who knows', establish the objects of knowledge at two different levels (*BG* 123,2-124,9; *SJC-III* 117,8-118,3). The highest level of knowledge is constituted by criteria 1 and 3: If the disciple knows the Father 'in pure knowledge', he or she 'will go to the Father and rest in the unengendered Father' (the Forefather), and knowing 'the immortal Spirit' brings existence 'in light'. The lower level of knowledge is described by criteria 2 and 4: If the disciple knows the Father 'in defect', he or she will 'rest in the Eighth', and only knowing 'the Son of Man' brings existence 'in the Eighth'.[26]

To reach the higher knowledge, an understanding of the Father's true nature is needed. As we saw earlier, the Father is also known as the Confronter and the immortal Man. In attaining heavenly existence, the disciple will go to the Father – or more accurately: to the place of the Confronter where the confronters or the Race with no reign over it exist. There the heavenly human beings stand face to face with the highest god (the unengendered Father), and there the spiritualised soul has its origin. Surprisingly, with inferior knowledge of the Father one can attain heavenly existence in the Eighth as well. As a heavenly dwelling place, the Eighth is brought forth by the immortal Man in the heavenly world, but is ruled by the Son of Man.[27] The Eighth is explicitly designated the Congregation (Ἐκκλησία) (*BG* 111,2-14; *SJC-III* 111,1-7). This perhaps points at the mainstream Church, where Christians – from our author's point of view – only possess defective knowledge of the Father. Notice, however, that *SJC* never enters the polemical discussion known in the writings of the Church Fathers, where the Valentinians (for instance) are described as looking down

---

26   Two similar knowledge levels are found in *Orig. World*, where the lower level is connected to heavenly existence in the Eighth, and the higher level to perfection 'in the unengendered Father' (II 125,3-11; 127,7-14).

27   *BG* 95,8-17; 101,6-12; 124,1-9; *SJC-III* 101,22-102,7; 105,19-24; 117,22-118,3.

on Church Christians.[28] Actually, the opposite situation is found here: Even though Christians in the Congregation only know the Father defectively, they are precisely included in the heavenly salvation of the Eighth.[29]

MODEL 3: Terrestrial function of the Son of Man and the twofold salvation

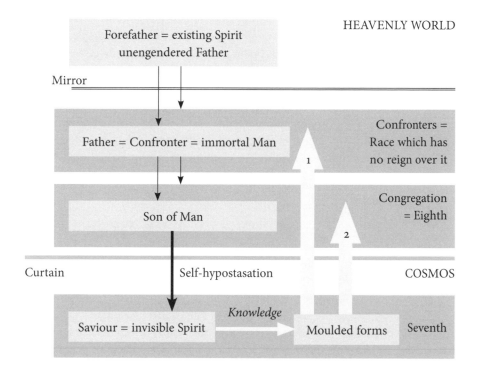

Model 3 recapitulates the triadic pantheon according to the present time of the revelation dialogue. In comparison with Model 2, two differences – both connected to the Son of Man – must be highlighted: (1) The Son of Man rules the heavenly dwelling place called the Eighth or the Congregation. This place is brought forth by Father / the Confronter / the immortal Man, and is therefore lower than the place of the confronters in the heavenly hierarchy. (2) In the time of the revelation dialogue, the Son of Man comes to the world as the Saviour / Christ (bold arrow in Model 3). The Son of Man's earthly hypostasis is also characterised as the invisible Spirit, and is therefore

---

28   In Irenaeus' account of the Valentinians, the defective knowledge suspends pleromatic redemption. The pneumatics (the Valentinians) reach the highest redemption, whereas the psychics (other Christians) only go to an ex-pleromatic place called the Middle (*Adv. Haer.* 1,7,5).

29   'In any case, the text does *not* say that individuals are predetermined to go to one level or the other, it only states what level will be achieved by this or that degree of knowledge' (Williams 1985, 170-171); 'Es sind in der *SJC* zwar Abstufungen im Heil zu erkennen, aber allen Genannten wird Heil zugesagt, es werden nicht etwa bestimmte Gruppen völlig ausgeschlossen' (Hartenstein 2000, 40).

connected to the ultimate spirit principle belonging to the Forefather / existing Spirit / unengendered Father.[30] The saving knowledge is instrumental in bringing about the spiritual principle inside the disciple, and it ('that Spirit') enables humankind to release the immanent Sophia power ('the breath') back to its original existence.

Thus, a Christian can reach two levels of heavenly existence. If you know the true nature of the Father / the Confronter / the immortal Man as an anthropological paradigm on both a heavenly and earthly plane, you are given access to the place of the confronters / the Race which has no reign over it (arrow 1 in Model 3). If you do not know the Father's anthropological double function, you are only given access to the realm of the Son of Man in the Eighth / the Congregation (arrow 2 in Model 3). Notice here – as pointed out by Judith Hartenstein – that *SJC* does not intend to offer a new and distorted teaching of Christian doctrine, but rather a teaching on a higher level.[31] Probably, the high-level teaching of *SJC* is not meant to leave out Christians that adhere to the common teaching of the Gospels in the Church, but to facilitate them with the author's alternative exegesis of the creation account from The Jewish Bible.

Conclusion

The pentadic pantheon of *Eugnostos* is reduced to a triadic one in *SJC*: The highest god is the Forefather, and is known as the ultimate spiritual principle; the second god is the Father, the Confronter, and the immortal Man; the third god of the heavenly world is the Son of Man, and his earthly hypostasis is the Saviour / Christ, who mediates the Forefather's spiritual principle to humankind.

The second god of the triadic pantheon is interesting. The immortal Man has a status as both a high god and a fallen entity. His history resembles the history of humankind, and he is therefore best understood as an anthropological paradigm on a heavenly and earthly level. Knowledge of this enables Christians to reach the highest possible level of existence; defective knowledge of the immortal Man also brings salvation, but on a lower level in the Congregation.

All this might be new to the letter of *Eugnostos*, which only seems to present an interpretation of the anthropogonic account from Gen 1:26-28: The (mirror) image of God is called the confronters (lit. 'the ones standing face to face' – with the godhead) (III 75,3-16); the first human beings meant to rule the creation are called 'the Race which has no reign over it' in order to signify its sovereignty (III 75,16-23); the first human being created as male and female is indicated in that the immortal Man, the Son of Man, and the Saviour have female Sophia figures as partners (III 77,3f.; V 9,3-6; III 82,3-6).

---

30   This explains the self-contradictory statements that the Saviour comes from both the Forefather and the Father (*BG* 81,17-19; 83,14-17; 87,13-14; 102,1-5; *SJC-III* 93,8-9; 94,11-13; 96,19-20; 106,5-7). The highest god sends him as the Saviour, his spiritual principle, whereas the Father / the Confronter / the immortal Man generates him as the Son of Man.

31   'Die SJC ist nicht eine neue, fremde Lehre, sondern die Fortsetzung des in den kanonischen Evangelien gebotenen auf einer höheren Stufe' (Hartenstein 2000, 62).

Apparently, this was not enough for the author of *SJC*, who added an interpretation of Genesis 2-3 in the process of rewriting *Eugnostos*: The breath that causes the first human being to become a living soul (Gen 2:7); the gender polarity (Gen 1:27) in connection with the principle of oneness (Gen 2:24), in that the breath will be fertilised through the Spirit in order to become one as from the beginning; fallen humankind (Gen 3) indicated by an immortal Man in need of the salvatoric act of Christ.

In her study, Judith Hartentein has already shown important connections between *SJC* and the Gospels of The New Testament. In addition, the author might also have had Paul in mind when the pentadic pantheon of *Eugnostos* was reduced to a triadic system in *SJC*. Basically, the triadic pantheon consisting of the Forefather – the immortal Man – the Saviour could be the equivalent of the more common system of God – Adam – Christ found in the Pauline letters. In *SJC*, the immortal Man as a fallen being is connected to the soul-endowed and earthly existence, and he is chronologically before the Saviour, who by means of the Spirit comes from the highest possible existence. In Paul, the soul-endowed and earthly Adam comes into existence before the life-giving spirit that represents Christ, who derives from heaven (1 Cor 15:45-47). If this is the case in *SJC*, the author used – besides an alternative Genesis interpretation – Pauline Adam christology to form the basis of *SJC*'s salvation system.

Bibliography

Barry, Catherine 1993. *La Sagesse de Jésus-Christ (NH III, 3 et V, 1). Texte établi et présenté.* (Bibliothèque copte de Nag Hammadi, section "Textes" 20). Québec: Les Presses de l'Université Laval.

Hartenstein, Judith 2000. *Die Zweite Lehre: Erscheinungen des Auferstandenen als Rahmenerzählungen frühchristlicher Dialoge.* (Texte und Untersuchungen zur Geschichte der altchristlichen Literatur, 146). Berlin: Akademie Verlag.

Krause, Martin 1964. 'Das literarische Verhältnis des Eugnostosbriefes zur Sophia Jesu Christi'. In: Alfred Stuiber, Alfred Hermann (eds.), *Mullus: Festschrift Theodor Klauser.* (Jahrbuch für Antike und Christentum, Ergänzungsband, 1). Münster, Westfalen: Aschendorffsche Verlag, 263-277.

Parrott, Douglas M. 1991. *Nag Hammadi Codices III,3-4 and V,1 with Papyrus Berolinensis 8502,3 and Oxyrhynchus Papyrus 1081. Eugnostos and The Sophia of Jesus Christ.* (Nag Hammadi Studies, 27). Leiden: E.J. Brill.

Pasquier, Anne 2007. 'Eugnoste (NH III,3; V,1)'. In: Jean-Pierre Mahé, Paul-Hubert Poirier (eds.), *Écrits gnostiques: La bibliothèque de Nag Hammadi.* 571-613. Paris: Éditions Gallimard; Québec: Les Presses de l'Université Laval.

Perkins, Pheme 1971. 'The Soteriology of Sophia of Jesus Christ'. In: *Society of Biblical Literature, 107th Annual Meeting Seminar Papers*, vol. I. Atlanta, Georgia: Regency Hyatt House, 165-181.

Pétrement, Simone 1984. *Le Dieu séparé: les origines du gnosticisme.* (Patrimoines-Gnosticisme). Paris: Les Éditions du Cerf.

Williams, Michael A. 1985. *The Immovable Race: A Gnostic Designation and the Theme of Stability in Late Antiquity.* (Nag Hammadi Studies, 29). Leiden: E.J. Brill.

Tardieu, Michel 1984. *Écrits Gnostiques: Codex de Berlin*. (Sources Gnostiques et Manichéennes 1). Paris: Les Éditions du Cerf.

Trakatellis, Demetrios 1991. *The Trancendent God of Eugnostos: An Exegetical Contribution to the Study of the Coptic Text of Nag Hammadi. With a Retroversion of the Lost Original Greek Text of Eugnostos the Blessed*. (Translated by C. Sarelis from the Greek publication, Athens 1977). Brookline: Holy Cross Orthodox Press.

JUSTIN AND TRYPHO IN THE CONTEST OVER MOSES AND THE PROPHETS

Jörg Ulrich

Justin's dialogue with the Jew Trypho[1] can be regarded as one of the most prominent texts of the second century in which one can see how early Christianity embarked on a controversial discourse concerning texts viewed as sacred. The conflict with Judaism is particularly relevant to the perception of such debates, as many of the texts the Christians viewed as normative were also sacred to the Jews. Viewed globally, the result of Justin's dialogue with the Jew Trypho is a fundamental disagreement about the interpretation of those texts recognised as being shared by both communities.[2] This means that it should be possible to identify implicit and explicit norms beyond the norms of those texts which both communities recognised as authoritative. Here, it is not important whether or not Justin's dialogue with the Jew Trypho actually reflects an historical discussion between Christian and Jewish teachers (admittedly transformed into the literary genre). It may have been created by Justin alone with the object of refuting Judaism without recourse to any real dialogues recording the disputes separating the two communities. Regardless of one's position on this issue,[3] it cannot be disputed that Justin's dialogue demonstrates the authenticity of Christian claims to one of the texts recognised and claimed by the Jews as part of the canon of their holy texts, and also underscores the Christian claim to the exegetical-hermeneutic method of argument.

---

[1]   Iustinus Martyr, *Dialogus cum Tryphone Iudaeo* (*Dial.*, CPG 1076). The most recent edition with a French translation and commentary is P. Bobichon 2003. *Justin Martyr, Dialogue avec Tryphon. Édition critique, traduction, commentaire*, 2 vols. Fribourg, Paradosis 47/1 and 47/2. M. Marcovich 1997. *Justini Martyris Dialogus cum Tryphone*. Berlin: Walter de Gruyter) is not unproblematic, due to the numerous rather arbitrary conjectures. German translations: P. Haeuser 1917. *Des heiligen Philosophen und Märtyrers Justinus "Dialog mit dem Juden Tryphon". Pseudo-Justinus, "Mahnrede an die Hellenen"*. (Bibliothek der Kirchenväter). Kempten BKV 33, 1-231; H. Ristow. *Die Apologeten*. Berlin: Evangelische Verlagsanstalt Berlin (excerpts). English translations: T. Falls 2003 2003. *St. Justin Martyr, Dialogue with Trypho*. (Ed. M. Slusser). Washington: Catholic University Press; A.L. Williams 1930. *Justin Martyr: The Dialogue with Trypho*. London: SPCK.

[2]   In the end, the two part in friendly disagreement. Trypho was extremely positive about the content of the discussion which has just ended, and raises the hope of an increasing mutual appreciation and understanding in a possible continuation (*Dial.* 142,1). Justin himself proclaims the wish to continue, without renouncing the missionary intentions of his arguments (*Dial.* 142,2f.).

[3]   I assume that the Dialogue with Trypho is a freely reworked literary version of actual debates between Jews and Christians. The fact that the Christian perspective comes out particularly well and the Jewish party is repeatedly impressed by the Christian, appearing to betray diminished certainty, is inevitable as part of the protreptic-apologetic intention of the Christian author. This does not necessarily mean, however, that the arguments did not actually relate to the real world of actual disputes between between Jews and Christians. The work of O. Skarsaune (1987) has shown that the Christian kerygma of the *Dialogue* must have been developed in intensive exchange with Judaism. Concerning the character of Trypho himself, the general consensus today is that this is only a straw man, cf. Lieu 1996.

Common sacred scriptures

The entire discussion in Justin's Dialogue with the Jew Trypho is founded on the condition that both partners appreciate that they both recognise a certain number of texts as normative.

This distinguishes this dialogue from other texts of the second century commonly described as apologetic: this condition was necessarily absent when debating with pagans.[4]

This mutual claim means that the debate is about the correct understanding of those texts known to the Jews as the Bible and the Christians as the Old Testament. At the time that Justin's dialogue was composed,[5] the debate was already ancient. Trypho notes, however, that the Christian argumentation had taken on new dimensions, both in intensity and detail.[6]

Arguing on the basis on the Scriptures is the *conditio sine qua non* of a useful debate.[7] Put in positive terms, the exegesis of the Holy Scriptures recognised by both means that it is possible to construct an argumentation which assumes the form of a proof – if certain conditions are met. Both parties initially agree that the texts which both recognise merit the highest authority, and both agree that Scripture is the decisive criterion in theological argumentation. The text is to be obeyed (*Dial.* 90,1), 'forcing' the two opponents to agreement or concession (*Dial.* 67,8). This consensus forms the foundation of the attempt to persuade the opponent of the veracity of one's own interpretation. This also necessarily means a willingness to be persuaded by the opponent's exegesis, and these conditions apply to both participants.

Trypho is explicitly introduced as a person who respects the texts (αἰδούμενος δὲ τὰς γράφας) (*Dial.* 79,1), and this is indeed why he is not only prepared to be taught by the texts, but views this as fundamental. He challenges Justin to justify the Christian interpretations through scriptural proofs. He states that the Jews would adopt Justin's position if it could be shown that this position emerges out of the text itself.[8] At the same time, he aims to refute Justin, using textual passages to argue against his interpretation (*Dial.* 35,1), expecting that Justin will follow the exegesis he proposes. Drawing on textual references, Trypho criticises the Christians for not observing the feasts or the Sabbath, and for not practising circumcision. This is contradictory, as all of these practices are imposed by the very Scriptures which both sides recognise as

---

4   From the second century until Late Antiquity, in the East (Eusebius, Theodoret) and the West (Lactantius, Augustine), the Christian Apologetics perfected a procedure claiming pagan texts. However, while parallelling the principle of our *Dialogue*, this really belongs to another level of analysis as these texts did not have the status of ultimate authority – they were not 'sacred' texts. Nevertheless, over time a canon of these pagan texts emerges that is relatively well established and fixed. This is an interesting phenomenon, which merits a thorough investigation.

5   The *Dialogue* was written after the *Apologies* (to be dated between 150 and 154). This follows from *Dial.* 120,6. The *Dialogue* thus belongs to the second half of the 150s.

6   *Dial.* 56,16: 'We have never before heard anyone who made such inquiries, examinations, or proofs.' This and the following quotes are from the translation by Falls 2003.

7   *Dial.* 56,16: 'In fact, we would not have listened to you thus far, had you not constantly cited the Scriptures in your attempts to prove your point.'

8   *Dial.* 10,4 and often – *Dial.* 90,1. 'Lead us forward, then, from the Scriptures, that we too may believe you!'

being the entire basis of their claims in their arguments (*Dial.* 10,3f). Supported by the texts, Trypho contends that the Christians set their faith on a mere man and 'have made themselves a Christ' (Χριστὸν ἑαυτοῖς τινα ἀναπλάσσετε).[9] This is incomprehensible, as it opposes the divine revelation which they themselves recognise as law. The fact that Jesus of Nazareth was the object of the prophecies of the Hebrew Prophets is a mere claim as far as he is concerned. This cannot be proven from the texts – and he demands that Justin demonstrates his claim on the basis of the texts (*Dial.* 36,1).

In the reverse sense, the same premises apply to Justin. He too recognises the texts as unavoidable authority. He uses the concepts of 'fact' and 'written proof' interchangeably.[10] He likewise declares himself prepared to be persuaded by exegetic arguments, yet here in the sense of the apologetic-protreptic intention of the *Dialogue*, it is decisive that his object is persuading Trypho and his like of the veracity of the *interpretatio Christiana*. With this goal, he immediately begins by citing the texts when developing a proof. He expects that his opponent will follow his exegesis. Justin suggests that the Jews do not understand their own sacred texts, and that the Jewish commentaries give erroneous explanations of the texts.[11] The exegesis he proposes aims at 'correcting' those 'wrong' interpretations. Justin's basic premise is that the Holy Spirit works through Scripture. For him, therefore, his own textual exegesis offers the possibility of freeing one's self from seduction by bad teachers depending on independent, mistaken authorities. This opens the route to an 'objective' judgement (*Dial.* 74,2).

Justin's contends that the Jews do not recognise Jesus as the Christ, and thus fail to recognise his teachings as the new law, although it is precisely this that is foreseen in the texts which the Jews themselves recognise as being divine revelation. He views it as a mistaken interpretation of the text if the Jews stick to the traditional law, and especially the rituals, even though both the law and the Prophets specifically refer to the finite and relative nature of the law. Both of the participants in the dialogue assume the self-evident power of the proof which arises from the texts which both of them recognise as authoritative.

This is the basis for a stimulating debate, which is superficially dominated by premises of openness and mutual interest.[12] Following the literary form of a Platonic dialogue, there is an intellectually demanding and exegetically complex contest about the correct understanding of those texts. It is interesting to note that there is no trace of a difference of opinion concerning the authoritative or canonical nature of any of the texts discussed. There is no dispute about *antilegomena* and *apocrypha*, as becomes the norm in the later debates about the canon in disputes between Jews and Christians arguing within their own communities. The dialogue centres on the argumentation of

---

9   *Dial.* 8,4. For the Jewish reproach that the Christians had made themselves a Messiah; cf. Setzer 1991, 315-328.

10 *Dial.* 93,2. In *Dial.* 67,3 'factual' proof referring to historical events appears alongside proof through text.

11 *Dial.* 9,1: 'You don't know what you are saying; you have been instructed by teachers who are ignorant of the meaning of the Scriptures'. The criticism that the Jews did not understand the text at all is raised by Justin also in *Dial.* 29,2; 34,1; 36,2, and frequently.

12 Admittedly, the missionary ambition of the Christian party is awarded a greater importance.

homologoumena, that is the five books of Moses, the great prophets, the Dodekapropheton, the Psalms and a few scattered references from historical tradition and wisdom literature. In these texts, both Justin and Trypho perceive potential proofs, as they agree on the issue of the canonical character. The course of the dialogue reveals that the mutual and agreed recognition of a clearly identified group of texts viewed as authoritative can indeed lead to a lively exchange. However, it cannot lead to a consensus, nor even to a convergence of perspective on the decisive points.[13]

Differing hermeneutical premises

The fact that both of the partners agree in recognising certain texts as divine revelation does not mean that the shared work on the texts can promise 'success' in the sense of a consensus. This is because the differences in the hermeneutical premises governing the approach to the texts separating the two partners are too great. These differences are: the authority of the texts of what later became the New Testament on the Christian side; the function of Jesus of Nazareth as the centre of Scripture amongst Christians; and the relative and finite nature of Moses and the Prophets, which is the consequence of the first two premises for Christians.

Since the texts of what became the New Testament ranked as divine revelation for the Christian Justin, he and his opponent Trypho do not actually share an identical canon of sacred texts, even though they agree about the authority of Moses and the Prophets.

For Justin, the 'teachings of the Saviour' (*Dial.* 8,2) recorded in the texts of what was becoming the New Testament merit the same, or indeed a higher ranking.[14] Trypho knows that these teachings are 'in what is called the Gospel' (ἐν τῷ λεγωμένῳ Εὐαγγελίῳ)[15] and he even suggests that he has read them. However, he thinks that on the one hand these are in reality too much for a human to obey;[16] and on the other hand he reveals that (however fascinating), the traditions about Jesus of Nazareth cannot be viewed as sacred teachings, and their written form cannot be viewed as sacred writings.[17] He thus refuses to recognise the texts of what was becoming the New Testament as being sacred. Ultimately this difference of opinion has a decisive influence on all of the individual exegetical decisions concerning the texts which they both recognise. Thus Justin endeavours to demonstrate the truth of Christianity on

---

13   Trypho places this at the centre in one passage of the *Dialogue*: 'The words of God are indeed holy, but your interpretations are not only artificial, as is evident from those you have given, but evidently even blasphemous...' (*Dial.* 79,1, translation by Falls). The texts are sacred, but the exegesis is wrong (cf. *Dial.* 32,1). This is a reversal of the reproach raised by Justin *Dial.* 9,1.

14   On Justin's memories of the Apostles, cf. Abramowski 1983. On Justin's Bible, cf. Skarsaune, 2007.

15   *Dial.* 10,2. In *Dial.* 100,1 Justin uses the designation 'Gospel' in a quote from Matth.

16   This certainly applies to the counsels of the Sermon on the Plain and the Sermon on the Mount, which Justin perceived as the ideal characterisation of the ethics of Jesus. For this see 1 *Apol.* 14-16. For Justin's ethics, see Ulrich 2006.

17   *Dial.* 10,3: 'You place your hope in a crucified man, and still expect to receive favours from God when you disregard his commandments'.

the basis of the texts recognised by both, and he also takes into consideration textual forms and translations preferred by the Jews (cf. below). Yet the other party perceives that Justin is reading the texts of the Jews' own Old Testament from the perspective of those 'Teachings of the Saviour'. However much Justin endeavours to persuade him, for Trypho these Christian texts simply do not have the same rank as the texts of the Jewish Bible.

This difference of opinion about the authority of the 'Teachings of the Saviour' is relevant not only to the issue of the different canonical texts recognised by the two, but also for the understanding of those texts which both agree in recognising their canonical character. As far as Justin is concerned, all of the textual passages of the Old Testament which he cites refer to Jesus of Nazareth as the Christ, and must be interpreted and understood in the Light of Christ, with this specific condition that Jesus of Nazareth was the Christ; for Trypho, the situation is the opposite, for he considers it to be contrary to Scripture that a crucified man could possibly be the Messiah promised in his Bible.[18] According to Justin, through Jesus – the Christ – it is the Christians who have the correct understanding of the texts recognised by both parties, and thus it is only the Christians who have achieved the correct understanding of God. For Trypho, the Christians have abandoned God.[19] Regardless of the exegetical wrestling in the details of a multitude of biblical references,[20] the fundamental issue is hermeneutic, and the resolution of this question determines the exegesis of all of the references discussed, leading one party in one direction, and the other in the opposite. In the literary form of the dialogue as composed by Justin, Justin has the Jew Trypho concede some exegetical details to his opponent, but the difference of opinion on the decisive issues remains. The Logophanies in the tradition were either manifestations of Jesus as Logos, or they were not (*Dial.* 60,1). The prophecies of the Prophets referred to Jesus as the Christ, or they did not (*Dial.* 36,1). The crucifixion of Jesus was the fate compatible with the Law and the Prophets, or it was not, etc. (*Dial.* 39,7; 89,1; 90,1).

In the first century these were the fundamental points, and Jews could decide to interpret their sacred texts in the one fashion or in the other, and become Christians or not. In the middle of the second century, each in their own consistent fashion, Justin and Trypho represent these two exegetical traditions. In this situation, an exegetical dialogue covering the content and details of the texts was always possible, but an 'agreement' was impossible. Among the positive theological aspects of the dialogue with Trypho, one must count the fact that Justin did not construct any kind of agreement with Trypho and his colleagues in the sense of a missionary programme, as do many later Christian texts.

---

18   *Dial.* 8,4: 'But you [Christians] have believed this foolish rumour, and you have invented for yourselves a Christ for whom you blindly give up your lives'.

19   *Dial.* 8,3: 'But, when you have turned away from God and have placed your hope in man, what chance of salvation do you have?'

20   Cf. below, next paragraph.

From the two initial and different hermeneutic premises, it follows in the third that the Holy Scriptures recognised by both are in fact ranked differently. Moses and the Prophets of the Holy Scriptures enjoy the highest authority (cf. above). But for Trypho these are the final documents and the absolute foundations of his Jewish religion, so that he can only admonish Justin to respect everything that stands in these texts.[21] For Justin, on the other hand, these texts are to a certain extent outdated: Moses and the Law have not led to hope.[22] Instead, they only had (and have) the role of pointing to Christ as the new and ultimate lawgiver, whose new law has abrogated the old, and furthermore Christ's new law is universal, whereas the old law had only applied to the Jews. Moses and the Prophets can now appear 'correctly' in the light of the revelation by the Christ, recognised as Jesus of Nazareth. In the light of the revelation of Jesus Christ, who had been foreseen in the 'Old Testament', this text is now shown to be temporally limited as the new text brings it up to date, since the older text served only as documentary proof of the truth of the 'Teachings of the Saviour'. The 'Old Testament' is shown to be ethnically specific, in contrast to the universality of salvation through Jesus Christ, which is valid for all of humanity.[23] Due to the three named aspects, the hermeneutic perspectives of the Jew Trypho and the Christian Justin on the texts which they both view as sacred are completely different. The result is contrasting judgements on the details of the exegesis of the relevant references.

Differences in the exegesis of specific passages

In Justin's dialogue Trypho clearly expresses his surprise that his Christian opponent reveals a mastery of the details in his arguments based on the text.[24] Philippe Bobichon (2003, 921-941) has recently published a synopsis which allows a survey of the individual textual passages discussed in the dialogue. Throughout the discussion of the correct understanding of the many individual textual passages, the fundamental exegetical questions constantly reappear. These problems concern the issues of the reliability of the text, the translation and the exegetical method – and this leads to differing and indeed contradictory interpretations of the various text passages discussed.

On the issue of the reliability of the texts, it becomes clear that both parties apparently assume that their opponent will deliberately manipulate the texts.[25] The heterogeneous character of the biblical corpus offers grounds for such suspicions in

---

21   *Dial.* 8,4: 'If you will listen to me (indeed I already think of you as a friend), first be circumcised, then observe the precepts concerning the Sabbath, the feasts, and God's new moons; in brief, fulfil the whole written law, and then, probably, you will experience the mercy of God.'

22   *Dial.* 11,1: 'But, our hope is not through Moses or through the Law, otherwise our customs would be the same as yours.'

23   Dial 11,2: 'The law promulgated at Horeb is already obsolete, and was intended for Jews only, whereas the law of which I speak is simply for all men.'

24   *Dial.* 56,16 (cf. above n. 6).

25   *Dial.* 120,5: Those textual passages which supported the Christian argument and are still supported by the texts used by the Jews would also have been struck out if the Jewish teachers had understood them correctly (that is, as proofs of the Christian position). Similarly Irenaeus of Lyon, *Adversus haereses* (*Adv. haer.*) 3,21,1.

the case of theological controversies. In a lengthy passage (*Dial.* 71-73), Justin criticises the alleged elimination of dogmatically difficult passages from the Septuagint translation by Jewish teachers[26] – an 'unbelievable' procedure (as Trypho confirms, *Dial.* 73,5). Checking the individual passages leads to a more nuanced appraisal. For example, Justin's claimed elimination of Jer. 11:19 by the Jews cannot be verified on the basis of the preserved biblical manuscripts, as the verse is clearly preserved (*Dial.* 72,2). In another case, Justin's claim that a passage was struck out of Jeremiah by the Jews is not supported by the manuscripts, meaning that Justin was simply appealing to a freely circulating Christian tradition.[27] For Psalm 95, 'The Lord has become king', Justin suggests that the Jews have suppressed the famous words 'from the wood' (ἀπὸ τοῦ ξύλου, *Dial.* 73,1f), which Christians interpret as related to the crucifixion of Jesus. This became a highly popular 'proof text' in the history of Christian exegesis, but as a matter of fact it is a Christian interpolation in the Old Testament known from only a few manuscripts. The debate over the authentic biblical text reveals two aspects. On the one hand, the abundance and diversity of the tradition opens the way to mutual recrimination in questions of forgery. On the other, it is clear that the very disparity is itself the result of the contrasting exegetical goals of the two contesting parties. According to his own testimony, Justin endeavours to construct his argument based exclusively on uncontested textual passages, specifically in order to avoid any threats to the success of his proof (*Dial.* 71,2; 120,5). When one examines the passages which he actually introduces into the dialogue, however, one must concede that for many of the references there was not in fact a consensus on the integrity of the text. In this sense, Justin's 'proofs' rebound on the problem of the textual authenticity of the sources.

The same applies to the question of the authentic Greek translation, which is necessarily intimately linked to textual reliability. In principle, Justin assumes the validity of the Septuagint translation[28] and accuses the Jewish teachers of not recognising the Septuagint, and preferring another translation.[29] As the Christians claimed the Septuagint translation as their Old Testament, and based their apologetic argumentation on the Septuagint, the Jews were supposed to have either forged parts of the Septuagint texts, or produced alternative translations. The historical truth is, however, more complicated. Research on the references to textual passages in the Dialogue has now clearly revealed that Justin frequently cites references from the Christianised Septuagint versions, which he then contends is the authentic Septuagint, the 'Text of the 70'.[30] Divergences from the text which he views as authentic – but which was already revised by Christians – must

---

26   The view that the Jews had deliberately made versions of the Septuagint which perverted the text had become part of common Christian tradition, as can be seen in Eusebius' *Church History* (Eusebius., *Historia Eccleastica* 4,18,8).

27   *Dial.* 72,4. This same passage also 'cites' Irenaeus, who assigns it once to Josiah (*Adv. haer.* 3,20,4), and once to Jeremiah (*Adv. haer.* 4,22,1). Such uncertainties in the identification make it probable that this was initially part of an oral tradition of Christian source texts, and these had to be integrated into the traditional texts.

28   *Dial.* 71,1; 137,3. On all the problems the Septuagint poses for scholarship, see the excellent survey in Tilly 2005.

29   *Dial.* 71,1. Bobichon 2003, 765 suspects that here Justin was referring to the Theodotion translation.

30   In 1 *Apol.* 31 Justin refers to the legend of the emergence of the Septuagint to underscore their authority.

have appeared to him as translations changed by the Jews. Nevertheless, even though Justin generally used the Christianised translation, his arguments involuntarily confirm his suspicion that Jewish revisions of the Septuagint were also in circulation. Thus, in discussing the Dodekapropheton, he uses a text which is quite similar to one of the known Jewish Septuagint revisions, named the καί γε-Text today.[31] Justin was thus conscious of the problem of the different strands of the Septuagint tradition, even though he was unable to accurately identify the origins of the versions which he had at his disposal. In the dialogue, he confronts variants which arise through the differences between a 'Jewish text' and the Septuagint used by the Christians.[32] However, even here he still makes the effort to rely on textual variants used by the Jews, in order to avoid endangering his arguments by using translations which were not recognised by the Jews.[33] Concerning the exegetical method and its application, we can also observe that both of the parties in the dialogue raise a number of questions and reproaches. It is to be assumed that both Justin and Trypho were aware of the rules of textual exegesis according to the standards of the day, as also used by pagan authors interpreting pagan texts.[34] Both of the parties demand respect for these rules, and note the failure to do so critically. The differences range across the board: the question of the use of complete citations (*Dial.* 98,1); the establishment of correct or incorrect references (*Dial.* 43,8; 67,1; 122,1); the respect for the contextual relations within the texts, and the failure to respect these;[35] the arbitrary eclectic choice of textual references;[36] and the drawing of correct and incorrect conclusions.[37] Drawing on textual references must follow critical examination, respecting exact criteria.[38] There are also differences of opinion on the issue of the suitability of allegorical interpretations and the correct understanding of figurative language.[39]

31   For the Kaige-Revision, see Tilly 2005, 83f.
32   *Dial.* 124,2f.: This refers to Psalm 81. Justin interprets the plural ἄνθρωποι (reading of the LXX) of Ps 81,7 in the sense of the possibility of understanding the Christians as the sons of God. The Jewish reading has the singular ἄνθρωπος. The basis of the Greek Jewish tradition cannot be established.
33   *Dial.* 124,4: 'Hold whatever interpretation of the psalm you please. It has been shown that they were considered worthy to become gods, and to have the capability of becoming sons of the Most High…'.
34   The difficulties of textual criticism, commentaries and judgements of the authors of the canonical texts used in teaching followed Quintilians *Institutio Oratoria*. In this method, the *emendatio* aimed at text-critical analysis, the *enarratio* was the commentary based on historical, mythological and rhetorical aspects, and the *iudicium* touched upon the actual meaning of the text. In the history of Christianity detailed rules specifically dedicated to biblical texts are found in Origen's *De principiis* book 4, in Tyconius' *Liber regularum*, and in Augustine's *De doctrina Christiana*.
35   At issue here, for example, is taking the preceding and following sentences into consideration: *Dial.* 65,2 'I answered: "If you quoted that passage honestly and without malice, Trypho, and stopped without adding the words which both precede and follow it, then you may be excused. But you are sadly mistaken if you did so in the hope of embarrassing me into admitting that some passages of Scripture contradict others, for I would not be so bold as to assert, or even imagine, such a thing."'
36   *Dial.* 27,1: 'Why', objected Trypho, 'do you quote only those passages from the Prophets which prove your point, and omit those quotations which clearly order the observance of the Sabbath?'
37   *Dial.* 20,3: 'Such a conclusion lacks credibility.'
38   *Dial.* 65,3: 'And, gentlemen, I will add a few words of the content of the passage quoted by Trypho, and also those which immediately follow them. The words which I cite will not be taken from another chapter, but only from the context.'
39   *Dial.* 57,2: 'Thus, if we are in a slight way familiar with the use of figurative modes of expression, even in this scriptural passage there should be nothing puzzling to us', says Justin – thereby suggesting that the Jews do not understand them.

The abundance of the criteria and rules of proper exegesis topicalised in Justin's *Dialogue* with the Jew Trypho reveals elevated interest in agreement on the exegetical method wherever the disputed texts are assigned an authoritative significance. The existing difficulties of textual understanding arising from the date, the content or the complicated history of the tradition are themselves enhanced whenever it is assumed that the texts have a central and religiously authoritative role.[40] This phenomenon becomes even more significant when the contestants lay claim to the very same text or a group of these texts. This is exactly what we see in Justin's *Dialogue* with the Jew Trypho. It is for this reason that the conflict over the proper application of exegetical methods takes on such an important role.

Conclusions and summary

A consensus or partial consensus on a canon of sacred texts can provide a useful basis for both a common search for the truth and also mutual attempts at conversion between and amongst the adherents of different religious entities. Where both parties lay claim to the texts in that canon and both recognise the same norms, these fulfil a central condition for the possibility of a contest in the form of a discussion. At the same time, the limits constricting such a discussion become immediately apparent. In the case of best conditions, mutual and reciprocal recognition of the texts as canonical and the discussion about these texts will promote a profound understanding of the opponent's position. This does not, however, guarantee unity on the part of those who agree on the texts and dispute the correct understanding of those texts. Differing hermeneutic premises and contexts guide the textual exegesis. Problems arise over accepting or rejecting additional texts as canonical. Exegetical differences appear over textual reliability, translation and the methodical treatment of those texts which both recognise as canonical. The disagreement over the correct understanding of the texts recognised by both parties as being religiously authoritative also demands the establishment of a nuanced instrumental method, which is then exploited by both parties to support their own positions. All of these factors meant that although Justin and Trypho both recognised Moses and the Prophets and had a fruitful discussion of the understanding of the texts, ultimately it was impossible for them to reach agreement. Instead, they separated in friendly disagreement.[41] And indeed it was a friendly disagreement, and one wishes to note this in the light of the later history of relations between Christians and Jews.[42]

---

40   In this case, the religious or confessional claims to these texts are of no importance, nor is their original background. It is as if these were recognised 'canonical' cultural property like Homer or Virgil, or law codes, or even texts which could be assigned to a canon of the texts of divine revelation.

41   Trypho summarises, *Dial.* 142,1: 'If we could meet more frequently and continue our study of the Scriptures, we certainly would profit even more by it'. Justin responds, *Dial.* 142,2: 'If I had stayed here, I would have liked to continue this discussion every day.' See the commentary on the closing passage, Bobichon 2003, 915-917.

42   One can easily gain a good impression of the darker side of this history, extending into the High Middle Ages, with a glance at Schreckenberg 1990.

In any case, the procedures illuminated in the case of Justin's *Dialogue* with the Jew Trypho later led to conflicts both between Christians and Jews and also in the internal history of both Christianity and Judaism. These were not prevented by the existence of a group of shared sacred texts, but rather exacerbated by them – in contrast to what was ultimately quite an irenic dialogue in the case discussed.

Bibliography

Abramowski, L. 1983. 'Die "Erinnerungen der Apostel" bei Justin'. In: P. Stuhlmacher (ed.), *Das Evangelium und die Evangelien. Vorträge vom Tübinger Symposion 1982*. (WUNT 67). Berlin: De Gruyter, 341-351.

Bobichon, P. 2003. *Justin Martyr, Dialogue avec Tryphon. Édition critique, traduction, commentaire*. (Paradosis 47/1 and 47/2). Freiburg: Academic Press.

Falls, T. 2003. *St. Justin Martyr, Dialogue with Trypho*. M. Slusser (ed). Washington: Catholic University Press.

Haeuser, P. 1917. *Des heiligen Philosophen und Märtyrers Justinus "Dialog mit dem Juden Tryphon". Pseudo-Justinus, "Mahnrede an die Hellenen"*. (Bibliothek der Kirchenväter 33, 1-231). Kempten: Verlag Kösel.

Iustinus Martyr, *Dialogus cum Tryphone Iudaeo*. (CPG 1076). Turnhout: Brepols.

Lieu, J.M. 1996. *Image and Reality. The Jews in the World of the Christians in the Second Century*. Edinburgh: T&T Clark.

Marcovich, M. 1997. *Justini Martyris Dialogus cum Tryphone*. Berlin: Walter de Gruyter.

Parvis, S. and P. Forster (eds.) 2007. *Justin Martyr and His Worlds*, Minneapolis: Fortress Press.

Ristow, H. 1963. *Die Apologeten*. Berlin: Evangelische Verlagsanstalt.

Schreckenberg, H. 1990 (2nd ed.) *Die christlichen Adversus-Judaeos-Texte und ihr literarisches und historisches Umfeld*. Frankfurt: Peter Lang.

Setzer, C. 1991. '"You invent a Christ". Christological Claims as Points of Jewish-Christian Dispute'. *Union Seminary Quarterly Review*, 44, 315-328.

Skarsaune, O. 1987. *The Proof from Prophecy. A Study in Justin Martyr's Proof Text Tradition. Text-Type, Provenance, Theological Profile*. (NT.S 56). Leiden: Brill

Skarsaune, O. 2007. 'Justin and His Bible'. In: Parvis & Forster (eds.), *Justin Martyr and His Worlds*. Minneapolis: Fortress Press, 53-76.

Tilly, M. 2005. *Einführung in die Septuaginta*. Darmstadt: Wissenschaftliche Buchgesellschaft.

Ulrich, J. 2006. 'Ethik als Ausweis christlicher Identität bei Justin Martyr'. *Zeitschrift für evangelische Ethik*, 1, 21-28.

Williams, A.L. 1930. *Justin Martyr: The Dialogue with Trypho*. London: SPCK.

NORMATIVE STRUCTURES IN ORIGEN'S BIBLICAL EXEGESIS

Anders-Christian Jacobsen

Introduction

In the following I want to present some ideas about the normative structures which are decisive for Origen's exegesis of biblical texts. As I will show below, Origen's exegesis goes beyond a literal interpretation of biblical texts. This raises the question about which guidelines Origen follows in his exegesis. Does he just say what first comes to his mind, or is his exegesis guided and perhaps restricted by some kind of norms? If so, is it possible for us to identify these norms? I think it is. As I will show, Origen's exegesis is controlled by a rather wide range of different norms which all refer to the complex network of beliefs and skills which have formed him through his education and experience. This range of norms is wide, covering a broad field from rather strong theological / dogmatic norms to weaker rhetorical norms. These quite different types of norms are all in one way or another decisive for the content and presentation of his exegesis.

My article has the following content: First I will very briefly describe the principles which Origen sets up for his biblical exegesis. After that I will try to identify some of the norms which control his exegesis. I will focus on theological norms such as rules of faith, the idea of divine inspiration of the biblical texts and of the interpreter, and the idea that the Bible interprets itself; on philosophical norms such as the theme of paideia; and finally I will point to some rhetorical norms which he employs in his exegesis. To avoid any misunderstandings, I must make it clear from the outset that my division between theological, philosophical and rhetorical norms is artificial, because they all belong to the same 'package' of education or paideia which makes Origen the person he is. He would never have distinguished between his work as a theologian, a philosopher, and a rhetorician.

Main lines in Origen's allegorical exegesis

The main idea of the hermeneutical theory which Origen outlines in *De principiis* (*De princ.*)[1] 4,2 is that the biblical scriptures contain a number of levels, corresponding to the levels in the process by which every human being moves from lower levels to

---

1   The standard edition of the Latin and Greek text of *De princ.* is P. Koetschau 1913. *Origenes Werke, fünfter Band, De principiis* (*Die Griechischen christlichen Schriftsteller*, 22). Leipzig: J.C Heinrichs'che Buchhandlung. Another version of the Greek and Latin text with a German translation can be found in H. Görgemanns and H. Karpp 1976 (and later). *Origenes. Vier Bücher von den Prinzipien*. Darmstadt: Wissenschaftliche Buchgesellschaft. A third and now much used version of the text with a French translation is H. Crouzel and M. Simonetti 1978-1980. *Origène. Traité des Principes* (4 volumes). Paris: Les editions du Cerf.

higher levels of spiritual education and perfection. According to Origen, this means that the Logos of God, who has inspired the biblical texts, has constructed the text of the Bible according to an allegorical hermeneutics which only allows spiritually educated Christians to understand the deepest levels of biblical texts. Origen develops this idea in a very schematic outline in *De princ.* 4,2,4.

In *De princ.* 4,2,4 Origen says that the Scriptures have three levels, corresponding to the construction of man and mankind: The first level is the corporeal level, which is the same as the literal meaning of the texts. The next level is the psychic level, although Origen does not say explicitly what the psychic level in the Scriptures consists of. The third and deepest level in the Scriptures is the spiritual level, which is where one finds the shadows of the coming blessings. According to Origen, these three levels in the biblical texts are related to the tripartite construction of man and mankind: A man consists of body, soul and spirit, and mankind consists of spiritual, physical and corporeal persons.

There are many problems related to Origen's explanation of his exegetical methods in *De princ.* 4.2: First, he does not explain all the details very clearly. For instance, the content and use of the second level of scripture is quite unclear; second, he does not always follow these ideas in his practical exegetical works. For instance, he often only finds two levels in the biblical texts – a literal and a spiritual. And third, he gives many other explanations of his exegetical methods in his other works which are different from the explanation in *De princ.* 4,2 – even though they are not diametrically opposed.[2] However, it is not my intention to discuss these difficulties now.[3] My intention is rather to discuss the problems of normativity which arise out of the fact that Origen always finds different levels of meaning beyond the literal surface in the biblical texts which he interprets.

Norms applied by Origen for his exegesis

Many of Origen's critics over the centuries have criticised his allegorical exegesis because it enables him to read into or out of the biblical texts all kinds of ideas which are not inherent in them.[4] Origen would not have accepted this critique. He would claim that he uncovers hidden meanings which are inherent in the texts, and that this process of uncovering is guarded by certain rules or norms. In the following I will describe some of these norms.

---

2   In the following passages Origen makes important claims about his exegetical methods: *Commentary on John* 13,26-39; *Commentary on the Song of Songs*, prologue and 3,12; *Contra Celsum* 4,36-53.

3   For more general information about Origen's exegesis, see Jacobsen 2007, 62-70; Lauro 2005; Hyldahl 2004; Vogt 2004; Chadwick 1998; Bostock 1987; Torjesen 1986; Hanson 1959.

4   Concerning the condemnations and rejections of Origen's allegorical exegesis, see Jacobsen 2008a, 214-216.

Theological norms

Origen sees himself primarily as a theologian who brings forward the orthodox Christian teaching which originates from the prophets and the apostles, who were in turn inspired by the Logos of God. Therefore he sets up theological norms for the theological and exegetical work carried out by himself and others. I will explore some of these.

The rule of faith:
The idea that true Christianity is governed by 'rules of faith' or 'rules of truth' is known well before Origen's time in second-century Christianity, especially in Irenaeus (e.g. *Adversus haereses* 1,10,1) and Tertullian (e.g. *De praescriptione* 1,13f). These rules were short expressions of the most important elements of Christian teaching. One of their functions was to avoid or detect misinterpretations of the biblical texts. If an explanation of a biblical passage, a word or the like was in conflict with the content of the rule of faith, one could be sure that this explanation was a misinterpretation.[5] These rules were not unknown to Origen. The passage which I will discuss now contains one of the most explicit uses of this idea in Origen, although he does not explicitly use the expressions 'rule of faith' or 'rule of truth'.[6]

In *De princ.* 1,praef.,2 Origen says that Christians disagree about fundamental dogmatic questions such as God, Jesus Christ and the Holy Spirit. The reason why seems to be that some Christians do not follow the teaching of their predecessors (*diversa a prioribus*). However, the true Christian teaching remains unshaken:

So, seeing there are many who think they hold the opinions of Christ, and yet some of these think differently from their predecessors, yet as the teaching of the Church, transmitted in orderly succession from the apostles, and remaining in the Churches to the present day, is still preserved, that alone is to be accepted as truth which differs in no respect from ecclesiastical and apostolic tradition.[7]

This quotation shows that Origen sticks to the common idea of the ancient church that the true Christian teaching is handed down from the apostles themselves to the church in Origen's own time without any adulterations. This is the idea of an unchanged ecclesiastical tradition (*ecclesiastica et apostolica traditione*). Whether theological ideas are true or not can be decided by a comparison with the content of this apostolic tradition. Origen thus presents a quite strong theological norm which is decisive for the evaluation of all kinds of Christian teaching. *Nothing* which diverges from this norm

---

5   Concerning the use of 'rules of faith' before Origen, see Jacobsen 2008b, 223-225.

6   Origen says in *De princ.* 1,praef.,2 that because of disagreement among Christians about main topics such as God, Jesus Christ, the Holy Spirit and the creation, it will be necessary first of all to establish a fixed rule about these topics: '...*prius de his singulis certam lineam manifestamque regulam ponere,...*' (*De princ.* 1,praef.,2). Here Origen does not point to 'rules of faith' but to the teaching of these topics, which he will present in the first chapters of *De princ.* before he moves on to other questions.

7   This and the following English quotations from *De principiis* are from *The Ante-Nicene Fathers*, Vol. 6, Grand Rapids, Michigan: Eerdmans.

can be true Christian teaching. The question for Origen is now: Who decides what the true ecclesiastical and apostolic tradition is? In this case it seems to be Origen himself, because he goes on to define what the content of this tradition is.

In *De princ.* 1,praef.,3-8 Origen explains which parts of the Christian teaching the apostles have defined clearly and precisely in their teaching; what they have touched upon, but not explained in detail; and finally what they have not commented on at all. There seems to be a certain tension between this and what he said in the first paragraphs of the introduction to the first book of *De princ.*: How can anything be a part of Christian teaching if it is not contained in the apostolic tradition, which Origen claimed is normative for true Christian teaching? The key to understanding this is to be found in the final word in *De princ.* 1,praef.,2: '*discordat*'. According to Origen, parts of Christian teaching have not been taught by the apostles, but must be added by wise Christians afterwards. The things added in this way must not *contradict* (cf. *discordat*) the content of the apostolic tradition. So things can be added to the tradition if they are in accordance with the tradition.

According to Origen, the following topics have been explained openly and in detail by the apostles: God is one, he is the creator of the world and the father of Christ; Christ has always existed, he was the mediator in the creation of the world, he was incarnated in human form at the end of times, he died and was resurrected and taken up into the heavens; there is a Holy Spirit, who partakes in the Father and the Son and who has inspired the prophets; souls have their own substance and life, and will be punished according to their works; bodies will be resurrected into glory; and finally souls have been bestowed with the freedom of will (*De princ.* 1,praef.,4-5).

The apostles have not spoken openly and in detail about how souls are united with bodies; what the devil, the angels and the hostile powers are; and finally what was before and what comes after this world. This means that the truth about these topics is hidden under the literal surface of the biblical texts, and is therefore only approachable for those who have been entrusted by the Holy Spirit with wisdom and knowledge enabling them to understand what is beneath the literal surface of the texts (cf. *De princ.* 1,praef.,6-7). I will return to this theme of inspiration later on.

Finally, there are some important topics about which the apostles have not spoken at all. For instance: what does it mean that something is without body; when were the angels and the positive powers created and what is their nature; and finally do the sun, the moon and the stars have souls? Wise Christians must investigate these things on their own (*De princ.* 1,praef.,7-10). So there is plenty of room for wise and creative Christians to use their wisdom and creativity in unfolding the Christian teaching. According to Origen, the criterion for this is that nothing of what is presented must contradict the apostolic tradition. According to Origen, the apostolic tradition is a stable and well defined entity, but some things have to be explained and added. This is the problem! These explanations and additions unavoidably change the apostolic tradition. And that is why Christians disagree about the content and the interpretation of the apostolic tradition in Origen's view.

It seems to be clear from this that norms – in this case norms for what is true and false apostolic teaching – are continuously being defined and redefined by never-ending dialogue and conflicts between Christians who are of different opinions. Thus we see that Origen in his introduction to his dogmatic treatise reacts against other Christians who he believes have misunderstood and misinterpreted the apostolic tradition. Origen intends to correct their misinterpretations. Since Origen countless numbers of theologians and other Christians have sought to correct Origen's definition of what true Christianity is. This is a never-ending story – norms are apparently negotiable.

Divine inspiration of the biblical texts and of the interpreter:
Origen also tries in other ways to solve the problems of normativity which arise from the idea that not all true Christian teaching is available at the literal surface of the biblical texts but must be searched for at deeper levels by an allegorical reading of the texts. One of the norms which Origen presents as a fence against random explanations of the apostolic tradition inherent but hidden in the biblical texts is the idea of divine inspiration.

The idea that a certain text has several levels generally implies the notion that the text was deliberately constructed with these different levels.[8] According to Origen, the text of the Bible is constructed and inspired with meaning by Logos and the Holy Spirit. This is the precondition for his development of the allegorical hermeneutics in *De princ.* 4,2. Origen therefore develops the idea of divine inspiration of the Bible in *De princ.* 4,1,6, where he claims that the prophecies in the Old Testament about Christ are inspired by God (συναποδείκνυμεν θεοπνεύστους εἶ τὰς προφητευούσας περὶ αὐτοῦ γραφάς). These inspired sayings about the coming and the work of Christ could not be understood before Christ actually came. But when he came, the prophecies about him were revealed first by himself and later on by his followers, who taught and preached about him all over the world. Like Origen himself, these teachers were inspired by Logos in a way which made it possible for them to reveal the hidden truth about Christ in the scriptures.[9]

However, this is not the only way in which Logos' construction of the biblical texts is to be seen. Very often Logos has constructed the text in such a way that the spiritual meaning of the text is hidden under the surface of the letter. Origen says this directly in *De princ.* 1,praef.,8:

---

8   J. Hyldahl, 2004, 117-129, especially 120-121 accentuates that allegorical hermeneutics is not only a question of interpreting the text at different levels, but also a question of constructing the text with more levels. The latter is the work of Logos, and the former is the job of the inspired reader.

9   Chadwick 1998, 14 points to the idea of inspiration as something fundamental to the allegorical exegesis, because it is this inspiration which secures the internal harmony between the different levels of the text. However, a fuller discussion of the idea of inspiration in the hermeneutics and theology of Origen is to be found in the much older but still very helpful book by R.P.C. Hanson, 1959, 187-209. Like Chadwick, Hanson finds that the function of the idea of inspiration is to secure unity in the Bible: unity between the different layers in the texts; between the different texts; and between The Old and The New Testament. Finally, see Nardoni 1984 and Vogt 1990.

Then, finally, that the Scriptures were written by the Spirit of God, and have a meaning, not such only as is apparent at first sight, but also another, which escapes the notice of most. For those (words) which are written are the forms of certain mysteries, and the images of divine things. Respecting which there is one opinion throughout the whole Church, that the whole law is indeed spiritual; but that the spiritual meaning which the law conveys is not known to all, but to those only on whom the grace of the Holy Spirit is bestowed in the word of wisdom and knowledge.

The aim of this hiding of the deeper mysteries is to prevent simple-minded Christians from getting in touch with these spiritual meanings, which they are not able to understand in a proper way. This means, however, that the uncovering of these hidden meanings is only possible for inspired interpreters who possess the code by which these hidden meanings can be revealed.

Origen thus claims that the text of the Bible is not the only thing to be inspired by Logos and the Holy Spirit. The interpreter of the texts must be similarly inspired in order to find the hidden meanings under the literal surface of the texts. Origen explains this in *De princ.* 1,praef,3:

Now it ought to be known that the holy apostles, in preaching the faith of Christ, delivered themselves with the utmost clearness on certain points which they believed to be necessary to every one, even to those who seemed somewhat dull in the investigation of divine knowledge; leaving, however, the grounds of their statements to be examined into by those who should deserve the excellent gifts of the Spirit, and who, especially by means of the Holy Spirit Himself, should obtain the gift of language, of wisdom, and of knowledge:...

It does not take much inspiration to realise that Origen implicitly claims that he himself is one of the inspired interpreters who are able to explain the meanings of the different levels in the biblical texts.

As far as I can see, the idea of inspiration can only fulfil its normative task in relation to the allegorical exegesis if everyone agrees that the biblical texts are inspired by Logos and the Holy Spirit and therefore contain several layers of meaning. Everyone must also agree that the interpreters of the texts must be inspired, and finally everyone must agree who these inspired interpreters are. Most ancient theologians agree on the first point, and many on the second as well. But then as now there is a huge and insurmountable disagreement about who can be counted as inspired interpreters. To be functional the norm of inspiration must also be negotiated, and the results of these negotiations will thus probably only cover a small number of the actual interpreters.

Interpreting the Bible by the Bible:
The fact that Origen interprets the Bible by the Bible itself is obvious. He always includes other biblical texts in his interpretation. The question is whether we can say that the Bible is normative for his biblical interpretation, and if so in which way it can be said to be normative. First, it is obvious that the text which Origen interprets is

normative for his interpretation of this text. However, as we have seen he often very quickly moves away from the literal level of the text to 'the inner meaning'. The text understood as the literal text thus only has a weak normative function in his exegesis of that text.[10] Secondly, when he moves from the interpretation of the literal level of the text to the deeper levels of the text he very often includes other biblical texts in his interpretation of the inner meaning of the concrete text which he is interpreting. So these other biblical texts are given a normative function for his interpretation of the first text, but what kind of normativity is this? Can we say that Origen exclusively interprets biblical texts by using other biblical texts? If we can, these other biblical texts would have a strong normative function. However, as far as I can see he does not exclusively interpret biblical texts by using other biblical texts. He also often includes other ideas which are not found in the Bible. Thus it can be concluded that the Bible itself has only a rather weak normative function in his biblical exegesis. Let me give an example of what I mean.

In his commentary on Romans (*CRom.*) 3,8 Origen presents his exegesis of Rom 3:25-26, where Paul speaks about Christ, whom God predetermined as a propitiation. This means, says Origen, that through the sacrifice of himself Christ made God propitious to man. This was necessary because the just God could not make unjust men righteous without some kind of mediator (*CRom.* 3,1). This is, however, only the literal meaning of the text. Having made this clear, Origen turns to the inner meaning. As usual he seeks to uncover this inner meaning by using other biblical texts which can lead him in the direction of the deeper meaning. This time he turns to Ex 25:10-22, where God instructs Moses how to build an ark. Upon this ark he is to place a propitiation of pure gold two cubits and a half high and one cubit and a half wide. According to Origen, this propitiation is a sign of Christ. The fact that the propitiation is to be made of pure gold 'indicates that holy and pure soul of Jesus which committed no sin nor was deceit found in his mouth' (Isa 53:9). Then Origen speculates on the meaning of the size of the propitiation. The height or length is to be two and a half cubits. This signifies that it is something more than human, because the height of normal humans could not be more than two cubits. But the height is not three cubits, which would be a totally superhuman height. So the height seems to be somewhere between human and divine. Therefore it must be signifying the soul of Christ, which is the mediator between God and man. The same can be concluded about the width of the propitiation. Origen concludes:

For that reason then the Apostle, when discussing the mediator, indicated this by a plain distinction by saying, 'the mediator between God and men, the man Christ Jesus' (1 Tim 2:5), by which he was obviously teaching that this 'mediator' must be referred not to Christ's deity but to his humanity, i.e. his soul. Both its length and its width are therefore recorded. The length signifies

---

10   It is, however, important to be aware that according to Origen the literal text has a weak normative function as pedagogical instruction for people who are still at the mere bodily level of human existence.

that which pertains to God and is associated with the Trinity; the width signifies that he abides among men who customarily go along the wide and spacious road (cf. Matth 7:13); and therefore he is rightly called by the name of 'mediator', since, as we have said, this holy soul was a certain mid-point between the divinity of the Trinity and the frailty of humanity.[11]

This example shows how in his exegesis of a certain word or expression Origen sometimes moves rather far from the text which he is actually interpreting. In this case Paul uses a word ίλαστήριον (propitiation), which is also found in the Greek version (LXX) of Ex 25:17. This is of course the reason why Origen includes this text in his interpretation. From the mention of the pure gold in Ex 25:17 Origen moves to Isa 53:9, where the servant of God is said to be without deceit, this means pure. Isa 53 has been taken from the Christian beginnings as a prophecy of Christ. In this way the propitiation is identified as Christ. So far Origen's exegesis is 'controlled' by the canonical scriptures. Establishing such chains of scriptural passages was a very widespread way of doing biblical interpretation in the early church. It was by no means only used by those whom we designate as 'allegorists'.[12] It can of course be discussed how stable and controlled this kind of interpretation is. The number of possible combinations of scriptural passages seems to be indefinite, even though some rules seem to be established. Furthermore, the precondition for this concept of 'interpreting the Bible with the Bible' is that a well defined biblical canon exists. In Origen's times the main outlines of such a biblical canon existed, but the final definition was not ready until 100 years later.[13]

However, as the example shows Origen includes ideas from outside the biblical canon in his creative exegesis. Having moved from Romans 3:25-26 to Ex 25:10-22 by means of the word 'propitiation', he goes on to interpret the measures of the propitiation which are mentioned in Ex 25:17. In this case he does not rely on other biblical expressions, but speculates as to the size of human bodies. He arrives at the conclusion that the propitiation signifies Christ as the mediator, and that 'mediator refers to the human part of Christ'. Having arrived at this conclusion, he justifies it by a reference to 1 Tim 2:5. Thus one could claim that in this example of exegesis Origen manages to stay inside a concept of interpretation which could be called 'the Bible interprets itself'. However, I would say that Origen tends to move outside this concept by applying speculations about figures and the size of human bodies. The conclusion must again be that the biblical canon only functions as a weak norm for his exegetical work.

What does Origen mean by the concept of 'the inner meaning' of scripture? It is obvious that he thinks that this meaning is contained in the biblical texts. However, the inner meaning is not to be found at the literal level of scripture (cf. *De princ.* 4,2). When

---

[11]   The best version of the text of Origen's commentary to the Romans is found in C.P. Hammond-Bammel 1990-1998. *Der Römerbriefkommentar des Origenes: Kritische Ausgabe de Übersetzung Rufins.* Freiburg in Breisgau: Herder. This and the following quotations from Origen's commentary on Romans are from Thomas P. Scheck 2001-2002. *Origen. Commentary on the Epistle to the Romans.* Washington, D.C.: The Catholic University of America Press.

[12]   One example among thousands is Irenaeus, *Adv. haer.* 5,13,3, where Irenaeus includes 1 Cor 15:53-55; Phil 3:20-21 and 2 Cor 5:45 in his argumentation that according to Paul flesh can inherit the kingdom of God.

[13]   Cf. the contribution of Nils Arne Pedersen in this volume.

Origen says in the preface to *De princ.* that he will continue the work of the apostles by seeking meanings which they have not expressed, he indicates very clearly that he will go beyond what the apostles have said explicitly and what is handed down in the biblical texts. At the same time, he indicates that what he says will be said in continuation of and not against what the apostles have said. We can thus conclude that the Bible has a normative function in Origen's biblical exegesis. It is debatable how strong this normative function of the Bible is. Origen's principle is that he will not go against what the apostles have said in the Bible, so one could conclude that the Bible has a strong normative function in his biblical exegesis. However, as we have seen above it is difficult for Origen to set up fixed norms which guarantee that he does not go beyond or even against what the apostles have said. I would therefore say that the principles and not least the practices of Origen's exegesis do not allow us to conclude that the Bible has a very strong normative function in Origen's exegesis, but rather that it has a weakened normative function.

Philosophical norms

It is well known and commonly accepted that Origen incorporates many ideas from his philosophical context in what is called 'Middle Platonism'. This is of course also the case in his exegesis. In my opinion we could even say that some very important principles in his exegetical work derive from his philosophical context. In the following I will point to one of these principles, namely the ideas of paideia and accommodation, which are combined in one exegetical principle. In short, this idea can be formulated this way: Humans are like children. They have to be educated (paideia). The wise teacher or pedagogue (Logos) addresses his pupils at the level at which they can be found at the moment. This means that the teacher accommodates his teaching to the specific pupils in question. This combination of ideas probably has different philosophical roots in Stoicism (logos) and in Platonism (paideia), but the ideas are combined in Middle Platonism, from where Origen knows them.[14]

Origen, as we have seen, generally finds two or three levels in the biblical texts (cf. *De princ.* 4,2). The texts are constructed like this by Logos, because the texts of the Bible have to speak to everybody at their own level. The literal level is directed at simple Christians, and the psychic level – if it exists in the text – is directed at those who are on their way to perfection but still need moral education. The spiritual level is aimed at spirituals who are morally clean and therefore able to look into the spiritual mysteries. The aim of these different levels in the texts is to bring about moral and spiritual education for everybody as they are able to receive it. This is the principle of *accommodation*. In connection with Origen's hermeneutics, *accommodation* means that

---

14   It is not possible here to be more detailed about the philosophical background. The ideas and Origen's use of them are well described in the literature, see e.g. Dillon 1977; Koch 1932. In this connection I also recommend a very interesting (but not yet published) Italian book on Origen's concept of the child, written by Chiara Barilli. Barilli shows that Origen's concept of the child is related to these ideas about paideia and accommodation, and that in these matters Origen draws upon Chrisippus and Philo.

Logos and the Holy Spirit inspiring the Bible present the messages in several ways so everybody can understand them. This is like parents or teachers talking baby language so young children can understand them:

After this because Celsus failed to understand them, he ridicules passages in the Bible which speak of God as though He were subject to human passions, in which angry utterances are spoken against the impious and threats against people who have sinned. I reply that, just as when we are talking with little children we do not aim to speak in the finest language possible to us, but say what is appropriate to the weakness of those whom we are addressing, and, further, do what seems to us to be of advantage for the conversation and correction of the children as such, so also the Logos of God seems to have arranged the scriptures, using the method of address which fitted the ability and benefit of the hearers. In fact, in Deuteronomy it is quite generally stated concerning this type of address which is attributed to God, in these words. 'The Lord thy God bare with thy ways, as a man might bear with his son' (Deut 1:31). The Logos speaks like this because he assumes, as it were, human characteristics for the advantage of men. There was no need for the multitude that the words put into God's mouth, which were intended to be addressed to them, should correspond to His real character. However, anyone interested in the exposition of the divine scriptures, by comparing spiritual things with spiritual, as it is said, will discover from them the meaning of the sayings addressed to the weak and of those spoken to the intelligent, while often both meanings lie in the same text for him who knows how to understand it.[15]

The idea of accommodation is also used by Origen to explain how in The Old Testament and especially by his incarnation Logos takes on a form which makes it able for men to grasp him. This shows that according to Origen it is basically the same thing which happens when Logos expresses himself in the Bible, and when he incarnates himself in the man called Jesus from Nazareth.[16]

As we can see, philosophical ideas play a rather strong normative role in Origen's exegesis. Thus it should be clear by now that Origen's exegesis is not only controlled by dogmatic 'rules of faith' or by other texts from the biblical canon, but also by philosophical norms which are decisive for the way in which Origen understands the construction of the biblical texts, and the way he presents the results of his exegesis to his different auditoria. In one sense, these pedagogical or philosophical norms turn into quasi dogmatic norms because they also become decisive for the way in which

---

15   *Contra Celsum (Cels.)* 4.71. The Greek text can be found in P. Koetschau 1899. *Origenes Werke*, vol. 1-2. *Die Griechischen Christlichen Schriftsteller*, Leipzig: J.C. Hinrichs'sche Buchhandlung; and in: Marcel Borret 1967-1976. *Origène. Contra Celse. Sources Chrétiennes* 132, 136, 147,150, 227. The English translation is from H. Chadwick 1965. *Origen: Contra Celsum*, Cambridge: Cambridge University Press. See further Origen's *Homily in Jeremia* 18.6 for a long and beautiful explanation of the idea of *accommodation*, where God is described as a father talking baby language to his child in order to be understood. Concerning the idea of Logos' accommodation in the scriptures, see Hanson, 1959, 224-231. Hanson's main interest is to use the idea of Logos' accommodation in the Bible to explain how Origen deals with all the sayings in the Bible which represent God in human form, which disagree with each other and so on. Hanson (210-231) shows that Origen explains all these kinds of saying by means of the idea of accommodation.

16   Cf. Origen, *Philocalia* 15.19; Origen, *Commentary on Matthew* 15.3. Also Hanson, 1959, 193-194.

he understands Logos and the work of Logos. However, I cannot deal with this theme here.[17] This leads us to the last group of norms which I will deal with, namely literary and rhetorical norms.

Literary and rhetorical norms in Origen's exegesis

When Origen writes his exegetical works, he follows some fixed literary and rhetorical rules which he knows from his own education in grammar and rhetoric, and from his time as a teacher in these topics. There are several examples of this in Origen's works, two of which I will mention here. The first is a rhetorical technique called 'prosopological exegesis', and the second is a rhetorical technique called 'quæstiones et responsiones'. In these matters I am heavily inspired by two of my Italian colleagues: Andrea Villani, who has written about the prosopological exegesis (Villani 2008), and Lorenzo Perrone, who has written about quæstiones et responsiones (Perrone 1994; 1995).

Prosopological exegesis:
Prosopopoiia is a rhetorical term which means that a writer can let persons or personified things speak in his text. When a writer does that he must take care to let these persons speak in a way which is proper for them. This means, for example, that a Jew must speak like a Jew and a Greek like a Greek, a philosopher like a philosopher and a fisherman like a fisherman. This rhetorical concept has a long history in the classical rhetorical tradition. Villani shows that Origen is very well acquainted with this concept and knows how to use it in different ways. Origen uses the concept several times in *Contra Celsum* as part of his apology against Celsus. In this case Origen shows that Celsus is unable to use the concept in practice. For instance, he puts words in the mouth of a Jew which a Jew would never utter (cf. *Cels.* 1.28). Origen also uses the concept in his exegesis of biblical texts. This is the case when he discusses how different statements in a biblical text are distributed to different speaking subjects: Is God or Logos or the Holy Spirit speaking? Do Logos speak through a prophet and so on (cf. e.g. *Philocalia* 7,1). According to Origen, the identification of the distribution of the words of a text to different subjects is a very important part of the exegesis of a concrete text. According to Villani, Origen links this rhetorical concept to the idea of the divine inspiration of the Bible. Thus it is ultimately always Logos or the Holy Spirit who speaks in the texts. Logos and the Holy Spirit act like a writer who is trained in rhetoric in that they distribute the words to various subjects in the texts in a proper way.[18] It is the exegete's job to identify these subjects in the biblical text.

---

17   This will be a main theme in my forthcoming book on Origen's christology and soteriology.
18   Cf. Villani 2008. Further Neuschäfer 1987.

Quæstiones et responsionis:

The rhetorical strategy called 'quaestiones et responsionis' is another example of the way in which Origen employs rhetorical strategies which were known to him from tradition. In this case the tradition goes back to antique rhetoric traditions, for example Aristotle.[19] The concept is also known to and used by Philo from Alexandria, and after Origen the concept seems to be very widespread among Christian authors in the fourth and fifth centuries such as Eusebius and Augustine. As far as we know, Origen has not written a treatise with the title 'Quaestiones in....', but as Lorenzo Perrone (1994; 1995) shows, he has used the method in all the different types of texts he has written such as treatises, commentaries and homilies. Perrone also shows that Origen used the strategy of quaestiones not only in apologetic contexts, but also in didactic contexts. Perrone points to several very clear examples of Origen's use of this rhetorical strategy. One is found in a long passage in *De princ.* 3,1,7-24, where Origen discusses the theme 'freedom of will'. This long passage is structured by questions and answers, revealing that this strategy can be used to create structure in a literary work of a systematic nature (Perrone 1994, 7-12). One could imagine that this part of *De princ.* was an independent speech or literary work with the title 'Questions in the freedom of will' before it was included in *De principiis*.[20] Another example is found in Origen's *Commentary on John* 28,15-17, where Origen comments on the conversation between Jesus and Martha after the death of Lazarus (Joh 11:1-44). This is an example of the use of the technique in a biblical commentary with a more didactic purpose (Perrone 1994, 19-21; 1995, 156-159). However, it is not my aim to present Origen's use of this rhetorical strategy. Instead, I merely wish to use it as an example of the way in which Origen employs rhetorical strategies in his work, thereby determining the way he discusses and presents his ideas.[21]

These two examples of Origen's use of common classical rhetorical concepts in his exegesis show us that he follows rhetorical rules and strategies which he knows from his own education as a grammarian and a rhetorician. It can thus be claimed that such rules and strategies have a normative function in his exegesis. These rules can be classified as weak norms for his exegesis. He uses them when he finds it useful to do so, not as norms that he must always attend to.

Conclusion

The conclusions which can be drawn after this survey of normative structures in Origen's exegesis vary depending on which perspective we choose. If we choose to look at it from Origen's own perspective (emic), the conclusion must be that Origen himself considers his exegetical work to be controlled by theological norms inherent in

---

19   Cf. Perrone 1995, 154.
20   Cf. M. Harl 1961, who tried to show that *De princ.* consists of 15 loosely connected lectures.
21   Concerning the rhetorical strategy 'questiones et responsiones', see the survey article Dörrie and Dörries 1964 and the collection of essays about the theme Volgers and Zamagni 2004.

tradition such as Logos' inspiration of biblical texts, the fundamentally fixed apostolic tradition; this tradition as it is summed up in the rule of faith etc. According to Origen himself, he follows strong theological norms which are set in advance. From a modern observer's perspective (etic), we can conclude that Origen's exegesis is controlled in various ways by a network of different norms ranging from rather strong dogmatic norms to weaker rhetorical norms. However, it is characteristic that Origen's allegorical exegesis is by no means totally decided by fixed norms which would decide the results of his exegesis in advance. Even though Origen recognises a fixed apostolic tradition, there are still some dogmatic questions left open to be discussed by wise and spiritually mature Christians like himself. Even though he is philosophically well trained and therefore adheres to basic philosophical truths of his own time, he is always able to use philosophical concepts in a way which suits his purposes. Even though he is a well trained rhetorician, he is able to use the rhetorical rules in a way which suits his exegetical purposes. We can thus conclude that Origen considers the theological norms to be very strong, while he probably considers his use of philosophical and rhetorical skills to be mere 'tools'. From an outsider's point of view, all the different norms which he applies to his exegetical work seem to be more or less weak because in his practice he does not feel strongly tied by any of them.

Bibliography

Bostock, Gerald 1987. 'Allegory and the interpretation of the Bible in Origen'. *Literature and Theology* 1, 39-53.

Chadwick, Henry 1998. 'Pagane und christliche Allegorise'. In: Christoph Markschies (ed.), *Antike Schriftauslegung, Hans-Lietzmann-Vorlesungen*, 3. Berlin/New York.

Dillon, John 1977. *The Middle Platonists*. London: Duckworth.

Dörrie, Heinrich and Dörries, Hermann 1964. 'Erotapokriseis'. In: *Reallexikon für Antike und Christentum*. Stuttgart: Anton Hiersemann, vol. 6, 342-370.

Hanson, R.P.C. 1959. *Allegory and Event*. London: SCM Press.

Harl, M. 1961. 'Recherches sur le Peri Archon d'Origène'. In: F.L. Cross (ed.), *Studia Patristica* vol. III (= *TU* 78). Berlin: Akademie-Verlag, 57-67.

Hyldahl, Jesper 2004. 'Origenes og Bibelen: Den fortalte historie og den skjulte betydning'. In: René Falkenberg and Anders-Christian Jacobsen (eds.), *Perspektiver på Origenes' Contra Celsum*. Copenhagen: Anis, 117-129.

Jacobsen, Anders-Christian 2007. 'Skriftsyn og metode i oldkirken'. In: Sigfred Pedersen (ed.), *Skriftsyn og metode*. Århus: Aarhus University Press, 46-85.

Jacobsen, Anders-Christian 2008a. 'Genesis 1-3 as Source for the Anthropology of Origen'. *Vigiliae Christianae* 62, 213-232.

Jacobsen, Anders-Christian 2008b. 'Sand og falsk kristendom i andet århundrede'. In: Anders Klostergaard Petersen, Jesper Hyldahl and Einar Thomassen (eds.), *Mellem venner og fjender. En folkebog om Judasevangeliet, tidlig kristendom og gnosis*. Copenhagen: Anis 2008, 207-230.

Koch, Hal 1932. *Pronoia und Paideusis. Studien über Origenes und sein Verhältnis zum Platonismus.* Berlin: Walter de Gruyter.

Lauro, Elizabeth Ann Dively 2005. *The Soul and the Spirit of Scripture within Origen's Exegesis.* Leiden: Brill.

Nardoni, E. 1984. 'Origen's concept of Biblical Inspiration'. *Second Century* 4, 9-23.

Neuschäfer, Bernhard 1987. *Origenes als Philologe.* Basel: Friedrich Reinhardt.

Perrone, Lorenzo 1994. '"Questiones et Responsiones" in Origene. Prospettive di un'analisi formale dell'argomentazione esegetica-teologica'. *Cristianesimo nella storia*, 15, 1-50.

Perrone, Lorenzo 1995. 'Perspectives sur Origène et la Littérature Patristique des "Quaestiones et Responsiones"'. In: G. Dorival and A. Le Boulluec (eds.), *Origeniana Sexta. Origène et la Bible.* Leuven: Peeters, 151-165.

Torjesen, Karen J. 1986. *Hermeneutical Procedure and Theological Method in Origen's Exegesis.* Berlin and New York: Walter de Gruyter.

Villani, Andrea 2008. 'Origenes als Schriftsteller: ein Beitrag zu seiner Verwendung von Prosopopoiie, mit einigen Beopachtungen über die prosopologische Exegese'. In: L. Perrone et al. (eds.). *Adamantius* 14, 130-150.

Vogt, Hermann J. 1990. 'Die Lehre des Origenes von der Inspiration der Heiligen Schrift. Ein Vergleich zwischen der Grundlagenschrift und der Antwort auf Kelsos'. *Theologische Quartalschrift* 170/2, 97-103.

Vogt, Hermann J. 2004. 'Origen of Alexandria'. In: Charles Kannengiesser (ed.), *Handbook of Patristic Exegesis. The Bible and Ancient Christianity.* Leiden: Brill, 536-574.

Volgers, Annelie, Claudio Zamagni (eds.), 2004. *Erotapokriseis: Early Christian Question-and-Answer Literature in Context.* Leuven: Peeters.

THE SONG OF SONGS AS NORMATIVE TEXT

Bart Vanden Auweele

Introduction

What does the Song of Songs mean? At first sight, the answer to this question seems quite evident. The Song is a poem about human heterosexual love. And yet, answering the question often seems a little more complicated than that. Hardly any biblical book has stimulated such a multitude of diverse interpretive approaches as the Song of Songs. The poem's meaning may seem obvious, and yet there is no scholarly agreement either on the literary unity or the structure of the text, or on its dating, its authorship, its literary sources, etc.

Moreover, what is this poem about human erotic love doing in the biblical canon? In the Canticle, no explicit reference is made to God. Besides, the text is everything but a normative text. It is poetry without any apparent didactic intention. Modern interpreters read the Song as a pure celebration of secular human love. Should the canonisation of the Song of Songs therefore be regarded as one of the practical jokes of history? Or does the text, as a book of wisdom, possess a genuine theological message in spite of appearances? Or, thirdly, should the poem's specific theological status be understood as a mere consequence of its insertion in the Canon of Scripture? In other words, is the Song of Songs' spiritual interpretation prior to or posterior to its canonisation?

Recent investigations have shown that there is no proof of a real debate in early Jewish or Christian milieus regarding the canonicity of the Song of Songs. It seems as if the canonical status of Salomon's Song has never really been doubted.[1] However, at the same time the recognition of the Song as part of Revelation implied tacitly a midrashic or allegorical reading of the text. For Christians as well as for Jews, the Song expressed their spiritual growth very well:

...the Song of Songs' own drama of love lost, found, and lost again, proved an endlessly powerful metaphor for these interpreters' description of the ever unresolved play of disclosure and concealment of the divine in their lives (Carr, 1998, 180-181).

---

1   As Barton and Broyde show, there was however a real discussion among rabbis about the extent to which the absence of any explicit mention of the divine name in Esther, Ecclesiastes and the Song influenced the sacred status of manuscripts containing copies of these texts. This debate about the question of whether these writings 'made the hands unclean', should therefore not be regarded as a discussion about the Song's status as a canonical text, but as a debate about the ritual treatment of the text. Amongst Christians, Theodore of Mopsuestia or Junilius Africanus, for instance, may be suspected of not fully recognising the canonicity of the Song, but their views do not seem to have been shared by other exegetes (see Auwers, 2002, 132-136).

Rabbi Akiba as well as Origen considered this love poem to be the 'Holy of holies' of the whole Bible.[2]

As long as the Song was read and understood allegorically, it was regarded as one of the most important, most inspiring and most used books of Scripture. Strangely enough, from the emergence of modern exegesis onwards, the poem fell gradually into a kind of oblivion as its *obvious* meaning became recognised. In the nineteenth and the first half of the twentieth century, the Song was scarcely read in Church and at university. The Song was regarded as yet another example of antique love poetry, totally comparable to other (e.g. Babylonian or Egyptian) love poems. Moreover, modern exegetes approached the Song as a collection of diverse short erotic poems instead of being a coherent story with a well-constructed plot. In other words, exegetes isolated the Song from its biblical context, fragmentised the poem, and read it like any other witness of a long outdated culture. At the same time, however, they were confident that their reading not only reflected the obvious meaning of the text, but also should be regarded as reflecting the *original* intent of the redactor of these poems, in spite of the lack of any historical proof of the existence of such an understanding.

In recent years, however, the possibility and legitimacy of a reading of the Song according to its so-called 'obvious and literal meaning' has been challenged. Modern interpreters such as Ricœur, Patmore and Berder have criticised secular erotic readings of the Canticle for representing modern reader expectations rather than expressing a genuine biblical view on sexuality. They regard the alleged opposition between the so-called secular message of the poem and its spiritual biblical context more as the result of a modern approach than as a reflection of the original understanding of the text.

The Songs of Songs, by reason of the non-evidence of its meaning as a biblical text, offers therefore ideal grounds for observation of the relationship between a biblical text and its readers. The poem remains a hermeneutical challenge for every exegete. What (if any) are the criteria making it possible to evaluate the validity of an interpretation that exceeds pure repetition and retranslation of the 'obvious meaning' of the text? In this way, the search for a theological evaluation of the Song of Songs seems to be not only an ancient but also an increasingly contemporary question, although the answers given are quite diverse. Can the Song, in spite of its appearance, be understood and read *as* a normative text? In the following pages, this article will first mention three modern attempts to read the Song as a theologically relevant text. I shall then try to formulate some parallels between these modern text approaches and patristic commentaries. More concretely, I will try to illustrate these similarities by analysing some fundamental principles of Gregory of Nyssa's exegetical method in his Sermons on the Song of Songs.

---

2   Cf. Mishna *Yadayim* 3,5; Origen, *Sermons on the Song of Songs* 1,1.

Some trends in newer commentaries
A renewed questioning of the literary genre of the text

One first tendency one can discover in recent interpretations of the Song is the critical distance exegetes take towards an excessively simple understanding of the so-called 'obvious meaning' of the Song. Most scholars recognise fully that this poem speaks poetically about human love. But at the same time, they refuse any opposition between an anthropological interpretation and a theological reading of the text. Among contemporary exegetes, a renewed interest in the poetic dimension of the Song can be noticed. Poetic language is by definition open to multiple interpretations. As a poem, the Song of Songs is metaphorical to such a degree that it is often impossible to distinguish between reality and dream, desire and realisation, sometimes even between male and female. In the Song, time and space seem frozen and evoke the desire of the lovers rather than functioning as categories for situating the events. Presence and absence, town and countryside, alternate continuously. In many cases the Song suggests the sexual encounter between man and woman, but these descriptions are never explicit. Some exegetes are therefore able to read the text as thoroughly pornographic (e.g. Boer 2000), while others can legitimately claim that there is no trace of any sexual encounter in the poem. As polyphony of metaphors, the Song of Songs remains a kind of riddle for its readers.

Furthermore, modern scholars are increasingly aware of the quasi-impossibility of tracing a uniform and all-encompassing narrative plot in the text. Not only is the Song fundamentally plurisignificant because of its poetic character. It cannot be read as a reflection of love, either (except Song 8:6-7). On the contrary, the Song is love language in its purest form. It evokes love by directly giving voice to the lovers themselves. By doing so, the Song creates an 'illusion of immediacy' (Exum 1999, 48). It is not a story *about* two lovers, but the direct rendering of their dialogue, or more precisely, their consecutive monologues. In this (pseudo-)dialogical aspect, the Song distinguishes itself from all other erotic poetry of the ancient East. It leaves the reader with the impression of being a silent witness of the dialogue of two lovers who continuously praise each other. In other words, the poem does not seem to contain a direct message to its readers. It does not even address itself to them. The reader constantly has the impression of overhearing private conversations of two lovers in their intimate encounter in a locked garden.

In many respects, the text can also be understood as a parody. Its main characters, male and female, describe each other as brother and sister (Song 8:1), king and queen (Song 3:9-11), shepherd and shepherdess (Song 1:7-8). Contrary to any ancient oriental convention, it is the girl who boldly takes the initiative (Song 1:2) and who, at the end, invites her partner to disappear again (Song 8:14). Moreover, the poetic description (*wasf*) of the girl often seems so unflattering that certain interpreters tend to read the Song of Songs on a whole as a grotesque, criticising every social convention. Instead, the descriptions of the woman seem to ridicule her, presenting her as a supernatural figure with gigantic and warrior-like dimensions (see e.g. Song 3:6; 4:4; 7:4). As a result, some scholars read the poem as a grotesque (Black 2000a; Whedbee 1993), while others claim that the text has hidden theophanic connotations (Müller 1984; 1997).

As a poem, a dialogue and a grotesque, the Song offers several interpretations and solicits its readers to the highest degree. In order to make sense of the text, exegetes are invited to enter the Song's poetical universe and to take a stand. As such, the Song is all but normative, but in being so, it precisely invites its readers to define the function they want to give the text. The Song can be read as a secular parody on love as well as a religious hymn on love's transcendence. Reading the text as one or the other (or as both at the same time) requires the reader to take part in the game of love, in the game of metaphor.

The Song in its canonical context

Other exegetes criticise a purely secular understanding of the Song by referring to the specific biblical context in which it has to be read. They try to establish a 'canonical reading' of the text. Some understand the Song of Songs as a critique of other biblical narratives. In their opinion, this poem is a kind of biblical anomaly, a 'counter-text' (see e.g. Ostriker 2000) that radically denounces other passages of Scripture, which are regarded as far too negative towards women and towards erotic love. The Song, written as a genuine and integral part of the biblical canon, should therefore be understood as a counterpart, as a liberating statement for those who are repressed by a male-dominated culture.

As such, the theological value of the Song should not necessarily be regarded as opposed to its 'obvious meaning'. In the opinion of these commentators, it is precisely the secular and erotic outlook of the text that can be regarded as the theological claim of the Song. Anthropocentric and theological interpretations of the poem are therefore two sides of the same coin. André LaCocque, for instance, considers the Song to be an iconoclastic work, a subversion of the nuptial imagery of the Prophets (LaCocque 1998a; 1998b). By placing the erotic metaphors used to describe the relationship between God and Israel back in their secular context, the Song deliberately criticises a far too disincarnated and spiritualised view on marriage and love. In this way, the provocative dimension of nuptial imagery is re-established and rediscovered by the Song.

However, other commentators refuse to understand the canonicity of the Song as an element already present at the level of the composition of the text. They tend to approach the Song as a (collection of) secular love song(s) that, being *read* in the context of the biblical canon, receives a surplus of meaning. In their opinion, it is first of all the reader who discovers and evaluates the elements of continuity and discontinuity between the Song and other biblical texts. As Paul Ricœur points out, 'The question for me is […] that of an intersecting reading that respects the difference in the setting of the texts under consideration' (Ricœur 1998, 301). In this intertextual dialogue, the Song is used as a hermeneutical key to interpret other biblical stories, just as those stories in return shed a new light on the Song of Songs.

This intertextual and metaphorical approach does not necessarily lead to an allegorical interpretation of the text. The secular aspect of the Song is not negated, but it forms the basis of an intertextual reading. Quite often, for instance, the Song is read in the light of the stories of creation (Cainion 2000; Landy 1983). By doing so, the Song's description of human love as a secular reality also becomes theologically relevant as a reflection on love as an element of creation. The Song expresses the way in which man and woman discover each other, and presents human love as an extremely powerful sentiment. In the context of Scripture, this dialogue between man and woman can be read as a prolongation and an answer to the unilateral jubilation of Adam in Gen 2:23. But there is also a certain discontinuity between both texts. Whereas female erotic desire is regarded as one of the consequences of the Fall (Gen 3:16: 'To the woman He said, "…Your desire will be for your husband, and he will rule over you"'), it is here regarded as mutual and as something positive (Song 7:10: 'I belong to my lover, and his desire is for me').

The effect of the text on its readers

A third critique of a one-sided non-theological reading of the Song is based on the fact that the song is read as a theological text. Although God is not mentioned in the Song of Songs, the poem is read by Jews and Christians *as* the Word of God. So by thoroughly studying the 'effects of the text' on its readers, some exegetes try to revisit the enigma of the theological meaning of the Song. For instance, some refer to the central role that the Song of Songs plays in the feminist critique of Scripture. According to some feminist exegetes, the poem contributes to the liberation process from a far too male-dominated religious language. The Song is a woman's text: not only is the woman the main character of the poem; she is also the one who takes the initiative and who, against all patriarchal traditions, expresses her autonomy: 'My own vineyard is mine' (Song 8:12). Other exegetes, on the other hand, claim that the writing is nothing else than a typical example of patriarchal contempt and that it presents the woman as an object of male gaze (Clines 1995). Here again, the text is open to very different interpretations. As a result, the feminist Bekkenkamp chooses to propose no less than four different readings of the Song, depending not only on the definition of feminism, but also on the degree of sympathy a feminist reader has towards the Song (Bekkenkamp 2000).

The absence of any explicit theological message in the Song paradoxically enables the reader to discover a liberating message in the text. Some even describe the process of interpretation as an erotic encounter with the text. The Song of Songs is not just erotic because it describes a love relationship, but also (and rather) because the metaphorical language of the Song attracts and rejects the reader in his/her attempt to make sense of the text, a sense continuously slipping out of the reader's desire to close his/her interpretation (Black 1999). Reading the Song resembles erotics: one tries time after time to understand the Song, but the meaning of the text cannot be defined, fixed. Just like the game of love: attraction – rejection / encounter – separation. Although these exegetes regard the poem as the revelation and celebration of the secular reality that is erotic love, they equally feel themselves personally implied by this poem. Reading the Song is not only reading a love story (not even reading the best of all love-stories), it is also a normative text. One is questioned by the text: one is changed by the text:

> Lured by its language, its assumptions of immediacy, its presumption of the female voice, we seem to lose our own. For me, this observation, if true, is another mark of an *inspired* text (however we may understand that term!) We do not simply read the Song; we are changed by it, coaxed and cozened, and left [...] with a song on our own lips. Shockingly partial to this little book, we are astonished to find ourselves in agreement from time to time with great rabbis and holy monks (Fontaine 2000, 182).

In contemporary exegesis, the Song is therefore more than ever regarded as an ambiguous text which commentators feel uneasy about. Confronted with the apparent absence of a theological 'message' in the Song, they refer to the specific poetic style, the canonical context and the expectations of the readers, with a view to seek a theological valuation of the text. In doing so, their approach resembles remarkably a patristic reading of the text, as an overview of Gregory of Nyssa's *Sermons on the Song of Songs* will illustrate.

Gregory of Nyssa's reading of the Song of Songs

As contemporary as these hermeneutical reflections may seem, they often find their corollary in patristic exegesis. For instance, modern readers are often astonished by the degree to which the interpretation of the Fathers in fact presupposes a highly erotic approach to the text (Cox Miller 1986; Laird 2002). According to Gregory, eroticism, precisely because it is the strongest and most radical of all human desires, functions in the Song as a metaphor for the desire of God.

The Song read as a metaphor

Gregory approaches the Song radically as part of Revelation. In other words, even if the Song can be read as describing erotic love, it is equally supposed to possess a message about God. If a biblical passage does not directly seem useful when interpreted according to its obvious meaning, then the reader has no other option than to understand it as a parable, a riddle or a metaphor (see *Sermons* Prologue, GNO 6, 4-5)[3]. This is clearly the case for the Song of Songs.

According to Gregory, human language has the ability to reconstitute metaphorically a linguistic space for the unutterable and uncreated reality of God (Douglas 2000, 465). This quality of language validates its use in an attempt to approach asymptotically the nature of God. The desire of the Bride in the Song of Songs is a metaphor for

3   GNO: Langerbeck, Hermann 1960. *In Canticum Canticorum* (Gregorii Nysseni Opera, 6). Leiden: Brill.

the desire for God. But it is only in and through this human desire that God can be represented. The Canticle is Revelation only because it creates a metaphorical space, in which the unutterable One can be thought, but only through an infinite deferral of linguistic meaning.

In other words, Gregory is very interested in the poetic genre of the Song of Songs, precisely because it creates a useful device to create metaphorically a language in which the Unspeakable can be – not expressed – but represented, or better: desired. As long as this criterion is fulfilled, multiple interpretations can be accepted.

The Song as part of Scripture

Reading the Song of Songs requires the reader, verse after verse, to pursue and to participate in the Bride's erotic journey. One can only grasp the spiritual meaning of certain biblical passages if one connects them with the general narrative structure of the text in which they are placed. In order to progress on the way towards perfection, a Christian reader has to follow this sequence of the narrative.

But the Song cannot be understood outside the context of the Bible in its entirety, either. To a Christian, and more particularly to the nuns for whom Gregory wrote his Sermons, the Song reveals what it means to love and to desire God above all. Its placement within the Christian canon is a precious aid to its understanding. According to Gregory, following here Origen, the three sapiential works attributed to Salomon (Proverbs, Ecclesiastes and the Song of Songs) have to be understood as proposing their readers a specific pedagogical-philosophical curriculum (see *Sermons* I, GNO 6, 17-25). In the context of the biblical canon, the Song of Songs should be considered and apprehended as a philosophical writing. By means of the three Books of Salomon, the reader is taught, step by step, not only a Christian language philosophy (the riddle-language of the Proverbs being understood as an introduction to logic and epistemology), but equally a moral philosophy (the Book of Proverbs again purifying the soul by indicating what is virtuous), and a philosophy of nature (Ecclesiastes as teaching the detachment of the world by demonstrating its vanity), as well as a mystical or inspective philosophy (the Canticle proposing the mystical union with God).

The Song and the spiritual growth of its readers

Gregory discovers in these three writings attributed to Salomon, Proverbs, Ecclesiastes and the Song of Songs a Christian pedagogical-philosophical programme. But in Late Antiquity, philosophy is above all regarded as a way of life whose main function is to guide the soul in its fight with the passions. So it is not surprising that Gregory highlights the protreptic and mystagogical implications of the Song of Songs. Gregory reads its poetic narrative not only as philosophical exercises in order to inflame desire for the divine. In his opinion, the Song equally indicates 'a journey in God's saving oikonomia' (Ludlow 2002, 62). The function of the text, its final utility, is nothing less than soteriological. In other words, the concept of utility is pivotal for a hermeneutics that reads the Canticle as a biblical, philosophical and religious text. The aim of the Song's love lyrics is to seduce the readers to real wisdom, which can only be obtained through the encounter with God.

Entering into the erotic world of the text is an absolute prerequisite for its understanding. The desire of the Bride is a catalyst for the reader's desire. Although the Song of Songs is apprehended spiritually and not bodily, it nevertheless gives expression to the *desire* for God. As Gregory of Nyssa puts it, 'through the words of the Song the soul is escorted to an incorporeal, spiritual, and pure union with God' (*Sermons* I, GNO 6, 15). Entering into the world of the text implies participating in its process of conversion and transformation. The text possesses a meaning only to the extent that it helps its readers in their continual growth. For the sake of utility, one cannot limit biblical interpretation to the quest of the obvious meaning of what is written. For the sake of utility, again, one cannot consider a biblical text to possess only a sole and unique meaning. As a result, Gregory of Nyssa writes in the prologue to his *Sermons on the Song of Songs*: 'there is nothing out of bound in searching with every means what is useful in the divinely inspired scriptures' (*Sermons* Prologue, GNO 6, 5).

Conclusion: The Song of Songs as a normative text

How should this erotic poem be read as part of Revelation, as a text with a theological message, as a kind of normative text? In the first part of this article, a paradox in the modern understanding of the Song of Songs was highlighted: 'no other biblical book is more "unbiblical" [...], and no other interpretive reading is more sacred' (LaCocque 1998a, 13). The tension between the text and its readers' horizon of expectations is striking. Only through interpretation can the Song be regarded as normative. However, this does not need to imply that every normative interpretation of the Song should be regarded as a denial of the poem's genuine function and meaning.

In order to make sense of this text in a Jewish or Christian context, contemporary exegesis is confronted with the need to take a stand. The Song has to have some theological relevance for the modern believer, in order to function as a real Christian or Jewish book. However, recent exegesis, influenced by literary, canonical and reader-response criticism, claims that the distance between reader and text should not be regarded as absolute. A text only possesses meaning when it is read. This implies that the 'world of the reader' belongs to the 'world of the text'.

It is precisely in the act of reading that a useful dialogue between the Church Fathers and modern interpretations can be established. Of course, many of the hermeneutical presuppositions and exegetical options of early Christian commentaries cannot be accepted in a modern context. But their option of reading the Song of Songs, in one way or another, as a theological text, is a possible and credible reading strategy even today. The Song of Songs, a metaphor about love, a part of the biblical canon and the writing of a religious community, can rightly be approached as a theological relevant text. However, this way of reading the Song is just one of many possible ways. Other readings are as legitimate and credible.

Nevertheless, a Christian understanding of the Song as a metaphor of love in the context of creation, revelation and salvation has the advantage of being in accordance with the poetical dimension of the text, its literary context, and its history of interpretation. In a Christian framework, the Song, as an eloquent expression of desire, the most profound human emotion, cannot be regarded as theologically meaningless, precisely because it expresses so well this fundamental dimension of the human heart. The incredible diversity of modern interpretations of the Song of Songs does not negate its normativity in a Christian context. The poem illustrates eminently what Gregory the Great regarded as the paradox of Scripture. Scripture resembles a 'river, shallow enough for the lamb to go wading, but deep enough for the elephant to swim' (Gregory the Great, *Letter to Bishop Leander* 4). Through an incredible variety of mutually conflicting interpretations, the Song remains the definitive prism through which Christians contemplate human love as a source of theological reflection.

Bibliography

Auwers, Jean-Marie 2002. 'Lectures patristiques du Cantique des cantiques'. In: Nieuviarts, Jacques & Pierre Debergé (eds.), *Les nouvelles voies de l'exégèse. En lisant le Cantique des cantiques*. (Lectio divina, 190). Paris: Le Cerf, 129-157.

Auwers, Jean-Marie (ed.) 2005. *Regards croisés sur le Cantique des cantiques*. (Le livre et le rouleau, 22). Brussels: Lessius.

Auwers, Jean-Marie 2006. 'Anciens et Modernes face au Cantique des cantiques. Un impossible dialogue?' In: André Lemaire (ed.), *Congress Volume Leiden 2004*. (Supplements to Vetus Testamentum, 109). Leiden / Boston: Brill, 235-253.

Auwers, Jean-Marie & André Wénin 2005. 'Problèmes herméneutiques dans l'interprétation du Cantique des cantiques'. *Revue théologique de Louvain*, 36, 344-373.

Barton, John 2005. 'The Canonicity of the Song of Songs'. In: Hagedorn, Anselm C. (ed.), *Perspectives on the Song of Songs. Perspektiven der Hoheliedauslegung* (Beihefte zur Zeitschrift für die alttestamentliche Wissenschaft, 346). Berlin / New York: Walter de Gruyter, 1-7.

Bekkenkamp, Jonneke 2000. 'Into Another Scene of Choices: The Theological Value of the Song of Songs'. In: Brenner, Athalya & Carole R. Fontaine (eds.), *The Song of Songs*. (The Feminist Companion to the Bible, Second Series, 6). Sheffield: Sheffield Academic Press, 55-89.

Berder, Michel 2002. 'La lettre retrouvée? Lectures actuelles du Cantique et sens littéral'. In: Nieuviarts, Jacques & Pierre Debergé (eds.), *Les nouvelles voies de l'exégèse. En lisant le Cantique des cantiques*. (Lectio divina, 190). Paris: Le Cerf, 103-128.

Black, Fiona C. 1999. 'What is my beloved? On erotic reading and the Song of Songs'. In: Fiona C. Black, Roland Boer, Erin Runions (eds.), *The Labour of Reading. Desire, Alienation, and Biblical Interpretation*. (Semeia Studies, 36). Atlanta: Society of Biblical Literature, 35-52.

Black, Fiona C. 2000a. 'Beauty or the Beast? The grotesque body in the Song of Songs'. *Biblical Interpretation*, 8, 302-323.

Black, Fiona C. 2000b. 'Unlikely Bedfellows: Allegorical and Feminist Readings of Song of Songs 7.1-8'. In: Brenner, Athalya & Carole R. Fontaine (eds.), *The Song of Songs*. (The Feminist Companion to the Bible, Second Series, 6). Sheffield: Sheffield Academic Press, 104-129.

Boer, Roland 2000. 'The second coming: repetition and insatiable desire in the Song of Songs'. *Biblical interpretation*, 8, 276-301.

Brenner, Athalya (ed.) 1993. *A Feminist Companion to the Song of Songs*. (The Feminist Companion to the Bible, 1). Sheffield: Sheffield Academic Press.

Brenner, Athalya & Carole R. Fontaine (eds.) 2000. *The Song of Songs*. (The Feminist Companion to the Bible, Second Series 6). Sheffield: Sheffield Academic Press.

Broyde, Michael J. 1995. 'Defilement of the Hands, Canonization of the Bible, and the Special Status of Esther, Ecclesiastes, and Song of Songs'. *Judaism*, 44, 65-79.

Cainion, Ivory J. 2000. 'An analogy of the Song of Songs and Genesis Chapters Two and Three'. *Scandinavian Journal of the Old Testament*, 14, 219-260.

Carr, David M. 1998. 'The Song of Songs as a Microcosm of the Canonization and Decanonization process'. In: Arie van der Kooij, Karel van der Toorn, Joannes Augustinus Maria Snoek (eds.), *Canonization and Decanonization*. (Studies in the History of Religions, 82). Leiden / Boston: Brill, 173-189.

Clines, David J.A. 1995. 'Why is There a Song of Songs and What Does It Do to You If You Read It?' In: David J.A. Clines, *Interested Parties: The ideology of writers and readers in the Hebrew Bible* (Journal for the study of the Old Testament, Supplement series 205; Gender, Culture, Theory, 1). Sheffield: Sheffield Academic Press, 94-121.

Cox Miller, Patricia 1986. '"Pleasure of the Text, Text of Pleasure". Eros and Language in Origen's Commentary on the Song of Songs'. *Journal of the American Academy of Religion*, 54, 241-253.

De Ena, Jean Emmanuel 2004. *Sens et interpretations du Cantique des Cantiques. Sens textuel, sens directionnels et cadre du texte*. (Lectio Divina, 194). Paris: Le Cerf.

Douglas, Scott 2000. 'A critical analysis of Gregory's philosophy of language: the linguistic reconstitution of metadiastemic intrusions'. In: Hubertus R. Drobner & Alberto Viciano (eds.), *Gregory of Nyssa. Homilies on the Beatitudes: an English Version with Commentary and Supporting Studies*. (Supplements to Vigiliae christianae, 52). Leiden / Boston / Köln: Brill, 447-465.

Exum, J. Cheryl 1999. 'How Does the Song of Songs Mean? On Reading the Poetry of Desire'. *Svensk Exegetisk Årsbok*, 64, 47-63.

Fontaine, Carole R. 2000. 'The Voice of the Turtle: Now it's *My* Song of Songs'. In: Brenner, Athalya & Carole R. Fontaine (eds.), *The Song of Songs*. (The Feminist Companion to the Bible, Second Series, 6). Sheffield: Sheffield Academic Press, 169-185.

Hagedorn, Anselm C. 2005. *Perspectives on the Song of Songs. Perspektiven der Hoheliedauslegung* (Beihefte zur Zeitschrift für die alttestamentliche Wissenschaft, 346). Berlin / New York: Walter de Gruyter.

LaCocque, André 1998a. *Romance She Wrote. A Hermeneutical Essay on the Song of Songs*. Harrisburg: Trinity Press International.

LaCocque, André 1998b. 'La Sulamite. Le Cantique des Cantiques'. In: André LaCocque & Paul Ricœur (eds.), *Penser la Bible*. Paris: Éditions du Seuil, 373-410.

Langerbeck, Hermann 1960. *In Canticum Canticorum* (Gregorii Nysseni Opera, 6). Leiden: Brill.

Laird, Martin 2002. 'Under Solomon's tutelage: The education of desire in the Homilies on the Song of Songs'. *Modern Theology*, 18, 507-525.

Landy, Francis 1983. *Paradoxes of Paradise. Identity and difference in the Song of Songs.* Sheffield: Almond Press.

Ludlow, Morwenna 2002. 'Theology and Allegory: Origen and Gregory of Nyssa on the Unity and Diversity of Scripture'. *International Journal of Systematic Theology*, 4, 45-66.

Munro, Jill M. 1995. *Spikenard and Saffron. A Study in the poetic language of the Song of Songs.* (Journal for the Study of the Old Testament, Supplement Series, 203). Sheffield: Sheffield Academic Press.

Müller, Hans-Peter 1984. *Vergleich und Metapher im Hohenlied.* (Orbis biblicus et orientalis, 56). Freiburg / Göttingen: Vandenhoeck & Ruprecht.

Müller, Hans-Peter 1997. 'Travestien und geistige Landschaften. Zum Hintergrund einiger Motive bei Kohelet und im Hohenlied'. *Zeitschrift für die Alttestamentliche Wissenschaft*, 109, 557-574.

Nieuviarts, Jacques & Pierre Debergé (eds.) 2002. *Les nouvelles voies de l'exégèse. En lisant le Cantique des cantiques.* (Lectio divina, 190). Paris: Le Cerf.

Ostriker, Alicia 2000. 'A Holy of Holies: The Song of Songs as Countertext'. In: Brenner, Athalya & Carole R. Fontaine (eds.), *The Song of Songs.* (The Feminist Companion to the Bible, Second Series, 6). Sheffield: Sheffield Academic Press, 36-54.

Patmore, Hector 2006. '"The Plain and Literal Sense": on contemporary assumptions about the Song of Songs'. *Vetus Testamentum*, 56, 239-250.

Pelletier, Anne-Marie 1989. *Lectures du Cantique des cantiques: de l'énigme du sens aux figures du lecteur.* (Analecta biblica. Investigationes Scientificae in Res Biblicas, 121). Roma: Editrice Pontificio Instituto Biblica.

Ricœur, Paul 1998. 'La métaphore nuptiale'. In: André LaCocque & Paul Ricoeur (eds.), *Penser la Bible.* Paris: Éditions du Seuil, 411-457.

Whedbee, J. William 1993. 'Paradox and Parody in the Song of Solomon: Towards a Comic Reading of the Most Sublime Song'. In: Brenner, Athalya (ed.), *A Feminist Companion to the Song of Songs.* (The Feminist Companion to the Bible, 1). Sheffield: Sheffield Academic Press, 266-278.

THE NEW TESTAMENT CANON AND ATHANASIUS OF ALEXANDRIA'S 39TH *FESTAL LETTER*

Nils Arne Pedersen

The 39th *Festal Letter* for the Easter of 367 by Athanasius, Bishop of Alexandria, is famous for containing the first extant list from the ancient church of precisely the 27 New Testament writings that are still held as the canonical New Testament today. Even though Athanasius only claims in the *Letter* that he is transmitting a received tradition of the Alexandrian Church, scholarship has regarded his list as a landmark in the history of the canon of the New Testament.[1] The reason for this is that the formation of the New Testament is normally interpreted as a gradual process which gained some initial demarcation back in the second half of the 2nd century but remained 'open' as regards the status of a number of texts until it was finally 'closed' when the list known from Athanasius was accepted in the Western and Eastern Churches during the 4th and 5th centuries.

Some years ago this consensus was challenged by a new approach in David Trobisch's *The First Edition of the New Testament* (2000, German original 1996). According to Trobisch, a complete archetype, a 'Canonical Edition' of the New Testament consisting of the 27 books, was deliberately edited about the middle of the 2nd century, and this means that the discussions about the canonicity of New Testament texts which can be found in patristic literature, including Athanasius' 39th *Festal Letter*, should only be seen as critical reflections in relation to an already existing publication, much like modern New Testament exegesis (2000, 34-38).

Although this is an interesting and stimulating new approach, it raises a number of questions, and it is worth mentioning here that when Trobisch *inter alia* uses *Codex Sinaiticus* and *Codex Vaticanus* to show that Athanasius' contemporary canon was no innovation because these codices already contain 'complete editions of the Christian Bible',[2] one speculates how he will explain the inclusion of *Barnabas* and the *Shepherd of Hermas* at the end of *Codex Sinaiticus*. His answer, that these texts are non-canonical additions in the manuscript (2000, 24), seems to presuppose what should firstly be established. Both the inclusion of these texts, now seen as 'Apostolic Fathers', in *Codex Sinaiticus* and also of similar texts in the somewhat younger *Codex Alexandrinus*, as well as the fact that there is no clear evidence of the alleged Canonical Edition in the

---

1 Especially the 19th century was the classical era of research in the history of the New Testament canon with eminent scholars like B.F. Westcott, A. Loisy, T. Zahn and A. von Harnack. Though recourse to these scholars is still necessary, newcomers could begin with H. von Campenhausen's *The Formation of the Christian Bible* (1972, German original 1968) and supplement with two recent volumes with articles covering most of the problems connected with the definition and history of Old and New Testament canons: McDonald and Sanders 2002; Auwers and De Jonge 2003.

2 Trobisch 2000, 36. Cf. below concerning the possible evidence of *Codex Vaticanus*.

patristic testimony before Athanasius, therefore still seem to give the 39th *Festal Letter* of Athanasius great importance in the history of the formation of the New Testament canon. Even though Athanasius speaks as if there never had been any doubts as to the question of the limits of the Bible, this also contradicts the testimony in the earlier Alexandrian Church Fathers as well as his own way (in his other works) of using and quoting texts like *Wisdom* or the *Shepherd of Hermas* as inspired texts. In the 39th *Festal Letter*, however, these texts are excluded from the list of canonised texts but allowed to be read for the catechumens. This important fact, to which Ruwet (1952) drew attention, is probably an expression of inconsistency and a testimony of the real tradition in which Athanasius stood. But it is hardly correct to use it, as Ruwet did, to misinterpret the clear wording of the 39th *Festal Letter* as if Athanasius in this *Letter* also regarded such texts as fully inspired. In the 39th *Festal Letter* Athanasius seems to present only the elements from tradition which he thought best fitted the present needs of the church as the sole tradition.

In this contribution an attempt will be made to shed light on two questions: Firstly what we can learn from the 39th *Festal Letter* about Athanasius' motives and arguments for producing this list; and secondly whether these motives and arguments, taken to-gether with Athanasius' whole story and importance in the church history of the 4th century, can explain why this was the list that provided the normative New Testament for all future Christian generations.

Even back in the 3rd century it was the custom of the bishops of Alexandria to write festal letters for Easter to the Egyptian congregations, probably in order to influence and dominate the Christians up the Nile; and this tradition was continued by Athanasius, from whose hand a large number of *Festal Letters* are preserved.[3] The 6th Canon of the Council of Nicaea (325) had even established that the see of Alexandria (according to 'the ancient customs') had authority over Egypt, Libya and Pentapolis; but these official rights – which were only later subsumed into the title 'Patriarch' – were threatened by the diversity of Egyptian Christianity, especially the existence of the Melitians, a regular counter-church with its own network of congregations, presbyters and bishops throughout Egypt (concerning the Melitians cf. especially Bell 1924; Crum 1927; Camp-lani 1989; and Martin 1996). One of the problems facing Athanasius was therefore how to maintain and re-establish his authority in Egypt – something which he attempted using many different means (pastoral visits, *Festal Letters*, theological and moral tracts, even violence). His other problem concerned the groups in Alexandria and outside Egypt which maintained subordinationist theologies, and which Athanasius referred to under the label 'Arians'. 'Arian' bishops like Eusebius of Caesarea and Eusebius of Nicomedia had sided with Arius against Athanasius' predecessor and spiritual father,

---

3   Except for Greek fragments, the first 20 *Festal Letters* are preserved in a Syriac translation (Cureton 1848), while fragments of *Letters* 1-2, 6, 24-29 and 36-43 are preserved in Coptic translation (Lefort 1955; Coquin and Lucchesi 1982; Coquin 1984). The primary purpose of the *Festal Letters* was not, as claimed by earlier scholars, to indicate the precise time to celebrate Easter for the congregations, since Athanasius did this for the following year in short notifications after the end of each Easter (cf. Barnes 1993, 183).

Bishop Alexander of Alexandria, but they had been seriously humiliated during the chain of events which had the Council of Nicaea as its zenith. Having the support of a number of emperors, they were able to take vengeance on Athanasius, who had to spend about half of his long episcopate (328-373) in exile from his office.

In 367, when Athanasius issued the 39th *Festal Letter*, he had finally prevailed in both conflicts. After returning from his second exile in 346, Athanasius had been able to make his peace with many of the Melitian bishops – they became Catholic bishops instead. During his subsequent exiles (356-361, 362-363 and 365-366) he may have lost touch with the general situation of the Egyptian church to some extent, but when he returned the Melitians were still without their old network of bishops, a movement without leadership.[4] At the same time the Emperor Valens – who otherwise supported the 'Arian' groups in the Roman Empire – did not dare to oppose Athanasius after his restoration as Bishop in 366. Outside Alexandria and Egypt the 'Nicene' party was growing in strength – and with it Athanasius' reputation as the staunch defender of Orthodoxy.

Unfortunately, the 39th *Festal Letter* is not preserved in its entirety, and is only partly in its original language, Greek. The greater part of the *Letter* is preserved in a Coptic (Sahidic) translation.[5] However, in spite of the lacunae it is possible to grasp much of the basic idea of the *Letter*. But firstly we should perhaps take a look at the New Testament canon in the part of the *Letter* that is preserved in Greek.

Here Athanasius establishes both the Old and New Testament biblical canons. We will not consider his list of Old Testament books here, but merely observe that while earlier canonical lists from the 4th century, like those of Eusebius of Caesarea and Cyril of Jerusalem, account for texts that are disputed or of secondary rank, Athanasius actually isolated the canonical books from all others. In this connection he is the first to use the technical term κανονιζόμενα, 'canonised, included in the canon of scripture'. 'The teaching of piety is solely preached in these books. No-one should add anything to them nor take anything away from them' (lines 52-54 in Zahn 1890, 212). Besides these there are two more categories, the ἀναγινωσκόμενα and the ἀπόκρυφα. The ἀναγινωσκόμενα are neither canonised nor rejected; they are books only to be read during the instruction of catechumens, and include five texts related to the Old Testament and two related to the New: *Didache* and the *Shepherd of Hermas*. The ἀπόκρυφα are totally rejected. Furthermore, Athanasius is not only interested in establishing which books are canonised and which are not. He also wants to produce the right sequence of all the books from Genesis to Revelation, and this feature must, as

---

4   This is the interpretation of the evidence in Camplani 1989, 263.

5   The Greek fragment is available (for instance) in *PG* 26, 1435-1440 and 1176-1180 or Zahn 1890, 203-12. Unfortunately, I have not had access to the edition in Joannou (1963, 71-76). A Syriac translation of the canon part of the *Letter* is edited in an appendix in Cureton 1848. Most of the Coptic fragments are edited in Lefort (1955, 15-22, 58-62; tr. 1955a, 31-40); two fragments were already edited in Schmidt 1898; 1902); another fragment in Coquin 1984. Brakke's English translation (1995, 326-32) is based on all the extant material.

observed by Zahn, presuppose the existence of enormous codices like *Codex Sinaiticus* or *Vaticanus* pretending to contain the whole biblical canon (Zahn 1901, 9-11).

There was nothing radically new in Athanasius' list. To say that he tried to close an open canon could give the false impression that a lot of texts still had a chance. Actually, as far as the New Testament is concerned the only thing which was undecided was the exclusion of a few of the 27 texts we now recognise, especially Revelation, and the inclusion of a few more texts like *Barnabas*, *Hermas*, *Didache* or 1 or 2 *Clement*. The widespread use of Apocrypha which is attested in Egypt and elsewhere both before and after 367 does not mean that the ecclesiastical authorities considered them authoritative or allowed them to be read in the churches at the Sunday service. Even though Athanasius' New Testament list won, his attack on the ἀπόκρυφα was surely also a failure. However, within the small group of books whose status was still undecided, we do not even know why Athanasius came to this or that decision because he does not explain his arguments. In the present context the interesting question is why he felt the need to decide the last open questions, why the canon had to be unambiguous.

The beginning of the *Letter* is lost, and the first part of the text that we do have centres on Christ as a *teacher*. Athanasius distinguishes sharply between teaching from human beings and teaching from God in accordance with his anti-Arian theology, which establishes an ontological gulf between Creator and created, placing Christ on the side of the Creator:

> So it is the nature of everyone who belongs to the creation to be taught, but our Lord and Creator is a teacher by nature, for He was not taught to be a teacher by anyone, but firstly, however, all men, even if they are called 'teacher', were disciples (Lefort 1955, 16.22-26).

Christ alone is 'the true teacher, for who is to be trusted to teach men about the Father if not He Who always is in His bosom?' (*IFAO, Copte* 25, f.1r in Coquin 1984, 138a.22-139a.3). Here the anti-Arian theme is clearly visible in the word 'always', and later on Athanasius actually mentions two Arian formulations which incidentally are among those condemned at the end of the Nicene Creed: 'the Son of God is a creature' and 'there was a time when He was not' (Lefort 1955, 17.20-21). Athanasius stresses this opposition between Creator and created by means of scriptural quotations, e.g. 1 Cor 2:9 about things unseen, unheard and not arisen from the human heart.

The linking of the title 'teacher' to this theological and ontological theme produces the problem of the *Letter* (cf. Camplani 1989, 206): According to Scripture only Christ ought to be called 'teacher' (Matth 23:8-11), but Scripture also refers to Christians as teachers in the plural (1 Tim 2:7; Eph 4:11; Jas 3:1). Athanasius' solution to the problem is to say that even though only Christ is the true teacher, since He is not taught by anyone, his disciples may be called teachers since they teach what they have been taught by their master.

According to Athanasius, there are, however, some who deny Christ and therefore wrongly call themselves teachers. Archetypical examples of these are the Jews; but

Pontius Pilate and Herod, who denied Christ or did not know the truth, are also mentioned. More in focus for Athanasius are their successors – his contemporary enemies 'the Arians and the Melitians' (Lefort 1955, 17.15-16). The Arians do not have Christ as their teacher because they make him a creature. As for the Melitians, Athanasius seems to imply that they share this Arian heresy but otherwise his argument is that they have left 'the spring of life' (Lefort 1955, 17.9), which in the nearest context means Christ but probably also alludes to the Scriptures, which Athanasius calls 'the springs of salvation' (line 51 in Zahn 1890, 212) later on in the *Letter*. For Scripture is 'divinely inspired' (line 13 in Zahn 1890, 210), and contains the revelations from God to men. So when the Melitians use a)po&krufa they are actually teaching what is not taught them by God, and therefore they are not true teachers.

Athanasius himself is only transmitting what he has been taught; he says that he has been 'taught from the beginning' (line 16 in Zahn 1890, 210), and towards the end of the *Letter* he declares in humility: 'For these things I have not written as if I teach, because I have not reached such a measure' (Lefort 1955, 21.11-12). On the contrary, Athanasius is merely announcing everything which he has heard from his father – his predecessor Alexander. On closer inspection, however, one observes that Athanasius' humble position here is actually everything that a Christian teacher could be: A disciple. In this way he actually maintains his own superiority as a Christian teacher.

In the 39th *Festal Letter* Athanasius is certainly not polemising against teachers as such, but against Arian and Melitian teachers. When he claims that these 'heretics' bring their own viewpoints forwards and do not have Christ as their teacher and consequently are not his disciples, these polemics do not reflect different social modes of producing or transmitting knowledge; they are simply dogmatic statements meaning that his opponents cannot have Christ as their teacher because they say that He is a creature or when they use a)po&krufa. In another way Brakke (1994) has tried to elucidate the 'teacher' theme of the *Letter* by means of a distinction taken from Williams' book *Arius* (2002, 82-91) between a so-called 'Academic' approach, with its focus on the personality of the teacher or the distinctive ideas of a school, and a 'Catholic' approach with the espiscopal authority operating within the sacramental context, representing a focus of unity in a common practice of worship with the bishop as the centre. Brakke (1994, 404) thinks that Alexander and Athanasius wanted 'to eliminate the academic mode of authority and spiritual formation from their parochial system'. Without taking into account whether or not Williams' two types could be helpful in connection with the showdown between Alexander and Arius, they are at least irrelevant for the time fifty years later. The simple fact that Didymus the Blind, the one person then who best fits Williams' description of the Academic approach, belonged to the 'Athanasian' and not the 'Arian' party in Alexandria shows that Athanasius did not have any intention of eliminating any academic mode of authority; instead, he wanted to eliminate theological and ecclesiastical enemies.

However, the real opponent of the *Letter* does not seem to be the 'Arians' but the Melitians.[6] Athanasius probably mentions Arianism partly as a short demonstration of his viewpoints, and partly in order to insinuate a connection between this heresy and the Melitian one – probably the accusation was only for tactical reasons without foundation in realities.[7] The Melitians are the ones who use ἀπόκρυφα, which is the theme Athanasius has chosen to deal with in 367.[8] Throughout the *Letter* Athanasius distinguishes between the Melitians and some simple persons from his own congregations who are victims since they are being seduced by the Melitians: The Melitians lead simple people astray with their books.

Athanasius claims that the a)po&krufa are the 'invention of heretics' (line 66 in Zahn 1890, 212), but it is certainly difficult – as stressed by Zahn – to believe that he was not aware that the texts mentioned by him were older than the Melitian schism[9]. But here we should probably assume that Athanasius is somewhat crude in order to reach his target group of simple believers. Furthermore, this claim is necessary for Athanasius since he seems to be interested in rejecting the argument that the ἀπόκρυφα are sanctioned because they are quoted in the New Testament. For instance, Athanasius says about the quotation in 1 Corinthians 2:9: 'But if it exists in the Apocrypha as the heretics say, then those who invented them stole from the words of Paul and wrote it down later on' (Lefort 1955, 60,b30-61,b5; 61,a8-12). The argument seems to presuppose that Paul was referring to his own text with the formula 'it is written'!

The hard line towards ἀπόκρυφα could simply be aroused by the Melitian interest in them and the parallel between the ambiguity of an 'open' canon and the ambiguity of Christianity in the light of the existence of heretics and counter-churches. But David Brakke's suggestion of a connection between ἀπόκρυφα joining martyrdom with visionary powers and Melitian divination at martyr tombs, attacked in the 41th and 42th *Festal Letters* (Brakke 1994, 410-17), also seems possible and ought to be further investigated. One wonders, however, whether it really was the final showdown with the Melitians in Athanasius' last years which gave rise to his closed canon in the *Letter*. It seems more probable that it was the Arian controversy which gave rise to such a canon, since during these disputes the Bible was regarded as the basis for arguments by all the parties. This situation would naturally make it difficult to retain categories of doubtful, disputed books since it would be uncertain whether arguments could be built on them (compare Zahn 1901, 1-2). Actually Athanasius himself informs us in the

6   Cf. Camplani 1989, 260-261 about the anti-Arian polemics becoming barren and clichéed in Athanasius' final *Festal Letters*.

7   The Melitians originated in disputes not about doctrine but about discipline, and despite their political alliance with the Eusebians Athanasius formerly distinguished them from the Arians: These were heretics, they were schismatics. The distinction is dropped in the late *Festal Letters*, where the Melitians are attacked for being heretics influenced by Arianism; cf. Camplani 1989, 266-270. For the viewpoint that the Melitians really became influenced by 'Arianism', cf. Bell 1924, 41f.

8   In other late *Festal Letters* the bishop deals with further practical aspects of Melitianism.

9   Cf. Zahn 1901, 14. Athanasius refers to a)po&krufa by Enoch, Isaiah and Moses. Besides the 39th *Festal Letter* there is a little more evidence which seems to confirm the correctness of Athanasius' claim that the Melitians had a special interest in ἀπόκρυφα (see Camplani 1989, 275-76).

Defence before Constantius ch. 4 from c. 353-57 that he had once sent volumes (πυκτία) of the divine Scriptures to Constans, the Emperor in the West 337-350, on his demand. It is probable, though not certain, that this took place during Athanasius' second exile, when he was in Constans' part of the empire. The important fact, however, is not only that *Codex Vaticanus*, which can be dated to the middle of the 4th century, contains the same books as the ones in the canon of the 39th *Festal Letter*, but that their sequence is identical. So the hypothesis that *Codex Vaticanus* was one of the copies that Athanasius made for emperor Constans seems highly probable,[10] and this hypothesis also places Athanasius' original limitation of the New Testament canon firmly in the context of the heated Arian controversies.

Assuming that it was Athanasius' canon which caused the permanent limitation of the New Testament, we may well ask how this was possible. We get some impression of the answer, though not an explanation, by looking at some known facts about the further influence of the 39th *Festal Letter:* In Athanasius' lifetime most of the *Festal Letters* were preserved in Alexandria, and after his death they were collected there while another collection was also made somewhere else, perhaps at Thmuis in Egypt. Later on an historical introduction or *Festal Index* was added to the Alexandrian collection which also mentions the 39th *Festal Letter*. Though we have some evidence of the Alexandrian collection, both the Syriac and Coptic versions are substantially translations from the non-Alexandrian collection. But the Alexandrian *Index* was later on prefixed to the non-Alexandrian collection, and is therefore preserved in the Syriac translation.[11] The part of the 39th *Festal Letter* containing the list of canonical Scriptures, however, soon began to circulate independently of the rest of the *Letter*. As such, we have it in a number of Greek manuscripts with collections of canon law, and in a Syriac translation.[12] According to Camplani, there is further evidence of this independent transmission of the 'canon part' in *The Bohairic Life of Pachomius* ch. 189, which contains a paraphrase of some clauses in that part of the *Letter* and the statement that Theodore, the successor of Pachomius, had it translated into Coptic to serve as a rule for the monks.[13]

This kind of independent transmission of the canon part of the *Letter* could explain the success of Athanasius' limitation of the New Testament, but Zahn argues that it was only late that it became part of canon law. He thinks that Athanasius' limitation of the New Testament had the greatest impact on the Western Church, though not via

---

10   Zahn 1901, 33. The hypothesis was originally advanced in Rahlfs 1899 and has been accepted by many modern scholars, and it still seems very probable in spite of the criticism of it in Skeat 1999.

11   Cf. the summary of scholarship about the *Festal Letters* in Barnes 1993, 183-191. A quotation from the 39th *Festal Letter* in Mar Jakob, Bishop of Edessa c. 700, is from the Syriac collection of all the *Festal Letters*, which was then complete (cf. Camplani 1989, 47).

12   Zahn 1901, 3-4; Camplani 1989, 31, 50-51. Because the Syriac and Greek excerpts are not precisely identical, Zahn doubts, however, that they have anything to do with each other.

13   Cf. Veilleux 1980, 230-32. Camplani (1989, 49, 51, 69) argues that this translation only concerned the canon section of the *Letter*. The reference in the chapter that the Lord 'raises up in each generation, and in ours as well, perfect teachers in whom he dwells, to preserve us from all the deceits of the devil' (tr. Veilleux 1980, 230) could otherwise be an allusion to the 'teacher theme' of the whole *Letter*.

the *Letter* (except in Egypt); but he also allows for his indirect but slower influence in the East, e.g. through Epiphanius or through cultural exchange between East and West (Zahn 1901, 3-4, 29-36).

At least Camplani is probably right that the translation which Theodore started had nothing to do with the present Coptic translation of the *Festal Letters*. In 5th century Egypt the 39th *Festal Letter* is quoted by the famous Coptic author and abbot Shenoute from the White Monastery in his treatise *Against the Origenists*. His quotation is not from the canon part, so probably he knew the entire *Letter*.[14] Probably the Coptic translation of the *Festal Letters* was done in the White Monastery, which is where the provenance of all the manuscripts is as well (cf. Camplani 1989, 52-53, 70-71).

But all of this hardly explains why Athanasius' decisions could succeed. Here I think we should look to the fact that Athanasius won for himself an authority which was not only bound up with his office or his direct power. He was the man who never compromised, and who suffered for what he believed in. The same reasons that made him a saint after his death made his canon a success. I think that we can sense how he plays on this kind of 'charismatic' authority in the 39th *Festal Letter* in not mentioning a fact that all his readers knew: his ordination as bishop of Alexandria made him the highest bishop in Egypt. Instead he refers to the tradition received from his predecessor, and points to his own unutterable greatness as the one who only wishes to be the disciple of Christ.

Bibliography

Auwers, J.-M. and De Jonge, H.J. (eds.) 2003. *The Biblical Canons.* (Bibliotheca ephemeridum theologicarum lovaniensium, CLXIII). Leuven: Leuven University Press.

Barnes, Timothy D. 1993. *Athanasius and Constantius. Theology and Politics in the Constantinian Empire.* Cambridge, Mass. and London, England: Harvard University Press.

Bell, H. Idris 1924: *Jews and Christians in Egypt. The Jewish Troubles in Alexandria and the Athanasian Controversy Illustrated by Texts from Greek Papyri in the British Museum,* ed. by H. Idris Bell. With Three Coptic Texts ed. by W.E. Crum. London: Printed by the Order of the Trustees, sold at the British Museum.

Brakke, David 1994. 'Canon Formation and Social Conflict in Fourth-Century Egypt: Athanasius of Alexandria's Thirty-Ninth *Festal Letter'. Harvard Theological Review,* 87(4), 395-419.

Brakke, David 1995. *Athanasius and the Politics of Asceticism.* (Oxford Early Christian Studies). Oxford: Oxford University Press.

Campenhausen, Hans von 1968. *Die Entstehung der christlichen Bibel.* (Beiträge zur historischen Theologie, 39). Tübingen: J.C.B. Mohr.

Campenhausen, Hans von 1972. *The Formation of the Christian Bible.* Philadelphia: Fortress Press.

Camplani, Alberto 1989. *Le lettere festali di Atanasio di Alessandria. Studio storico-critico.* Rome: C.I.M., Unione Accademica Nazionale, Corpus dei Manoscritti Copti Letterari.

14   More precisely, the title is *I Am Amazed*; cf. Camplani 1989, 49 concerning Shenoute's use of the *Letter*.

Coquin, R.-G. 1984. 'Les Lettres festales d'Athanase (CPG 2102). Un nouveau complément: Le
    manuscrit IFAO, Copte 25 (Planche X)'. *Orientalia Lovaniensia Periodica*, 15, 133-158.

Coquin, R.-G. and Lucchesi, E. 1982. 'Un complément au corpus copte des *Lettres festales* d'Athanase
    (*Paris, B.N., Copte 176**) (Pl. III)'. *Orientalia Lovaniensia Periodica*, 13, 137-142.

Crum, W.E. 1927. 'Some Further Meletian Documents. With plate X'. *The Journal of Egyptian
    Archaeology*, 13, 18-26.

Cureton, William (ed.) 1848. *The Festal Letters of Athanasius, Discovered in an Ancient Syriac Version*.
    London: Printed for the Society for the Publication of Oriental Texts.

Joannou, Péricles-Pierre (ed. and tr.) 1963. *Fonti: Discipline générale antique, IVᵉ-IXᵉ siècle. II. Les
    Canons des pères grecs*. Rome: Grottaferrata.

Lefort, L.-Th. (ed.) 1955. *S. Athanase Lettres festales et pastorales en copte.* (Corpus Scriptorum
    Christianorum Orientalium, 150. Scriptores Coptici, 19). Louvain: Imprimerie orientaliste L.
    Durbecq.

Lefort, L.-Th. (tr.) 1955a. *S. Athanase Lettres festales et pastorales en copte.* (Corpus Scriptorum
    Christianorum Orientalium, 151. Scriptores Coptici, 20). Louvain: Imprimerie orientaliste L.
    Durbecq.

Martin, Annick 1996. *Athanase d'Alexandrie et l'Église d'Égypte au IVᵉ siècle (328-373).* (Collection de
    l'École Française de Rome, 216). Rome: École Française de Rome, Palais Farnèse.

McDonald, Lee Martin and James A. Sanders, (eds.) 2002. *The Canon Debate.* Peabody, Mass.:
    Hendrickson Publishers.

Rahlfs, A. 1899. 'Alter und Heimat der vaticanischen Bibelhandschrift'. *Nachrichten von der Königl.
    Gesellschaft der Wissenschaften zu Göttingen.* Philologisch-historische Klasse, aus dem Jahre
    1899, 72-79.

Ruwet, Jean 1952. 'Le canon alexandrin des écritures. Saint Athanase'. *Biblica*, 33, 1-29.

Schmidt, Carl 1898. 'Der Osterfestbrief des Athanasius vom J. 367'. *Nachrichten von der Königl.
    Gesellschaft der Wissenschaften zu Göttingen'.* Philologisch-historische Klasse, aus dem Jahre
    1898, 167-203.

Schmidt, Carl 1902. 'Ein neues Fragment des Osterfestbriefes des Athanasius vom Jahre 367'.
    Nachrichten von der Königl. Gesellschaft der Wissenschaften zu Göttingen. Philologisch-
    historische Klasse, aus dem Jahre 1901, 326-349.

Skeat, T.C. 1999. 'The Codex Sinaiticus, the Codex Vaticanus and Constantine'. *The Journal of
    Theological Studies*, 50, 583-625.

Trobisch, David 1996. *Die Endredaktion des Neuen Testaments. Eine Untersuchung zur Entstehung der
    christlichen Bibel.* (Novum Testamentum et Orbis Antiquus, 31). Freiburg: Universitätsverlag
    Freiburg Schweiz, Göttingen: Vandenhoeck & Ruprecht.

Trobisch, David 2000. *The First Edition of the New Testament.* Oxford/New York: Oxford University
    Press.

Veilleux, Armand 1980. *Pachomian Koinonia, the Lives, Rules, and Other Writings of Saint Pachomius
    and his Disciples.* In: *The Life of Saint Pachomius and his Disciples.* Translated, with an
    introduction by Armand Veilleux. Foreword by Adalbert de Vogüé. (Cistercian Studies Series,
    45). Kalamazoo, Michigan: Cistercian Publications.

Williams, Rowan 2002. *Arius. Heresy and Tradition,* (rev. edn., Originally published 1987), Grand
    Rapids, Michigan/Cambridge, UK: Eerdmans.

Zahn, Theodor 1890. *Geschichte des Neutestamentlichen Kanons. II,1: Urkunden und Belege zum ersten
    und dritten Band.* Erlangen and Leipzig: A. Deichert'sche Verlagsbuchhandlung Nachf.

Zahn, Theodor 1901. *Athanasius und der Bibelkanon.* Sonderabdruck aus der Festschrift der
    Universität Erlangen zur Feier des achtzigsten Geburtstages Sr. königlichen Hoheit
    des Prinzregenten Luitpold von Bayern. Erlangen und Leipzig: A. Deichert'sche
    Verlagsbuchhandlung Nachf.

THE INFLUENCE OF ISLAM ON THE DEVELOPMENT OF MANDAEAN LITERATURE

Jennifer Hart

So far the essays in this collection have thoughtfully considered the processes, conflicts, motivations and other various intricacies that accompanied the normativising of Jewish and Christian literature. And while much more remains to be said about the quest for literary normativity in Judaism and Christianity, my essay momentarily shifts the attention away from these two traditions towards that of Mandaeism and the development of its literary canon. An investigation of normativity in relation to Mandaean literature presents a valuable interlude because the formative stages of Mandaeism, especially as regards their literature, are roughly contemporaneous with those of Rabbinic Judaism and early Christianity, which means that a discussion of the emergence of an official literary corpus in Mandaeism is poised to add another dimension to our overall understanding of the process of canonisation in Late Antiquity.

The inclusion of Mandaeism in this study contributes two pieces to the mosaic of knowledge that underpins the topic of canonisation. Its first contribution is that of introducing Mandaean literature as a non-biblical comparison of a model of literary normativity. The second contribution comes from the fact that while functioning as a comparative model, the normativising process found in Mandaeism manages to bring the sometimes overlooked tradition of Islam into discussions of canonisation in later antiquity. Islam finds a foothold here because it is, I contend, imprudent to speak of the development of a Mandaean canon without simultaneously considering the influence of Islam. More specifically, this essay seeks to demonstrate that exposure to Islam had a formative impact upon the Mandaean move towards canonisation. In terms of timing, content, structure and desire it is possible to discern the imprinture of Islam throughout the process Mandaeism followed while creating its canon.

Mandaeism, despite its relatively small size, boasts an extensive and impressively diverse collection of literature. The corpus of Mandaean literature includes elaborate treatises on cosmology and mythology; detailed doctrinal and liturgical writings; ritual manuals; esoteric texts; quasi-historical records; instruction for charms and magical aids, as well as scrolls of actual spells; and a guide to astrology.[1] All the various forms of Mandaean literature contribute to the overall formation of Mandaeism as a religion, but out of this comprehensive collection two books (the *Ginza* and the *Book of John*) stand out as the primary texts of Mandaeism. Taken together they are the source for much of Mandaean theology, doctrine, liturgy and ritual. Furthermore, they are among

---

1   For a more detailed description of the various genres of Mandaean literature, see either Buckley (2002, 10-16) or Lupieri (2001, 54-59).

the best known and most widely distributed Mandaean texts both within and outside the Mandaean community. For these reasons the *Ginza* and the *Book of John* are useful focal points for investigating the evidence of Islam's influence upon the normativising of Mandaean literature.

First we will examine how the content and timing of the initial composition of the *Ginza* suggests that this formative work of Mandaean religious identity seems to have taken shape at least partially in response to Mandaeism's exposure to Islam. Next, a similar study of the *Book of John* will reveal that it too owes some of the motivation for its inception to the Mandaeans' early exchanges with their new Muslim neighbours. And finally, a survey of extra-textual material from the *Ginza*, *Book of John*, and other Mandaean texts will highlight the fact that in the wake of Islam's incursion into Mandaean territory an unprecedented call for the production and dissemination of standardised, authoritative versions of Mandaean texts arose among the religious leaders of the Mandaean community.

The Ginza

The *Ginza* lays claim to the position of the most revered work in the literary corpus of the Mandaeans. It is a lengthy tome, constructed from a conglomeration of numerous once individual works of prose and poetry.[2] Structurally the *Ginza* is divided into two parts, known as the *Right Ginza* (GR) and *Left Ginza* (GL) respectively. The two parts of the *Ginza* are identified by the right and left sides because the scroll form in which the *Ginza* is written is always designed so that upon reaching the end of the GR the text must be turned 180 degrees and the GL read with the upside down.[3] The two parts of the *Ginza* are further subdivided within each side. The GR is comprised of eighteen tractates, many of which contain various, sometimes repeated, mythic narratives about creation; hero journeys; the deeds of various Lightworld beings; and the evil schemes of the minions of the Darkness. Additional material found in the GR covers moral teachings; polemics; some liturgical traditions; and apocalyptic histories. On the flip side – literally – the GL consists of just three tractates, all of which are unified by a thematic focus on the fate of the soul after death.[4]

---

2   There is evidence that as individual poems etc., some parts of the *Ginza*, including most of the GL, predate the composition of the *Ginza* as a whole, see Buckley (2002, 10-11; 2006, 17-24).

3   Jorunn Buckley (2002, 10) has observed that this peculiar structure allows the *Ginza* to mimic Mandaean prayer bowls, which are traditionally buried in front of Mandaean homes to ward off evil. The bowls are positioned prior to burial so that one is inverted atop the other, causing the inscriptions on the edge of the two bowls to touch. Similarly when the *Ginza* is folded over vertically the two sides of text are placed face to face. Buckley believes that this trait is intentionally reminiscent of the prayer bowls, the existence of which seems to predate the composition of the *Ginza*.

4   The material in the GL is older than that of the GR. Much of the GL may be from as early as 270 C.E. (Buckley 2006, 35-37; 39; 43-44; 51-52). However, because the *Ginza* as a book contains all of the Left and Right sides, when speaking of a composition date for the *Ginza* as a whole we can only go back as far as both sides are present. So while the material in the GL may originate in the third century C.E., the *Ginza* does not originate until the mid-600s C.E.

The contention that the *Ginza* was first compiled at some point during the early Islamic period derives first of all from the observation that references to Muslims and the religion of Islam pepper the *GR*. Examples of the Muslim presence in the books of the *GR* take a multitude of forms. Some are just brief allusions, the content of which acknowledges a familiarity with Muhammad and his role in the promulgation of Islam. For example *GR* 1,203[5], somewhat cryptically, reports:

> Then came Ahmat, son of the sorcerer Bizbat. He propagates a shout that is not a shout, he does much evil in this world and leads the stock of souls[6] astray, into error (*GR* 1,203, Lidzbarski, 1925, 30).

Ahmat[7] is one of the many variations on Muhammad's name found in Mandaean literature, and the 'shout that is not a shout' is a reference to Islam, which the Mandaeans regard as a false religion. Islam is a 'shout' that does not emanate from the true teachings of the Lightworld, and therefore it is not a real 'shout'. In another short reference to Muhammad, the Mandaeans demonstrate that they possess knowledge of the Islamic understanding of the history of prophethood and Muhammad's place in it:

> After all the prophets a prophet will rise up from the earth. The Arab prophet comes and rules over all the peoples. Thus wretchedness is great in the world. After that dominion the world will be in confusion. After the Arab Mhamat, son of Bizbat, no prophet will come into the world, and the faith will disappear from the earth (*GR* 2,1,164, Lidzbarski 1925, 54).

Although it is filtered through a decidedly anti-Islamic polemic, this Mandaean description of Muhammad clearly echoes the Islamic notion of Muhammad as the seal of the prophets, the last messenger needed to communicate the will of the divine to humanity. This suggests that by the time these sections of the *Ginza* were composed Mandaeism was familiar with Islam as a competing religious tradition and cognizant of key aspects of Islamic belief.

Interestingly, most of the other references to Muhammad and Islam found in the *Ginza* concentrate on how the coming of Muslim domination heralds the culmination of an apocalyptic history[8], or on how Islam's religious identity is integral to its perpetuation of violent persecution. *GR* 9,1 speaks of Ruha, the traditional source of false religion according to the Mandaeans, giving the Arab 'Abdallah' (Muhammad) 'the book and

---

5   Citations from the *Ginza* are given by book number and verse (i.e. GR X,YYY), sometimes a section number will be given prior to the verse (i.e. GR X,Z,YYY) but since not every book is divided in the same manner not all citations include a section number. For clarity in the footnotes I will also give the page number(s) from Lidzbarski's translation of the *Ginza* (*Ginza: Der Schatz oder das grosse Buch der Mandäer* Göttingen: Vandenhoeck and Ruprecht, 1925).

6   'The stock of souls' is a phrase commonly used in Mandaean literature to designate the Mandaean religious community.

7   He is also known as Mhamat, M(u)habit, Muhammad, Abdula/Abdala/Abdallah, and Son of the Arab Butcher.

8   See all of *GR* 18, especially *GR* 18,384-390, Lidzbarski 1925, 412-416.

discourse', which he used to rally his servants around him and which allowed him to invade and overtake all of Tibil (earth), subdue 'every divinity' and sack 'every people, borders and languages.' The message in this passage is that the religion of Islam is the underlying force behind the violent spread of Arab rule. It also shows that once again the Mandaeans who composed the material in the *Ginza* have an awareness of Islam and its place in the unfolding of worldly events. And perhaps more significantly, the Mandaean imbrication of Islam with the Arab conquest indicates that the writers of the *Ginza* had given enough thought to the nature of the Muslims to assign them the status of a dangerous, rival religion.

One final observation about *GR* 9,1: in the course of describing the circumstances of Islam's rise to power Ruha notes that Muhammad, here conflated with Allah, inspired Islamic conquest by telling the Muslims that: 'There is no god stronger than I; I shall give you beautiful women.'[1] Like the Mandaean description of Muhammad as the Islamically defined seal of the prophet recorded in *GR* 2,1,164, these two motivational statements reproduce distinctive elements of Islamic doctrine. The first being Islam's profession of belief in a single, omnipotent god. While this belief is not unique to Islam, the declaration that there is no god but Allah – implying that all power therefore resides in Allah – is the foremost devotional conviction and act of Islam.[2] Similarly, the idea that those who fight for the propagation of Islam will be rewarded with beautiful women is part of the prevailing mythology surrounding martyrdom and Islam. The inclusion of a key piece of Islamic doctrine and what is perhaps a well known but secondary teaching of Islam in the polemic of *GR* 9,1 indicates that the Mandaeans had a familiarity with Islam that extended beyond simple knowledge of its existence into the realm of meaningful engagement with the essential religious ideals of Islam.

The references to Muhammad, Islam and most especially particular elements of Islamic belief found in the *Ginza* substantiate the notion that the spread of Islam made an impression on Mandaeism. The Muslims were, as evidenced by their appearance in the *Ginza*, a force with which to be reckoned. Islam's rise to power necessitated that the Mandaeans make an effort to integrate the Muslims into the Mandaean world view. Moreover, it would seem that while they were trying to explain the existence of Islam and its place in the unfolding of cosmic history the Mandaeans developed a familiarity with fundamental aspects of Islamic doctrine. Knowledge of the Muslim belief in the seal of the prophet, the omnipotence of Allah, and the reward for martyrdom in the name of propagating Islam influenced the Mandaeans to the extent that all three ideas found their way into Mandaean literature. Given Mandaeism's awareness and internalisation of these elements of Islamic theology, it is reasonable to assume that other Muslim ideals, particularly those which contend that each legitimate religion possesses a foundational book containing the message of god, also exerted an influence over the

---

1   *GR* 9,1,231-233, Lidzbarski 1925, 232-234.
2   Recitation of the Shahada, 'There is no god but Allah and Muhammad is his prophet' is the first Pillar of Islam. See Turner, 2006, 100-101.

Mandaeans. In the same sense that the manifestation of Islamic themed content within the *Ginza* speaks to Islam's impact on Mandaeism, the very existence of the *Ginza* as a book may owe something to Mandaean exposure to Islamic doctrine.

The possibility that the composition of the *Ginza* (and other critical pieces of Mandaean literature) resulted at least partially in response to the sacred book tradition of Islam is bolstered by the chronological information contained in the *Ginza* colophons. Colophons are lists of scribes or copyists, sometimes including their lineages and benefactors, appended to most Mandaean texts. The colophons provide a historical record of the transmission of Mandaean literature by listing all the scribes that copied a given manuscript and from whom or upon which manuscripts they based their copy, tracing the text back to its origin source.[3]

A study of colophons associated with all the available extant *Ginza* manuscripts reveals that the earliest versions of the *Ginza* date to approximately 650 to 700 C.E.[4] The *Ginza* colophons do not all end with the same scribe, but as the lists are followed back through history the colophons often culminate at a point during which a cluster of scribes were active. Ram Šilai; Qaiam of Zindana; Bayan Hibil; Šadan, Banan, Bihram initiates (and sons) of Brik Yawar are some of the most commonly found names at or around the terminal position of the *Ginza* colophons (Buckley 2006, 25-110). Painstaking analysis by Jorunn Buckley (2006, 275-296) has demonstrated that all of these scribes are roughly contemporaneous and often interrelated, suggesting that while the colophons may end with different names their point of origin belongs to essentially the same period.

Owing to a dearth of historical material independent from the colophons themselves, pinning down clear chronological parameters during which these initial *Ginza* scribes were active can be challenging. The exact dates are not available, but using a complex network of information about biological, initiatory, and scribal relationships, Buckley has been able to confidently identify time parameters during which the various scribes were working. For example, Ramuia, a scribe not mentioned in the *Ginza* colophons but who is a prominent copyist of the *Canonical Prayerbook of the Mandaeans*

---

3   Structurally this practice of appending a list of transmitters to the narrative text recalls the *isnad* (chain of transmission) that accompanies the Hadith (stories of the prophet) collections found in Islam. Usually a brief story recounting either the words or actions of the prophet Muhammad, each Hadith also includes a list of those who have passed the story along, i.e. …ibn Hassan who heard it from Ahmed who heard it from Ali Assad who heard it from…usually culminating with the name of a well known companion of Muhammad, whose proximity to the prophet lends the Hadith an air of authority. It is tempting to see these structural similarities as further evidence of Islamic influence upon Mandaeism, but it must be cautioned that a couple of Mandaean scribal lists associated with the *GL* and parts of the *Canonical Prayerbook* (*CP*) go back to scribes dateable to a period before Islam, and that the inclusion of the *isnad* is considered a relatively later development in the Hadith tradition. This suggests the possibility that the perceived similarity between the Mandaean colophons and Muslim *isnad* reflects the transmission of Mandaean practice into Islam. An intriguing notion, well worth pursuing but unfortunately beyond the scope of what is possible here. Regarding the Hadith and *isnad,* see Rahman 2002, 63-67.

4   For a detailed account of this study, including the availability and nature of the *Ginza* manuscripts and their colophons, see Buckley 2006. It should also be noted that as individual texts some sections of the *GL* have colophons that reach back to the mid-first century C.E., but that as a whole the *Ginza* with both complete right and left sides does not exist prior to 650 C.E.

(*CP*),[5] can be shown – thanks to references to dateable non-Mandaean events cited in a postscript he wrote – to have been working as a copyist in 638 C.E. (Buckley 2006, 192). This is significant, because elsewhere in the *CP* colophons Ramuia appears as the predecessor of Brik Yawar and as an immediate source of material for Bayan Hibil (Buckley 2006, 260; 278). Using this information about Ramuia's dates of operation and his placement relative to that of Brik Yawar and Bayan Hibil, it is possible to conclude that the latter two scribes were active sometime after 638 C.E., which is also subsequent to the establishment of the Arab Muslims' initial settlements in Iraq.[6] Taking into consideration the father-son relationship of Brik Yawar and Bayan Hibil (as well as Šadan, Banan, and Bihram), the timeline for the early production of the *Ginza* can be further refined. Based on his identity as a successor to Ramuia, Brik Yawar probably worked sometime between the late 640s and early 660s C.E., which means that his sons/initiates (Bayan Hibil, Šadan, Banan, and Bihram) probably produced texts a generation after him, between approximately 670 and 690 C.E.[7] This indicates that the *Ginza* colophons that terminate with the sons of Brik Yawar originated sometime during the late seventh century C.E.

The *Ginzas* in which Ram Šilai holds the terminal position in the colophons may be slightly older than those traced to the sons of Brik Yawar, but they also belong to the second half of the seventh century. Based on his position with respect to Qaiam, son of Zindana, and Bayan Hibil, Ram Šilai appears to have been active a little more than a generation before Bayan Hibil (Buckley 2006, 27). Following the timeframe sketched above, this places Ram Šilai and the *Ginzas* accorded to him somewhere in the 650s C.E., possibly a little earlier or later. And as there are no *Ginza* scribes earlier than Ram Šilai[8], one can conclude that at the very earliest the first *Ginza* appeared during the period after the Muslims had gained a definitive foothold in Mandaean territory.

The evidence garnered from the colophons roughly establishes the latter five decades of the seventh century C.E. as the epoch during which the *Ginza* emerged as a focal text for Mandaeism. When considered in context with the possibility of Islamic influence upon Mandaeism, the timing of the *Ginza's* emergence is conspicuously positioned to be read as a response to Mandaean exposure to Islam. Taking into consideration that independently verifiable historical records acknowledge that Islam had secured itself as a presence in the Mandaeans' homeland by the mid to late 630s C.E. (Choksy 1997, 14-30), it can be stated that by the time the first copies of the *Ginza* started to appear in the 650s through the 670/90s, the Mandaeans and Muslims would have had the opportunity for 20 to 40/60 years of exchange – more than enough time for

---

5   The *Canonical Prayerbook* or the *Qulasta* is the corpus of Mandaean liturgies. It contains over 400 prayers and is regularly used in the devotional life of all Mandaeans. For the text, see Drower, Ethel S. 1959. *Canonical Prayerbook of the Mandaeans*. Leiden: Brill.
6   For information on the timeline of expansion of Islam into the regions of Iraq and Iran, see Choksy 1997, 14-30.
7   Assuming as Buckley (2006, 28 note) has concluded that one generation between scribes is approximately 30 years.
8   Sections of the *GL* have scribes that predate Ram Šilai, but since the *Ginza* as a whole encompasses both the *GR* and *GL* Ram Šilai is the earliest scribe for the complete *Ginza*.

the Mandaeans to realise the religious importance that Muslims assign to foundational literature and respond accordingly. In other words, the *Ginza* surfaces in the Mandaean community in accordance with a trajectory that would have allowed the Mandaeans to become familiar with Muslim opinion about the need for a foundational book and then produce one of their own.

Book of John

All the arguments suggesting that Islam exerted an influence upon Mandaeism that caused the *Ginza* to undergo a move towards official codification reappear in conjunction with an examination of the *Book of John*. Like the *Ginza*, the *Book of John* is another lengthy religious tome of central importance to the devotional life of the Mandaeans.[9] Also like the *Ginza*, content clues from the *Book of John* and the colophons attached to it indicate that Islam may have left an imprint on the inception of this work.

The eponymous John of the title is John the Baptist, known from Christianity. According to Mandaeism John, Yahia or Yuhana as he is called by the Mandaeans is actually a devout Mandaean and gifted member of the Mandaean priestly community, who trained Jesus only to have Jesus betray him and corrupt the tenets of Mandaeism.[10] Despite its name, only one of thirty-seven tractates that comprise the *Book of John* actually contains material dedicated to Yahia.[11] The rest of the tractates are divided among stories about the deeds of various Lightworld beings; moral teachings and exhortations; polemics; and one tractate devoted entirely to an exemplary figure of Mandaean piety, Miriai (nominally the same figure as the Christian Mary, the mother of Jesus, although the stories about her in the *Book of John* make no mention of Miriai as a mother to Jesus). Interestingly, Mandaean scholarship generally maintains that the naming of this book after Yahia may reflect a conscious effort to appeal to Muslim authorities by emphasising the book's association with John the Baptist, a figure whom the Muslims revered and already regarded as a prophet.[12]

Mixed throughout the range of material in the *Book of John*, but especially apparent in the sections from the tractate on Yahia, are references to Islam. In one particularly notable instance acknowledgement of Islamic conquest comes directly from Yahia, who tells his disciples:

When all the priests are murdered and no more exist, [and] the Israelites are murdered, then Muhammad, the Arab, will be born, the son of a slave of 'Abdallah'. He called out to the world; he

---

9   Buckley has speculated that the *JB* is of greater importance to Mandaeism than has been recognised by scholars (Buckley 2004, 13).

10   For the Mandaean story of Jesus' baptism and training by Yahia, see *JB* 30, Lidzbarski 1925, 103-109.

11   The material on Yahia is found in tractate 6, Lidzbarski 1925, 70-123.

12   Buckley 2006, 225. The other name for the *JB* is *Drašia d-Malkia* (The Teaching of the Kings), an intriguing alternative because it seems to be more descriptive of the majority of the rest of the content in the *JB*.

disposed of all the temples; and great numbers of mosques in the world (*JB* 22.84-85, Lidzbarski 1925, 87-88).

Because Yahia was understood to have lived well before the birth of Muhammad, the text presents these events as predictions about the future, a prophecy put in the mouth of Yahia. But it is clear from the description he gives in addition to the subsequent detailed account of how the Muslims wash their bodies and hair, and then dye their beards with henna in preparation to pray in the mosques (*JB* 22,85-86, Lidzbarski 1925, 88-89), that these are practices with which the Mandaeans are familiar rather than speculations about what may happen in the future. Yahia's foresight is really hindsight born of Mandaeism's experience with Islam's expansion and having been exposed to Muslim customs. The text could not include this knowledge of Islam's rise to power or its traditions unless the story was composed sometime after the initial spread of Islam.

In addition to his familiarity with the history of Islam's expansion and its ritual practices, Yahia also demonstrates an intimate awareness of particular elements of Muslim theology. Specifically Yahia describes how the Muslims quiz the Mandaeans by asking 'Who is your prophet?' 'What is your holy book?' and 'How do you pray?' In response to these questions, Yahia observes that 'the condemned' (by which he means the Muslims) do not know and do not understand that the Mandaean 'Lord of the Lightworld is the highest, is the One' (*JB* 22,86, Lidzbarski 1925, 89-90). This is an interesting and telling exchange, firstly because it reveals that the Muslims have apparently engaged the Mandaeans with regard to inquiring about what the Muslims consider the primary tenets – prophet, holy book, manner of prayer – of one's theology; and secondly because Yahia's response indicates he recognises that Islam is using these three questions to assess the legitimacy of Mandaean religious beliefs. In fact the three questions Yahia claims the Muslims pose are remarkably similar to the three questions Islamic tradition contends every soul will be asked after death in order to judge whether they will be saved or condemned.[13] Yahia's answer seems to stand as a reprimand of the imposition of Muslim theological criteria upon the religion of the Mandaeans, especially since it ironically fails to properly gauge the truth that Mandaeism possesses. Both parts, the questions and the response, demonstrate that the Mandaeans knew Islam well enough to understand what Islam considered theologically important, and that the Mandaeans had assessed the value of Islamic beliefs in comparison to Mandaean doctrine. In other words, there is evidence in the *Book of John* that the Mandaeans and Muslims may have engaged in theological dialogue.

The possibility that some of the content of the *Book of John* records moments of religious interchange between Mandaeism and Islam is supported by the dates between which its colophons suggest the book was compiled. Most of the *Book of John* colophons list its earliest scribe as Sku Hiia (Buckley 2006, 227). Sku Hiia does not appear as a copyist in any colophons other than those of the *Book of John*, but three *Ginza*

---

13   The questions are: Who is your god? Who is your prophet? What is your qibla (direction of prayer)?

colophons mention a copyist called Haiašum, who is identified by the *Ginza* colophons as the student of Sku Hiia. Based on the position that Haiašum occupies on the *Ginza* scribal lists, Buckley determines that he and Sku Hiia are roughly contemporaneous with Qaiam, son of Zindana (Buckley 2006, 227). The identification with Qaiam dates Sku Hiia to approximately 670 to 700 C.E., meaning that the *Book of John*, for which Sku Hiia is the earliest listed scribe, was most likely originally assembled during the latter part of the seventh century C.E. This comfortably postdates the time when the Muslims had a sustained and influential presence in the region that is home to the Mandaeans. By the time the *Book of John* emerges there would have been ample opportunity for Islam to assume an influential place in Mandaean consciousness.

Expressing a desire for standardised literature

Scholarship on Mandaean literature persuasively maintains that at least some of the material found in the *Ginza* and perhaps the *Book of John* was authored before the mid 600s C.E. (Buckley 2004, 13-23), and yet the colophons connected to these works reveal that the *Ginza* and the *Book of John* were, in all likelihood, products of an era that immediately postdates Mandaeism's initial sustained exposure to Islam. It should hardly be dismissed as coincidental that within a generation or two of encountering a religion that valued highly the possession of a foundational book, the focus of Mandaean literature should shift from a loose library of disconnected texts to a collection of obviously collated, purposefully structured and thoughtfully named books. It should also be noted that despite the apparent familiarity of Mandaeans with Judaism and Christianity at a time when these two religions were codifying their literature, neither the effort nor the motivation to consolidate their texts appears within Mandaeism until after they encountered Islam. But something changed in the Mandaean community with regard to their thinking about the disorganised nature of their literature during the latter half of the seventh century C.E., and even the Mandaean colophons themselves begin to attest to a self-conscious need for an official literary tradition just as Islam's position as a religious authority in the former Persian Empire was solidifying.

A noticeable upsurge in Mandaean scribal activity, as well as a self-reflexive preoccupation with the legitimacy and ordered dissemination of Mandaean literature, occurred following the arrival of Islam. Comparing evidence of scribal production dating to the early Islamic period to that of other stages in Mandaean development, Buckley observes that there is a significantly larger amount of simultaneous copying happening between 650 and 700 C.E. Texts are not being copied once a generation, as is often the case during other periods. Instead, during this fifty-year span near the beginning of Islam's reign a number of scribes are producing multiple copies of a variety of works. The colophons record the existence of a practice which Buckley calls 'copying in circles', in which the copying of a single text 'circles' back and forth between different scribes within the same generation (Buckley 2006, 28). Notably, some of the scribes belonging to these copy circles are Bayan Hibil, Šadan, Banan, Bihram, Qaiam, Brik

Yawar, Ram Šilia, Ramuia, Haiašum, and Sku Hiia, all of whom are associated with the early production of the *Ginza* or the *Book of John*.

This increase in scribal activity seems emblematic of a corresponding internal increase in the interest in and emphasis on the material being copied. The fact that the Mandaean scribes active during the early Islamic period were so busy copying and recopying the texts of the *Ginza* and the *Book of John* suggests that this is a moment in Mandaean history when concern for these particular works of literature was especially pronounced, a moment when the significance of these texts was at the forefront of Mandaean consciousness. The attention given to the *Ginza* and the *Book of John* – as evidenced by the intensity with which they were copied and recopied – implies that this literature enjoyed a heightened level of importance within the Mandaean community at this time. It was the thing with which Mandaeism was actively concerned.

Interestingly, during this period of apparent heightened attention to Mandaean literature the colophons also record that the prolific scribes were grappling with establishing the legitimacy and orthodoxy of the texts they were copying and disseminating. In a postscript to a colophon for the *Canonical Prayerbook*, which like the *Ginza* and the *Book of John* experienced a surge in scribal interest during the late seventh century C.E., Bayan Hibil recounts that he has undertaken a survey of all available Mandaean texts, and fortified with this knowledge he proceeds to record the most legitimate versions of the texts:

I purified myself when I got possession of these mysteries. And I myself traveled around and went on foot to Nasoraeans[14] and took many diwans [scrolls] place to place. And nowhere did I find "mysteries" as reliable as the Mysteries of Baptism and Oil of Unction. I have written them here and have distributed them to a hundred Nasoraeans, so that they may hold on to and be staunch to them.[15]

The underlying message in this passage is that at the time Bayan Hibil was active as a scribe multiple, perhaps even competing versions of Mandaean texts were in circulation. He regarded it as part of his scribal duty to collect these texts, assess their legitimacy, and produce a single authoritative version that was to be disseminated among the priestly caste of the Mandaeans. By his own admittance he is attempting to codify and institute an official edition of the text which future Mandaeans are advised to faithfully maintain and follow. According to Buckley, Bayan Hibil even 'exhorts his fellow priests to adhere to his version of the baptismal liturgy' (Buckley 2006, 191).

---

14   This is the term that Mandaean literature uses to refer to the priestly class of the Mandaeans.

15   *Canonical Prayerbook* 71-72 (also quoted in Buckley 2006, 190-191). Oddly, Buckley introduces this passage by suggesting that Bayan Hibil lived just at the 'cusp of Islam' or that he is even pre-Islamic, which does not make sense given that elsewhere she repeatedly identifies Bayan Hibil as active around the 700s. Although this may be a nascent period for Islam, it does postdate the time when Islam, including traditional elements of Islamic theology, is demonstrably present in the former Persian Empire.

Bayan Hibil clearly regards himself as responsible for the task of establishing textual and doctrinal orthodoxy within Mandaeism.

This move towards producing an orthodox standard for Mandaean literature is perpetuated in the work of Ram Ziwa Bihram, an initiate of Bayan Hibil, whose post-script to a different *Canonical Prayerbook* colophon threatens 'dire consequences' for anyone 'who removes *zharas*,[16] changes the texts, cuts off part of the copy, or removes the name of the owner'.[17] This admonition echoes the curse found at the end of the Christian book Revelation:

> I warn everyone who hears the words of the prophecy of this book: if anyone adds to them, God will add to that person the plagues described in this book; if anyone takes away from the words of the book of this prophecy, God will take away the that person's share in the tree of life and in the holy city, which are described in this book (Rev 22:18-19).

Both warnings invoke the notion of a closed canon, an official compilation of texts which have received authoritative sanction and which therefore no-one may rightfully alter or amend. The postscript written by Ram Ziwa Bihram reveals that the desire to assign Mandaean texts the status of a closed literary tradition was of obvious concern to the Mandaean scribes operating during the early period of Islamic rule. Like his initiator, Bayan Hibil, Ram Ziwa Bihram seems intent on establishing a single, unal-terable version of Mandaean literature that would normativise Mandaeism's canon.

At roughly the same time as Bayan Hibil and his pupil were advocating for ortho-doxy and a closed canon, the scribe Ramuia assures Mandaeans that after careful study he too has assembled disparate Mandaean writings and turned them into a unified scroll that will benefit future Mandaean priests:

> When I wrote this Diwan[18] it was in separate treatises. I wrote them down and collected these reliable mysteries one by one, and combined them into fourteen writings…I have preserved it so that its beauty, fame and honor may be yours, and forgiveness of sins.[19]

Here again is a scribe who is known to be working in the aftermath of Islam's expansion to the Mandaean homeland acknowledging his efforts to transform a disorganised mass of Mandaean texts into a coherent, unified whole. Moreover, he regards the produc-tion of a single, composite text as a boon for the Mandaean priesthood, indicating that their religious health (with regard to the 'forgiveness of sins') will be better for it. There

---

16   Name insertions that identify individual(s) for whose benefit the text was copied.

17   Drower, Ethel S. 1959. *Canonical Prayerbook of the Mandaeans*. Leiden: Brill, 72

18   He is referring here to a text known as the *Alf Trisar Šuialia* (A Thousand and Twelve Questions), which is clearly a composite text dealing primarily with instructions to priests for the correction of ritual errors.

19   *ATŠ* § 434. For the text see *Drower, Ethel, S. 1960. The Thousand and Twelve Questions: A Mandaean Text (Alf Trisar Šuialia)*. Berlin: Akademie Verlag.

can be little doubt that Ramuia sees his efforts to unify its literature as advancing the underlying strength of Mandaeism.

As the testimony of Bayan Hibil, Ram Ziwa Bihram and Ramuia demonstrates, the urge to move Mandaean texts towards a canonised corpus of literature is a recurrent theme among scribes at work during the early Islamic period. The fact that a widespread concern for consolidation and refinement of Mandaean literature should appear in the generations that were the first to know and interact with Islam invites speculation that the standardising of Mandaean texts was a reaction to Islam. But the timing is not the only or even most substantial aspect of the scribal postscripts that suggests a link to Islam. The contention that Bayan Hibil and Ramuia gathered and surveyed multiple versions of their text in order to compile an authentic and authoritative edition of their particular piece of literature mirrors Islamic tradition regarding the origin of the Uthmani redaction of the Qur'an. According to Islamic records the Caliph Uthman, concerned by the uncoordinated circulation of multiple versions of the Qur'an during the initial phase of Islam's expansion, entrusted a Muslim scholar and scribe named Zayd ibn Thabit with the task of producing a definitive copy of the Qur'an. Tradition maintains that in order to accomplish this Zayd ibn Thabit painstakingly gathered all the written and oral material associated with the Qur'an, which he then compared and assessed for authenticity. From this vast collection Zayd ibn Thabit issued a single text, the Uthmani codex, copies of which were sent to important centres throughout the Muslim Empire and became the standard edition of the Qur'an for all of Islam (Turner 2006, 65-66). This process of collection, informed redaction and purposeful dissemination credited withcreating the official version of Islam's most sacred text follows the same pattern as the descriptions of the efforts of Bayan Hibil, Ram Ziwa Bihram, and Ramuia to develop their own corpus of sacred literature. The Mandaean scribes are represented as undertaking the task of redacting Mandaean literature in a manner that accords with a model established by the Muslim production of the Uthmani codex. The idea that the Mandaeans may have been inspired by Muslim example is made even more plausible by the fact that Zayd ibn Thabit's project occurred between 644 and 656 C.E. (the years of Uthman's reign), a period approximately contemporaneous with the time that Ramuia was active and immediately prior to Bayan Hibil and Ram Ziwa Bihram. All three scribes could potentially have had first-hand knowledge of Muslim efforts to officially organise and distribute their sacred text, in addition to an awareness of the significance that Islam assigned to the need for a single corpus of devotional literature.

The idea that Mandaeism's desire for a standardised corpus of literature was sparked by their exposure to Islam finds a final additional ally in the quasi-legendary record of Mandaean history itself. A Mandaean scroll known as the *Haran Gawaita* contains a strange and fractured account of what appears to be an active attempt on the part of the Mandaeans to present their religious literature to the Muslim authorities so as to receive the status of a protected people. In the story the primary Mandaean actor vacillates between the mythic Lightworld being, Anuš Uthra and the human Anuš-son-of-Danqa, whose existence as an actual leader of the Mandaean community during the early Is-

lamic period is confirmed elsewhere in Mandaean literature.[20] Through the agency of
Anuš, the Lightworld being and Anuš, the human, Muhammad is 'instructed' about
the 'Book (*compiled*) by his [Anuš-son-of-Danqa] fathers, upon which all kings of the
Nasoraeans stood firm' so that 'owing to the protection afforded by these explanations
of the Great Revelation' the Muslims were not allowed 'to harm the Nasoraeans who
lived in the era of his [Muhammad, meaning Islamic] government.'[21] This story indicates that soon after their initial encounters with the Muslims the Mandaeans actively
sought the status of ahl al-kitab (people of the book). This means that the Mandaeans
understood that the Muslims used the literary tradition of a religion and especially
their possession of a theologically sound sacred book as a criterion for determining
the status and treatment a religion would receive under Islamic rule. In other words,
the Mandaeans knew that Islamic perceptions of Mandaean literature would influence
the way in which the Muslim authorities would deal with Mandaeism. Given that the
Mandaeans realised the importance Islam assigned to literature as a means of calculat-
ing the validity and status of other religions, it seems reasonable to conclude that the
scribal efforts to standardise Mandaean literature during the late 600s C.E. were at least
partially motivated by the goal of achieving the benefits that came from conforming
to Islamic ideals.

Conclusion

In his observations on the formation of Mandaean literature, Rudolf Maçuch insists
that internal pressure percolating within Mandaeism itself holds the sole responsibility
for the late-seventh-century C.E. surge in scribal activity that led to the production
of key Mandaean texts.[22] I agree with Maçuch that at the heart of the creation and
standardisation of the *Ginza*, the *Book of John*, and other pieces of Mandaean literature
was a thoroughly Mandaean enterprise, born of the thoughts, concerns, debates and
desires of the Mandaean community. But unlike Maçuch I am not willing to dismiss
the influence of Islam as a factor in the equation that resulted in the development of
the Mandaean canon. However else the Mandaeans came to consolidate and codify
their literature, the evidence compellingly demonstrates that in terms of timing and
motivation the production of the *Ginza*, the *Book of John*, and others owes something
to Islam. Their colophons date the initial compilation of Mandaeism's major works to
the period immediately after the Mandaeans were first exposed to Islam. The content of

---

20   In a colophon to the *CP* Ramuia informs us 'I wrote this Diwan in the town of Tib in the years when Anuš,
       son of Danqa, departed with the heads of the people in the years when the Arabs advanced.' Quoted in Buckley
       2006, 192.
21   Drower 1953, 15-16. Emphasis in text.
22   Maçuch 1965. Owing to a desire to emphasise the existence of Mandaeism prior to Islam (in response to a
       scholarly debate in which others suggested that the Mandaeans were post-Islamic) I think Maçuch is overly
       dismissive of the Islamic influences found in Mandaean literature. While the Islamic references may be part of
       a later layer incorporated into material partially composed prior to Islam, the dimension that such references
       add to the overall picture of the composition of Mandaean literature cannot be deemed inconsequential.

these same texts reveals that the Mandaeans were knowledgeable about Islamic theology and the criteria used by Islam to judge the veracity of other religions. In the generations contemporaneous with Islam's rise to power, Mandaean scribes expressed a concern for establishing standardised Mandaean texts which echoed the Muslims' approach to the formulation of an official version of the Qur'an. And finally, Mandaean legend records an apparent attempt by the Mandaeans to present themselves to the Muslims as a religion with a literary tradition worthy of *ahl al-kitab* status. These are just a few of the many Mandaean-Muslim connections that prove that exposure to Islam had an influence on the development of Mandaean literature. It may not be the sole cause for the creation of a Mandaean canon, but Islam was certainly involved in shaping the trajectory of Mandaeism's literary corpus. In the larger context of thinking about the processes by which literature in Late Antiquity was canonised, the Mandaean example encourages us to seriously consider Islam as part of the discussion.

Bibliography

Buckley, Jorunn J. 2002. *The Mandaeans: Ancient Texts and Modern People*. Oxford: Oxford
    University Press.

Buckley, Jorunn J. 2004. 'A Re-Investigation of the *Book of John*'. ARAM 16, 13-23.

Buckley, Jorunn J. 2006. *The Great Stem of Souls: Reconstructing Mandaean History*. Piscataway, New
    Jersey: Gorgias Press.

Choksy, Jamsheed 1997. *Conflict and Cooperation: Zoroastrian Subalterns and Muslim Elites in
    Medieval Iranian Society*. New York: Columbia University Press.

Drower, Ethel S. 1953. *The Haran Gawaita* and *the Baptism of Hibil Ziwa*. (Studi e Testi, 176). Vatican
    City: Biblioteca Apostolica Vaticana.

Lidzbarski, Mark 1925. *Ginza: Der Schatz oder das grosse Buch der Mandäer*. Göttingen: Vandenhoeck
    and Ruprecht.

Lupieri, Edmondo 2001. *The Mandaeans: The Last Gnostics*. Translated by Charles Hindley. Grand
    Rapids, Michigan: Eerdmans.

Maçuch, Rudolf 1965. 'Anfange der Mandäer.' In: Franz Altheim and Ruth Stiehl (eds.), *Die Araber in
    der alten Welt*, 2:76-190. Berlin: Walter de Gruyter.

Rahman, Fazlur 2002. *Islam*. Chicago: University of Chicago Press.

Turner, Colin 2006. *Islam: The Basics*. New York: Routledge.

UNUM AND UNUS SPIRITUS:

THE NORMATIVE IMPACT OF AUGUSTINE'S INTERPRETATION OF 1 COR 6:17 ON BERNARD AND WILLIAM

Carmen Cvetkovic

The monastic revival in the early 12th century was accompanied by a renewed interest in the study of the Bible. In these monastic communities the reading of the biblical text was not merely a process of solitary scrutiny with the purpose of the simple acquisition of knowledge as in the emerging town schools. Read, memorised and ruminated on during *lectio divina*, the biblical text served here as a means for reflection, meditation and mystical prayer. Moreover, solid knowledge of the sacred text was perfected through extended exposure to the celebration of the liturgy and through the assiduous and detailed study of the Church Fathers. Reading Scripture through patristic lenses was a method that enabled the monastic interpreters to approach the biblical text in the spirit of the Christian tradition established by the Fathers without deviating from their teaching.

The two medieval monastic authors studied in this article, Bernard of Clairvaux (1090-1153) and William of St Thierry (c.1075-1148) had a profound sense of pertaining to an uninterrupted tradition which they had both to protect and to continue. As an illustration of their devotion towards and preservation of the teaching of the early Christian writers, they energetically militated against the novelties introduced in the Christian doctrine especially by the town school masters of their own time. Bernard declared that his intention was not to add anything new to the teaching of the Fathers[1]. In the same way, William never failed to mention that he said nothing of his own but merely reproduced the sayings of his more prestigious Christian predecessors. William's depiction of his work as largely attributable to the writings of the Fathers remained famous: it is like a little bird covered in brightly coloured feathers borrowed from many other birds; if these birds were to claim back their plumage, 'our little adornment would remain naked'[2].

And yet, in spite of these major concerns not to add anything new to the teaching of the Fathers, Bernard's and William's uses of the biblical and patristic sources were in no respect rigid or narrow. They took liberties *vis-à-vis* the biblical and patristic authority, and adjusted them to suit their own agenda. Bernard justified his freedom

---

1 *Epistola 77, SBO 7,184: Ideoque non quaerimus pugnas verborum, novitates quoque vocum iuxta apostolicam doctrinam evitamus. Patrum tantum opponimus sententias, ac verba proferimus, et non nostra: nec enim sapientiores sumus quam patres nostri.*

2 *Expositio super Epistolam ad Romanos, CCCM 86,3: Secundum poeticam fabulam aviculam nostra diversarum plumis avium et coloribus sollemniter vestivimus. Quae si venerint et abstulerint singulae quae recognoverint sua, nuda vel nulla remanebit nostra cornicula.*

in using the sources by declaring that: 'If something is said after the Fathers, which is not against the Fathers, I do not think it ought to displease the Fathers or anyone else.'[3]

The purpose of this article is to explore the edges of this limited freedom that the monastic authors seemed to have been aware of when they interpreted the Bible with the assistance of the Church Fathers. Instead of contrasting the teaching of an 'orthodox' monk with that of a 'heretic' town schoolmaster, which would probably be expected when identifying the borders of an elusive tradition, I decided to focus my attention on two close friends, Bernard and William, both of whom are recognised as great authorities of the Church and who occasionally differ a great deal in the way they treat their themes even though these themes are similar. It has been argued convincingly by Paul Verdeyen (1990, 73) that Bernard's and William's different views concerning the *unitas spiritus* might have led to a controversy that undermined their friendship towards the end of their lives. As there is no historical evidence available for such a disagreement between the two friends, Verdeyen relies in his assumptions mainly on their different theological accounts of the mystical union. No matter how attractive such a theory of controversy would seem, the intention of this paper is to argue against it for a freedom in dealing with the biblical and patristic sources that allows different views to coexist within the same theological tradition.

Both Bernard and William grounded their doctrine of the union of the soul with God biblically in the Pauline verse *Qui adhaeret Domino, unus spiritus est* (1 Cor 6:17), and in the Pauline expression *unitas spiritus* (Eph 4:3). This paper will concentrate mainly on the exegesis of 1 Cor 6:17 as it is most frequently quoted by both authors. Their patristic guide to the understanding of this Pauline verse, although not named by any of the two medieval authors, is Augustine. Both read the Bible through Augustine's eyes, but the results of their Augustinian reading are substantially different. To understand better who followed Augustine more closely and who felt freer in the company of this illustrious guide, I will first look at Augustine's exegesis of 1 Cor 6:17. Next I will move to Bernard's view of the mystical union as he presented it in his famous Sermon 71 *On the Song of Songs* (written between 1145 and 1148). Finally, I will examine William's view of the union of the soul with God as it was presented in one of his last works, *The Golden Letter* (written in c. 1144), although references to earlier texts dealing with the same subject might also be needed for the clarity of the argument.

Augustine

Augustine quotes 1 Cor 6:17 frequently throughout his career (for those interested in statistics, more than 30 times). In a small number of occurrences it is coupled with the preceding Pauline verse 1 Cor 6:16: 'He who is joined to the harlot is one body' (*Qui adhaeret meretrici unum corpus efficitur*), in order to underline the contrast between

---

3   *In Laudibus Virginis Matris* 4,11, SBO 4,58: *Sed si quid dictum est post Patres quod non sit contra Patres, nec Patribus arbitror, nec cuiquam displicere debere.*

the life of virtue on the one hand and fornication and lust on the other. However, a significant number of times 1 Cor 6:17 is yoked with Jn 10:30: 'I and the Father are one' (*Ego et Pater unum sumus*). Thus, the biblical texts offer a solid basis for the distinction between the summit of the virtuous life represented by the union of the human soul with God and the consubstantial unity of the Father and the Son.

For the first time in Augustine's works, the latter distinction is to be found in the great doctrinal treatise *De Trinitate*.[4] In Book 6, speaking of the unity between the Father and the Son, Augustine argues that only in their case is it possible to assert that they are 'one' (*unum*). For this claim, he adduces as biblical evidence the Johannine quotation 'I and the Father are one' (Jn 10:30). In Augustine's view two things are 'one' only 'by way of being not by way of relationship'.[5] Moreover, when several things are described in the Scripture as 'one' without further specification, the 'one' refers to the 'sameness of nature and being without variance or disagreement'.[6] When a specification is added to 'one', the united things must be understood as having different natures (*De Trinitate* 6,4, CCL 50, 231). When he speaks of nature or substance, Augustine does not have a fixed terminology. He uses as synonyms the terms *natura, essentia* and *substantia*, without any intention of making a rigorous distinction between these concepts.

Then he illustrates the distinction between *unum* and *unus spiritus* with two biblical passages. When the Apostle Paul says that: 'He who is joined to the harlot is one body' (*Qui adhaeret meretrici unum corpus efficitur*, 1 Cor 6: 16), he adds the word *corpus* so as to make clear that they are not 'one', which implies the same nature or substance. *Unum corpus* renders the idea that it is 'one body composed by being joined together of two different bodies, masculine and feminine' (*De Trinitate* 6,4, CCL 50, 232). Augustine claims that the Pauline verse that follows, that is *Qui adhaeret Domino unus spiritus est,* must be understood in the same way. Again the apostle does not say *unum*, an expression reserved only for the union of the same natures, because the spirit of God and the spirit of the human being are different in nature, but by being joined they become one spirit (*unus spiritus*) of two different spirits, so that the spirit of God is blessed and perfect without the human spirit, but the spirit of the human being cannot be blessed without God (*De Trinitate* 6,4, CCL 50, 232). Therefore, *unum* represents the union between the Father and the Son, who are consubstantial, while *unus spiritus* represents the union of different natures between the spirit of God and the human spirit.

Augustine also adds that the Father and the Son are not only 'one' but also 'one God', *unus Deus* (*De Trinitate* 6,4, CCL 50, 232), thus making it plain that he is addressing potential Arian readers, who understood the expression *unus Deus* as referring to the Father alone. The Arians were mentioned at the beginning of book 6, and it is certain that Augustine develops this interpretation with them in mind. The passage from *De*

---

4   A standard translation of *De trinitate* can be found in: *The Works of St. Augustine. A Translation for the 21st Century*. vol. 5. *The Trinity* (trans. Edmund Hill.) New York: New City Press 1991.
5   *De Trinitate* 6,3, CCL 50, 231: *Secundum essentiam, non secundum relativum.*
6   *De Trinitate* 6,4, CCL 50, 231: *Eadem natura atque essentia non dissidens neque dissentiens.*

Trinitate, Book 6, concludes with some final remarks on the union of the human soul with God, with Augustine having little to add of his own and seeming to prefer to express himself on this subject by combining several biblical quotations:

with him we are one spirit (1 Cor 6:17), because our soul is glued on behind him (*agglutinatur enim anima nostra post eum*) (Ps 63:8). And for us it is good to cling to God (*et nobis haerere Deo bonum est*) (Ps 72:28) (*De Trinitate* 6,7, CCL 50, 235).[7]

Although Augustine does not, unlike the later mystics, discuss at length the union of the soul with God, he certainly mentions it and speaks of it using words of Scripture. In addition, he equates the union of God with the vision of God, saying in *Letter* 147 (*On seeing God*) that 'the one, who is united with God spiritually, sees God invisibly' (*Epistola* 147,37, CSEL 44, 312). This affirmation is sustained again by the Pauline verse from 1 Cor 6:17.

Augustine returns to the distinction between *unum* and *unus spiritus* in two polemical works written towards the end of his life, the *Collatio cum Maximino episcopo Arrianorum* (14, PL 42, 722) and the *Contra Maximinum Arrianum* (1,10, PL 42, 751).[8] In general they repeat the exegesis present in the *De Trinitate*. However, in his answer to the Arian bishop Maximinus reflecting again on the meaning of 1 Cor 6:17 and Jn 10:30, Augustine has to take into account a new element in the interpretation of the Pauline verse: the will. The Arians interpret the Johannine verse 'I and the Father are one' like 1 Cor 6:17 as referring merely to unity of will (*unitas voluntatis*) and not to unity of essence. According to Augustine, the unity of will comes about where there is a difference in nature, as the human nature and the divine nature are distinct (*Contra Maximinum Arrianum* 1,10, PL 42, 751). The intention of Augustine in this text is not so much to distinguish between the different types of union, as to make the Arians accept that the Father and the Son are 'one God' (*unus Deus*). He then incorporates the expression *unitate voluntatis* into the Pauline verse, and claims that as it is possible to say that as through the unity of will, 'one becomes one spirit with God' (1 Cor 6:17), in the same way *unitate voluntatis*, the Father and the Son are one God, *unus Deus* (*Contra Maximinum Arrianum* 1,10, PL 42, 751).

It is obvious that Augustine's interpretation of 1 Cor 6:17 was shaped by his polemic against the Arians, in which he strongly affirms the Nicene orthodox position of the consubstantiality of the Father and the Son, and the fact that the Trinity is *unus Deus*. As Jaroslav Pelikan has remarked, 'the statement "I and the Father are one" brought together all the basic components of the Nicene Creed, in opposition both to the Arian and Sabellian heresies' (1990, 336). In addition, Augustine carefully preserves the ontological gap between human nature and divine nature, underlying their distinction

---

7   These are not integral quotations of the psalms, but as usual with Augustine he adapts the biblical passages to his own style.

8   Translations of these treatises can be found in: *The Works of St. Augustine. A Translation for the 21st* Century. vol. 18. *Arianism and Other Heresies*. New York: New City Press 1995.

even in their union which he biblically terms as *unus spiritus*. Augustine developed the distinction between *unum* and *unus spiritus* not in order to look in a systematic way at the difference between the two types of union, but in order to refute the Arian heretical claims that the Father and the Son do not share the same essence and that they are not one God. Therefore, Augustine's main interest in elaborating this interpretation was to define the inter-Trinitarian relationships which at that time constituted the reason for many heretical divisions in the body of the church.

Bernard

It is widely acknowledged that 1 Cor 6:17 is one of the most significant texts in Bernard's mystical theology, his 'signature text' (McGinn 1994, 213) for describing the union between the human soul and God. For the purposes of our article we will limit our investigation to several passages from Bernard's richest text on union, *Sermon on the Song of Songs* 71.[9] Explaining how eating is to be understood as a metaphor for uniting with or being in other person, Bernard pauses in order to make a comparative digression on the way in which the Father and the Son are in perfect mutuality in each other. In the same way, the soul 'whose good is to cleave to God' (Ps 72:28) will not consider itself united with him unless it perceives that it is in God and God in it. But like Augustine, Bernard is careful to underline that the unity of the Father and the Son, expressed in the text *Ego et Pater unum sumus* (Jn 10:30) is not identical with the union of the human soul with God as expressed in the text *Qui adhaeret Deo unus spiritus est* (1 Cor 6:17).[10]

Bernard insists that nothing can be more different than the unity of many and the unity of one[11], the unity of one mode of being and the unity of different modes of being. The Father and the Son have the same nature or substance and the same will.[12] Like Augustine, Bernard is not preoccupied with differentiating between *natura*, *substantia* and *essentia*. He uses these terms alternatively. The divine unity does not become (*fit*), therefore it is not temporal, it simply exists (*est*). It is not brought about by the act of uniting, but it exists from all eternity.[13] The Father and the Son are in one another in an ineffable and incomprehensible way.[14] Having one essence, they are consubstantial and have one will. It is possible to refer to their unity as a unity of will (*unitas voluntatis*), but not as unity of wills.[15] The term that designates this unity is *unum*. Like Augustine, who argued against the Arians that the Father and the Son is

---

9   A translation of Bernard's sermons on *The Song of Songs* can be found in: *On the Songs of* Songs, vol. 4. (trans. Irene Edmonds.) Kalamazoo: Cistercian Publications 1980.

10   In quoting 1 Cor 6:17, Bernard frequently replaces *Domino* with *Deo,* probably under the influence of Ps 72:28: *Mihi autem adhaerere Deo bonum est.*

11   *Sermo* 71,9, *SBO* 2, 220: *Unitas plurium et unius.*

12   *Sermo* 71,8, *SBO* 2, 221: *Est Patri Filioque natura, essentia voluntas, non modo una sed unum.*

13   *Sermo* 71,9, *SBO* 2, 220: *Non unitione constat, sed exstat aeternitate.*

14   *Sermo* 71,7, *SBO* 2, 219: *Non solum ineffabili sed etiam incomprehensibili modo.*

15   *Sermo* 71,9, *SBO* 2, 221: *Unitas voluntatum.*

unus Deus, Bernard claims that through an extension of meaning it is possible to say that the Father and the Son are not only *unum* but also *unus Deus,* in that there is one Lord, one God, and in that there are other characteristics which may be attributed to each and not to one in particular (*Sermo* 71,9, *SBO* 2, 220).

The union between the human soul and God differs from the divine unity because the former supposes two radically distinct substances and two drastically distinct wills (*Sermo* 71,10, *SBO* 2, 221). There is an ontological gap between creation and Creator. In the mystical union there is no confusion of the divine substance and of the human substance (*Sermo* 71,10, *SBO* 2, 221). Bernard understands the union between the human soul and God as the perfect agreement of the wills[16], whose intention and object coincide, while they continue to be distinct in their substances. The union and unity of the Father and the Son is described by Bernard as *consubstantiale,* whereas the mystical union of wills is merely *consentibile* (*Sermo* 71,7, *SBO* 2, 219):

Between the human person and God, on the other hand, there is no unity of substance or nature and it cannot be said that they are One, although it may be said with certainty and perfect truth that if they are attached to each other and bound together by the glue of love then they are one spirit (*unus tamen spiritus certa et absoluta veritate dicuntur, si sibi glutino amoris inhaereant*). But this unity results rather from a concurrence of wills (*conniventia voluntatum*) than from a union of essences (*Sermo* 71,8, *SBO* 2, 220).

To the Augustinian distinction between the unity of substance (*unum*) and the agreement of wills (*unus spiritus*) Bernard adds another Augustinian element: the glue of love (*gluten amoris*)[17]. The mystical union between God and creature is achieved by and through love. It is love that enables us to be in God and God in us. The biblical passages enumerated in Augustine, *De Trinitate,* Book 6, included Psalm 63:8 *agglutinatur anima mea post te.* The Augustinian expression *gluten amoris* (the glue of love) used by Bernard may very well be a reminiscence of the biblical text quoted by Augustine, or, to push our speculation further, even a deliberate replacement with an expression that explicates the meaning of the biblical text and that Bernard might have considered more appropriate for the spiritual edification of his brethren monks. In fact, Augustine himself explicates exactly the same biblical line by arguing that the glue is the charity itself in his *Enarratio in Psalmum 62*[18], a commentary that Bernard was likely to hear either read during the liturgical services or read during the meals, which was customary in the monasteries. However, no matter whether Bernard's reasons in using this expression were pedagogical concern, or an interpretative technique in which biblical passages are explained through words of patristic authorities, or simply an association triggered by the presence of a similar word, it is clear that Bernard reads and com-

---

16   *Sermo* 71,10, *SBO* 2, 221: *Communio voluntatum.*
17   In Augustine's writings this expression is mainly used in the ablative such as *glutino* or *glutine.* See *De Trinitate* 10,11, *CCL* 50, 324; *Enarratio in Psalmum* 62,17-18, *CCL* 39, 805-806.
18   *Enarratio in Psalmum* 62,17, *CCL* 39, 805. *Ipsum gluten caritas est.*

ments on the Bible with Augustine's assistance. At the same time he uses Augustine as a patristic support in the articulation of his view of the mystical union. Exegesis and mystical theology are closely connected.

Finally, the third psalm quoted by Augustine in his succinct enumeration 'For me it is good to cleave to God' (Ps 72:28) also figures in Bernard's text. Michael Casey (1988, 201) has observed that Bernard regularly joins 1 Cor 6:17 with Ps 72:28 and occasionally adds Ps 63:8, although in quoting the latter he replaces the verb *agglutinatur* with *adhaesit*. Thus, 'adhesion' becomes the theme connecting all these biblical quotations (Leclercq 1982, 73-74). Ps 72:28, apart from being applied like 1 Cor 6:17 to the union of the soul with God, serves to emphasise the actual experience of the mystical union.

Happy is this union if you experience it (*si experiaris*), but compared with the other it is not union at all. There is a saying by one who experienced it (*vox experti*): For me it is good to cleave to God (*mihi autem adhaerere Deo bonum est*) (Sermo 71,10, SBO II, 221).

The emphasis on the experiential dimension of the mystical union is the distinctive hallmark of Bernard's mysticism and in a certain way marks a new departure in the history of western mysticism. Although accounts of mystical experience were present in the Latin patristic literature beginning with the famous Augustinian passages from *Confessions* Books 7 and 9, Bernard accentuated the experiential aspect of the mystical union much more than Augustine. He differs from the previous patristic tradition in his insistence that what he says is deeply grounded in his own experience.[19] At the same time, he frequently urges his brethren monks to consult the book of their own experience.

To sum up, it is clear that in his reading and exegesis of 1 Cor 6:17 Bernard is greatly indebted to Augustine's interpretation of the same biblical passage. The distinction between *unum* and *unus spiritus* on the one hand, and *unum* and *unus Deus* on the other, the use of the same fluid terminology regarding the substance, the use of the same biblical quotations Jn 10:30 (in order to refer to the divine unity), 1 Cor 6:17 and Ps 72:28 (in order to refer to the union between the soul and God) cannot merely be disparate elements that Bernard could have plucked from a more or less lively Augustinian tradition. It is highly likely that Bernard had a profound knowledge of the Augustinian texts that deal with these issues, either from a direct reading of Augustine's works or through the use of one of the many glossed bibles which could have gathered together scattered Augustinian passages interpreting the same biblical passage.

There are of course differences between the accounts of the two authors, but these consist more in a different emphasis than in a contrasting content of their teaching. Augustine was more preoccupied with settling doctrinal matters concerning the inter-Trinitarian relationships against the Arians. Only incidentally does he deal with the mystical union in this context. On the other hand, Bernard's main purpose is to

---

19   *Sermo 51,3, SBO 2, 85: Loquor vobis experimentum meum quod expertus sum.*

stress the difference between the two types of union. He regarded the teaching on the consubstantiality of the Father and the Son as central to the Christian doctrine, and he repeats it faithfully for the theological edification of his monastic community. But more than Augustine, although following his example, Bernard balances his account on the divine unity with a more articulated and systematic teaching on the mystical union which represented the goal of the cloistered life. The emphasis on the importance of experience represents Bernard's original contribution to the traditional Augustinian view on the mystical union.

William

William discusses the union of the human soul with God constantly throughout his writings, from his earliest works such as *On Contemplating God* and *On the Nature and Dignity of Love* (c. 1120)[20] to his works of maturity such as *The Golden Letter* (c. 1144).[21] It is important to notice that although in each situation he might highlight different aspects of the mystical union, overall his teaching does not undergo considerable changes over time. An analysis of one particular paragraph dealing with this subject should not ignore the existing links with other passages from William's works treating the same topic. Jean-Marie Déchanet (1971, xx) was absolutely right when he observed that William's work *The Golden Letter* cannot be understood without recourse to his other writings.

William's treatment of the mystical union in *The Golden Letter* occurs in the context of the discussion of the three levels of likeness between the human being and God. The highest level is something so extraordinary and such a close resemblance with God that a more appropriate name for this state is *unitas spiritus,* which means that:

It makes the human being one (*unum*) with God, one spirit (*unus spiritus*), not only with the unity which comes of willing the same thing but with a greater fullness of virtue as has been said: the inability to will anything else.

It is called unity of spirit (*unitas spiritus*) not only because the Holy Spirit brings it about or inclines a human being's spirit to it, but because it is the Holy Spirit himself, the God who is Charity (*quia ipsa ipse est Spiritus, Deus Caritas*). He who is the Love of the Father and Son, their unity, Sweetness, Good, Kiss, Embrace and whatever they can have in common in that supreme unity of truth and truth of unity, becomes for the human person in regard to God in the manner appropriate to him (*suo modo fit*) what he is (*est*) for the Son in regard to the Father or for the Father in regard to the Son through unity of substance (*consubstantiali unitate*). The soul in its

---

20   These two treatises are translated in: *On Contemplating God. Prayer. Meditations* (trans. Penelope Lawson). Kalamazoo: Cistercian Publications 1970; and *The Nature and Dignity of Love* (trans. Thomas X. Davis). Kalamazoo: Cistercian Publications 1981.There is still ongoing controversy among scholars about which of these two treatises was written first. The majority of scholars seem to admit that *On Contemplating God* precedes *On the Nature and Dignity of Love*, since William himself in listing his own works in the *Prologue* of *The Golden Letter*, begins by mentioning *On Contemplating God*.
21   Translated in: *The Golden Epistle* (trans. Theodore Berkeley). Kalamazoo: Cistercian Publications 1971.

happiness finds itself standing midway in the Embrace and the Kiss of the Father and the Son. In a manner which exceeds description and thought, the divine human being is found worthy to become not God (*Deus*), but what God is (*quod Deus est*) – that is to say he becomes through grace (*ex gratia*) what God is by nature (*ex natura*).[22]

It is important to notice first that William uses the same technical terms as Augustine and Bernard, namely *unum* and *unus spiritus*. But he differs from them in that he does not attach *unum* strictly to the divine unity. Even in his early work *On Contemplating God*, William assigns *unum* both to the divine unity and to the mystical unity, quoting the words of Christ as they were reproduced in Jn 17:21: 'I will that, as you and I are One, so these also may be one in us'.[23] *Unus spiritus* deriving from 1 Cor 6:17 always designates for William the union of the human soul with God. When William juxtaposes the terms *unum* and *unus spiritus* in the passage quoted above in order to refer to the unity of the human being with God, he does so in accordance with his earlier interpretations and not necessarily as a reaction against Bernard's distinct use of *unum* and *unus spiritus*.

Bernard showed that the unity of spirit is realised through the bond of love (*glutino amoris*). But while for Bernard love is the intermediary that enables God and the human being to unite their wills, for William love is the unity itself. Furthermore, using a famous Augustinian idea[24], William strongly emphasises that the Holy Spirit is love and therefore that the unity of spirit is the Holy Spirit himself, the God who is charity. Although there is evidence that Bernard was familiar with Augustine's teaching on the Holy Spirit as love, since he referred to the third person of the divine Trinity as the 'kiss of the Father and the Son'[25] and also as the love of the Father and the Son[26], he never engages in theological explorations of this idea. Contrastingly, William bases his entire mystical theology on the identification of the Holy Spirit with love. This will take William a step further than Bernard, who remains confined to the spiritual level. However, while engaging in speculative theology William does not exceed the boundaries of 'orthodox' theology, and remains firmly grounded in the Augustinian tradition as he carefully preserves the ontological gap between the human being and God.

William finds himself in agreement with Augustine and Bernard in the distinction between the temporal character of the mystical union conveyed by the verb *fit* and the eternal aspect of the divine and consubstantial unity expressed by *est*. In the human

---

22   *Epistola ad Fratres de Monte Dei* 262- 263, CCCM 88, 285.

23   *De Contemplando Deo* 14, CCCM 88, 163: *Volo ut, sicut ego et unum sumus, ita et ipsi in nobis unum sint.*

24   On Holy Spirit as love or charity, see *De Trinitate* 6, 7, CCL 50, 235; *De Trinitate* 15,27-31, CCL 50, 502- 506; *In Epistulam Iohannis ad Parthos tractatus decem* 7,5-6, PL 35, 2031.

25   *Sermo* 8,2, SBO 1, 37: *Nempe si recte Pater osculans, Filius osculatus accipitur, non erit ab re osculum Spiritum sanctum intelligi, utpote qui Patris Filiique imperturbabilis pax sit, gluten firmum, individuus amor, indivisibilis unitas.*

26   *Sermo* 8,4, SBO 1, 38: *Utriusque siquidem amor et benignitas Spiritus Sanctus est.*

being the Holy Spirit becomes (*fit*) what he is (*est*) in the consubstantial union between the Father and the Son. More than that, the Holy Spirit becomes for the human being *suo modo* in a manner appropriate to him, while in the divine unity he represents the consubstantial bond of the Father and the Son. *Suo modo* indicates that the human being becomes merely by participation and through the grace of adoption what God is by nature.

One passage from *The Mirror of Faith* (1140-1143) confirms that William was preoccupied with these ideas before writing *The Golden Letter*: here William distinguishes between the Holy Spirit in God and the Holy Spirit in the human being, as there is a difference between the Holy Spirit as the consubstantial unity of the Father and the Son and the Holy Spirit in the inferior nature, between the Holy Spirit in the Creator and the Holy Spirit in creature, between what he is in his own nature and what he is in grace, between what he is in the Giver and what he is in the recipient, between what he is in the eternity and what he is in time. In God, the Holy Spirit is naturally and consubstantially mutual love, unity, similitude, mutual knowledge, and everything that is common for both Father and Son. The Holy Spirit bestows all these things by grace on the human being, and in doing so he dwells in the human being. In turn the human being, in whom all these things occur and who is thus transformed, dwells in the Holy Spirit (*Speculum Fidei* 107, CCCM 89,122). This indwelling does not entail a transformation of the human soul into divine nature, but William admits that while not reaching the divine beatitude this is nevertheless a state that surpasses exceedingly the human beatitude (*Speculum Fidei* 101, CCCM 89,102).

William tackled similar ideas even in one of his first works, *On the Nature and Dignity of Love*, where in a famous paragraph (which inspired Bernard as well[27]) commenting on the Johannine verse *Deus caritas est* he argues that both charity and God must be considered according to the nature of the Giver (*donans*) and the Gift (*donum*)[28], thus echoing Augustine's exegesis of the same Johannine verse from the *Tractates on the First Letter of John*. While in the Giver charity is substance, in the gift charity is mere quality. But the gift of love (*donum caritatis*) is said (*dicatur*) to be also God. From this short survey of some of William's writings it appears that William was constantly preoccupied with reflecting on the idea of God and especially the idea of the Holy Spirit as charity. Relying to a certain extent on Augustine's authoritative support, he confidently draws distinctions between God as the Giver and the Gift, while also going further than his predecessor on the solid ground of the patristic tradition.

Returning to the passage from *The Golden Letter*, William continues with the claim that the soul in this state of happiness finds itself included in the Embrace and

---

27 *De diligendo Deo* 35, SBO 3, 149. The dependence between William's text and the Bernardine passage is quite apparent, and since William's treatise on love was written around 1120 (several years earlier than Bernard's own treatise on love) it is highly likely that Bernard uses this idea directly from William, unless both of them draw on a common source.

28 *De Natura et dignitate amoris* 12, CCCM 88, 187.

the Kiss of the Father and the Son, being deigned worthy of a taste of the Trinitarian life. Exactly the same idea was exposed earlier in the same treatise *The Mirror of Faith*:

THE GOLDEN LETTER:	THE MIRROR OF FAITH:
Cum in osculo et amplexu Patris et Filii mediam quodammodo se invenit beata conscientia.*	(…) in amplexu et osculo Patris et Filii qui Spiritus Sanctus est, hominem quodammodo invenire se medium et ipsa caritate Deo uniri qua Pater et Filius unum sunt. **

*   *Epistola ad Fratres de Monte Dei* 263, CCCM 88, 282.
**   *Speculum Fidei* 111, CCCM 89, 123.

William is careful to add that being worthy of such a dignity does not equate with being God. The human being can only be what God is (*quod Deus est*), he cannot be God (*Deus*). This distinction is extremely audacious and needs to be understood in a larger context. Earlier in the same text, William explained that to be what God is signifies 'only to be able to will what God wills, that is, already to be what God is'.[29] Bernard referred to the mystical union as an agreement of wills, but William goes a step further by claiming in pure Augustinian fashion[30] that to be what God is presupposes the inability to will anything else but what God wills. William does not follow Augustine *ad litteram*. Instead he alludes through the alternative use of *posse* and *non posse* to the well known Augustinian pattern that opposes the paradisiacal state corresponding to Adam designated as *posse non peccare* to the state of the *renovatio in melius,* described as *non posse peccare* (*De correptione et gratia* 12,33, CSEL 92, 259). By echoing Augustine, William does not oppose the Bernardine view of the mystical union as that of the human and divine will in harmony; he simply adds an authoritative specification by insisting that in the mystical union the human soul is able not to will anything else but what God wills. Bernard himself made use of this Augustinian pattern in one of his earliest works, which he dedicated to William: *On Grace and Free Choice.* Moreover, in Bernard's view the state of *non pose peccare* corresponds to that of the mystical union.[31] The passage from *The Golden Letter* ends with a clear statement identical with the arguments of William in *The Mirror of Faith*: the mystical union does not affect human nature so as to transform the human being into God by nature. As a result of the *unitas spiritus*, the human being becomes 'what God is' (*quod Deus est*), but through grace (*ex gratia*), while God is God by nature (*ex natura*).

29   *Epistola ad Fratres de Monte Dei* 258, CCCM 88, 281: *Non posse velle nisi quod vult Deus, hoc est iam esse quod Deus est.*
30   *De correptione et gratia* 12,33, CSEL 92, 259.
31   *De gratia et libero arbitrio* 7,21, SBO 3,182. The inability to sin (*non posse peccare*) is termed by Bernard *liber complacitum*, and he admitted that although this state is reserved for the life to come, a few perfect souls enjoy it rarely for a fleeting moment in this life.

In the light of these textual parallels, William's teaching on the mystical union seems to have been consolidated long before he returned to it in his *Golden Letter*. Moreover, he shows a consistency in dealing with this subject which can be traced back to his first works, such as *On Contemplating God* and *On the Nature and Dignity of Love*, where all these ideas are already present.

Conclusion

In conclusion, although William goes much further than Augustine and Bernard in his interpretation of the mystical union, he remains nevertheless firmly grounded in the Augustinian tradition because in spite of the audacious terminology he preserves the ontological gap between God and the human being, who remain distinct even in the *unitas spiritus*. Apart from the similar terminology, there are two elements that occur in both William's and Bernard's treatments of *unitas spiritus*: love and will. But William's way of dealing with these concepts is theological, while Bernard remains on the spiritual level, that of the powers of the soul. The main difference between the two medieval accounts is that Bernard insists that the mystical union is a vague imitation of the consubstantial union between the Father and the Son, a conclusion to which he is led mainly because of the distinction between *unum* and *unus spiritus*. On the other hand, the core of William's argument is not this distinction but the Augustinian idea of the Holy Spirit as love; and this assumption leads him to a more optimistic view of the union of the human being with God, in which the former is granted the dignity of participating in the Trinitarian life by grace.

It is difficult to see here the grounds for a controversy between Bernard and William, as Paul Verdeyen has argued. The two accounts are visibly different, but they do not stand in stark opposition. As Bernard put it in answering the attacks of some adversaries who accused him of inconsistency, they are *diversa sed non adversa* (*Sermo* 81,11, *SBO* 2, 291). Moreover, William's ideas about the *unitas spiritus* seem to be constant throughout his career. He expresses himself in the same audacious way even in his earlier works without attracting the critique of his friend. It is highly unlikely that suddenly, towards the end of their lives, Bernard could have changed his position regarding William's longstanding attitude toward the mystical union. It is more likely that both Bernard and William, who were constantly alert to any novelties corrupting the Christian tradition, were very much aware of the freedom existing within the boundaries of their theological tradition which allows different views to coexist. Moreover, relying safely on the authority of Augustine, whose presence can be sensed behind almost every turn of phrase, Bernard and William assemble the elements of a mystical theology which does not simply repeat Augustine even though it is Augustinian by nature.

Bibliography:

Bell, David N. 1984. *The Image and Likeness: The Augustinian Spirituality of William of St. Thierry*. Kalamazoo: Cistercian Publications.

Casey, Michael 1988. *A Thirst for God: Spiritual Desire in Bernard of Clairvaux's Sermons on the Song of Songs*. Kalamazoo: Cistercian Publications.

Déchanet, Jean-Marie 1971. *The Golden Epistle* (trans. Theodore Berkeley). Kalamazoo: Cistercian Publications.

Evans, Gillian Rosalind 1983. *The Mind of Bernard of Clairvaux*. Oxford: Clarendon Press.

Gilson, Etienne 1940. *The Mystical Theology of Saint Bernard* (trans. A.H.C. Downes). London: Sheed&Ward.

Leclercq, Jean 1969. 'From Gregory the Great to St. Bernard.' In: G.W.H. Lampe (ed.), *The Cambridge History of the Bible*. Vol. 2. Cambridge: Cambridge University Press, 183-197.

Leclercq, Jean 1982. *The Love of Learning and the Desire for God: a Study of Monastic Culture* (trans. Catharine Misrahi). New York: Fordham University Press.

McGinn, Bernard 1994. *The Growth of Mysticism*, vol. II of *The Presence of God: A History of the Western Mysticism*. New York: The Crossroad Publishing Company.

Pelikan, Jaroslav 1990. 'Canonica Regula: The Trinitarian Hermeneutics of Augustine.' In: Joseph C. Schnaubelt, Frederick van Fleteren (eds.) *Augustine: 'The Second Founder of Faith'* (Collectanea Augustiniana). New York: Peter Lang, 329-345.

Pennington, M. Paul 1980. 'Two treatises on Love'. *Studia Monastica* 22, 273-285.

Verdeyen, Paul 1990. *La Théologie Mystique de Guillaume de Saint Thierry*. Paris: FAC-éditions.

ABOUT THE AUTHORS

Bart Vanden Auweele is a PhD scholar connected to the Faculty of Theology, Aarhus University. The theme of his PhD dissertation is Gregory of Nyssa's interpretation of the Song of Songs. Auweele is also a Minister in the Evangelical Lutheran Church of Denmark.

Carmen Cvetkovic is a PhD fellow at the Department of Classics at the University of St Andrews in Scotland. In 2007 she was a visiting PhD fellow at the Faculty of Theology, Aarhus University. She is writing her PhD dissertation on the theme: Reception of Augustinian theology by medieval theologians. She is part of the 'After Augustine Project' conducted by Professor Karla Pollmann.

Jakob Engberg is a postdoc fellow in the Department of Church History at the Faculty of Theology, Aarhus University. In the summer term of 2008 he was a visiting professor at the Faculty of Theology in Kiel, Germany. Engberg has an MA in History and Classical Philology. His research interests are Greco-Roman history and archaeology and early church history, especially persecutions of Christians, martyrdom and Christian apologetics. He gained his PhD in 2004 following a dissertation about reactions to Christianity in the Roman Empire from 50-250 C.E. In 2007 he published an English version of this dissertation under the title *Impulsore Chresto. Opposition to Christianity in the Roman Empire c. 50-250 AD* (Peter Lang, Frankfurt am Main). In addition, Engberg has published a number of articles in journals and anthologies.

René Falkenberg is a PhD fellow at the Department of Biblical Studies at the Faculty of Theology, Aarhus University. His forthcoming dissertation is entitled *Adam and Christ in Early Christianity*, and concerns anthropology and Adam christology in selected texts from The New Testament, the Nag Hammadi Codices, and the Church Fathers. He has translated a number of Coptic manuscripts into Danish, recently the *Gospel of Judas* from Codex Tchacos. In addition, he has published articles on various aspects of Gnostic Christianity.

Jennifer Hart teaches at Whitman College in Walla Walla, Washington. She did her PhD in Religious Studies at the Department of Religious Studies at Indiana University, Bloomington, Indiana and as a visiting PhD fellow at the Faculty of Theology, Aarhus University. The topic of her PhD studies was the influence of Islam on the formation of Mandaean identity.

Else K. Holt is an associate professor at the Department of Biblical Studies at the Faculty of Theology, Aarhus University. Her main research interests are the Book of

Psalms, Hosea and Jeremiah. She is also interested in theoretical aspects of biblical exegesis such as the normativity of the Old Testament and cultural and social anthropology. Holt gained her PhD degree in 1991 following a dissertation about the Book of Jeremiah. Since then she has published a commentary on the Book of Jeremiah, a three-volume commentary on the Psalms (in cooperation with her colleagues at the department), and several articles on Old Testament topics.

Jesper Hyldahl is a former assistant professor at the Department for Systematic Theology at Aarhus University. Hyldahl finished his PhD dissertation on philosophy and hermeneutics in Clemens of Alexandria in 2003. Since then he has written several essays on various hermeneutical problems in Philo and the Greek Church Fathers, and among Gnostic theologians.

Anders-Christian Jacobsen is an associate professor at the Department of Systematic Theology, Aarhus University. His main research interests are in Dogmatics and Patristic Theology. He finished his PhD in 1999 on the topic 'Anthropology and Eschatology in Irenaeus and Origen'. Since then he has published several articles and essays on dogmatic and patristic themes. Most recently he has published the articles 'Freedom and Providence in Origen's Theology', *Church Studies*, vol. 4, Nis 2008, 65-77; and 'Genesis 1-3 as Source for the Anthropology of Origen', *Vigiliae Christianae*, vol. 62, 2008, 213-232.

Gitte Lønstrup is a PhD fellow at the Department of Church History at the Faculty of Theology, Aarhus University. Lønstrup has an MA in History of Art and Classical Archaeology. During her MA and PhD studies Lønstrup has studied in Rome and Oxford. The title of her PhD project is 'Memory & Oblivion: Roman Past and Constantinopolitan Present (324-519)'.

Nils Arne Pedersen is an associate professor at the Department of Church History at the Faculty of Theology, Aarhus University. His main research interests are Church Fathers, Christian heresy (Gnosticism and Manichaeism), haeresiologists, Coptic and Syriac literature, and the church history of Syria and Egypt. He defended his doctoral thesis on Manichean text, 'The Great War', in 1996. Since then he has published several editions of Manichean texts and a monograph on Titus of Bostra. In addition, he has published many articles in Danish and English.

Anders Klostergaard Petersen is an associate professor at the Department of the Study of Religion at the Faculty of Theology, Aarhus University. His main fields of research and teaching are early Christianity, Judaism, and theoretical aspects of religious studies. Among his latest articles are 'Rewritten Bible as a Borderline Phenomenon-Genre, Textual Strategy, or Canonical Anachronism?', in Hilhorst, A., Puech, É., Tigchelaar, E. (eds), *Flores Florentino. Dead Sea Scrolls and Other Early Jewish Studies in Honour of Florentino Garzía Martínez*, Brill, Leiden 2007, 285-307; and numerous essays and reviews in Danish journals and anthologies. In 2007 he edited and contributed to a Danish anthology about Jewish Apologetics, and in 2008 he edited and contributed to another anthology about the Gospel of Judas. Both in the series 'Antikken og Kristendommen' (Antiquity and Christianity).

Karla Pollmann is Professor of Classics at the University of St Andrews in Scotland and a distinguished visiting professor at the Faculty of Theology in Aarhus. Pollmann has held several visiting professorships in Europe and Canada. Her research interests are Latin and Greek literature especially from Late Antiquity, patristics, the history of exegesis and hermeneutics, and pagan and Christian relations in literature and art. Pollmann is currently conducting a large research project on the reception of Augustinian literature, philosophy and theology called 'The After Augustine Project'. In 1991 Pollmann finished her doctoral dissertation with the title *Das Carmen adversus Marcionitas*; and in 1996 she finished her habilitation, which has the title *DOCTRINA CHRISTIANA. Untersuchhungen zu den Anfängen der christlichen Hermeneutik unter besonderer Berücksichtigung von Augustinus, De doctrina christiana* (Fribourg (CH) 1996). Since then she has published several books and articles.

Jörg Ulrich is Professor of Early and Medieval Church History at the Faculty of Theology at Martin-Luther Universität Halle-Wittenberg and a distinguished visiting professor at the Faculty of Theology, Aarhus University. His main research interests are Christian apologetics in the second century, Christianity and Judaism in the first centuries C.E., and theology and church in the twelfth century. Ulrich has published *Die Anfänge der abendländischen Rezeption des Nizänums* (PTS 39, Berlin New York 1994), which is his PhD dissertation; and *Euseb von Caesarea und die Juden. Studien zur Rolle der Juden in der Theologie des Eusebius von Caesarea* (PTS 49, Berlin, New York 1999), which is his habilitation. His latest monograph is a translation of and commentary on Augustine's *Confessiones*, which was published in 2008. In addition, Ulrich has published a great number of articles and essays in journals and anthologies.